Study Guide

MACROECONOMICS

Study Guide

MACROECONOMICS:
Principles and Tools
Fourth Edition

Arthur O'Sullivan
Steven M. Sheffrin

Janice Boucher Breuer

PEARSON
Prentice Hall

Upper Saddle River, New Jersey 07458

VP/Editorial Director: Jeff Shelstad
Executive Editor: David Alexander
Acquisitions Editor: Jon Axelrod
Manager, Print Production: Christy Mahon
Production Editor & Buyer: Wanda Rockwell
Printer/Binder: Courier, Bookmart Press

Copyright © 2006 by Pearson Education, Inc., Upper Saddle River, New Jersey, 07458.
Pearson Prentice Hall. All rights reserved. Printed in the United States of America. This publication is protected by Copyright and permission should be obtained from the publisher prior to any prohibited reproduction, storage in a retrieval system, or transmission in any form or by any means, electronic, mechanical, photocopying, recording, or likewise. For information regarding permission(s), write to: Rights and Permissions Department.

Pearson Prentice Hall™ is a trademark of Pearson Education, Inc.

10 9 8 7 6 5 4 3 2 1
ISBN 0-13-153621-4

Contents

Chapter 1	Introduction: What Is Economics?	1
Chapter 2	The Key Principles of Economics	9
Chapter 3	Exchange and Markets	22
Chapter 4	Supply, Demand, and Market Equilibrium	34
Chapter 5	Measuring a Nation's Production and Income	52
Chapter 6	Unemployment and Inflation	65
Chapter 7	The Economy at Full-Employment	79
Chapter 7	*Appendix*	93
Chapter 8	Why Do Economies Grow?	97
Chapter 9	Aggregate Demand and Aggregate Supply	111
Chapter 10	Fiscal Policy	124
Chapter 11	The Income-Expenditure Model	137
Chapter 12	Investment and Financial Intermediation	154
Chapter 13	Money and the Banking System	167
Chapter 14	Monetary Policy In the Short Run	178
Chapter 15	From the Short Run to the Long Run	194
Chapter 16	The Dynamics of Inflation and Unemployment	206
Chapter 17	Current Issues in Macroeconomic Policy	217
Chapter 18	International Trade and Public Policy	230
Chapter 19	The World of International Finance	243

CHAPTER 1
INTRODUCTION: WHAT IS ECONOMICS?

I. OVERVIEW

In this chapter, you will be introduced to economics. You will learn about the basic economic problem of scarcity and how it relates to what products a country produces, how it produces them, and who consumes them. You will be introduced to questions that economists answer and how economic analysis can be used. You will also learn about some of the terms and techniques economists use for thinking about problems that an individual, a firm, or a government faces.

II. CHECK LIST

By the end of this chapter, you should be able to:

- Explain the concept of scarcity and provide examples of it.
- Describe the difference between positive and normative economics.
- List the three basic economic questions that individuals, firms, and the government must answer.
- Describe the usefulness of making assumptions.
- Explain what is meant by "*ceteris paribus.*"
- Explain what a "marginal change" is.
- Explain the concept of rationality used by economists.
- Describe ways in which economic thinking can be used.
- Distinguish between microeconomic and macroeconomic issues.

III. KEY TERMS

ceteris paribus: the Latin expression meaning other variables being held fixed.

economics: the study of choice when there is scarcity, that is, a situation in which resources are limited and can be used in different ways.

marginal change: a small, one-unit change in value.

macroeconomics: the study of the nation's economy as a whole.

microeconomics: the study of the choices made by households, firms, and government and of how these choices affect the markets for goods and services.

normative economics: Analysis that answers the question, "What ought to be?"

positive economics: Analysis that answering the questions, "What is or what will be?"

scarcity: a situation in which resources are limited in quantity and can be used in different ways.

variable: a measure of something that can take on different values.

IV. PERFORMANCE ENHANCING TIPS (PETS)

PET #1

The term 'ceteris paribus' means 'holding other factors constant', i.e. keeping other factors at the same level before and after a change in a relationship between two other variables.

For example, you may read an article in the newspaper that says "student test scores rise by 10 points from reading 3 more hours a week." The relationship between tests scores and reading assumes some other factors are held constant. For example, the relationship between reading and test scores may be based on students getting eight hours of sleep a night before and after the additional reading time is logged. Let's put some numbers to the example to illustrate the point. Suppose that on a standardized verbal test, students score 78% based on reading five hours a week. Further suppose that when students increase their reading to eight hours a week (three more hours), standardized verbal test scores rise to 84. The relationship assumes that nothing else relevant to the relationship has changed. For example, it assumes that students get the same hours of sleep per night in the case where they were reading five hours a week and in the case where they were reading eight hours a week. If this was not assumed, then the article would have to indicate that student test scores rise when students read three more hours a week and, say, get more than eight hours of sleep a night.

For another example, you may hear an ad on the radio that says that "walking 3 miles a day four days a week will, over the course of a year, lead to weight loss of 10 pounds." The relationship between walking and weight loss assumes some 'other factors held constant.' Those 'other factors held constant' might be that eating habits remain unchanged over the year and/or that no diet supplements are taken.

V. PRACTICE EXAM: MULTIPLE CHOICE

1. Economics is:
a) the study of money.
b) the study of financial decisions.
c) the science of choice in the face of limits.
d) the study of production.
e) the science of efficiency.

2. Limits or constraints on the resources we have:
is defined as 'scarcity.'
a) forces individuals and society to make tradeoffs.
b) prevent an economy from growing.
c) create inefficiencies in production.
d) (a) and (b).

3. Which one of the following does NOT represent the concept of "scarcity"?
a) a decision by your parents to put more of their savings to fund college expenses and less to life insurance.
b) public policy in the state of Washington to reduce timber production so that more wildlife species will be preserved.
c) a decision by a company to increase advertising expense for a new board game by decreasing its budget for telephone expense.
d) a decision to commit more time to perfecting your volleyball serve and more time to perfecting your tennis serve.
e) a decision by a student to spend more time studying and less time partying.

4. Which one(s) of the following questions is an example of normative economics?
a) by how much will spending on housing decline when interest rates rise?
b) if an electronics store lowers the price of DVD players, how many more will be sold?
c) should lottery money be used to fund scholarships to attend college?
d) should I start saving now for my retirement?
e) (c) and (d).

4   Chapter 1

5. Which one(s) of the following questions is an example of positive economics?
a) health care costs will rise by 7% if universal health insurance is adopted.
b) countries that adopt free-market policies should grow faster than those that do not.
c) the government should increase the minimum wage to reduce poverty.
d) the central bank should lower interest rates to get the economy out of recession.
e) banks should be permitted to sell mutual funds.

6. All of the following are elements of the economic way of thinking EXCEPT:
a) simplifying assumptions.
b) individuals acting in their self-interest.
c) thinking at the margin.
d) the need for government intervention.
e) all of the above.

7. Which of the following statements illustrates the use of the *ceteris paribus* assumption?
a) "If I increase the amount of time spent reading my economics textbook and working through the study guide, my course grade in economics should improve."
b) "If the U.S. budget deficit was reduced, then interest rates would be lower."
c) "If the tax on cigarettes was increased, fewer packages of cigarettes would be sold."
d) "If my company lowers the price of its product, it should sell more, assuming that our competitors don't do likewise."
e) "Lower interest rates will lead to consumers taking out more car loans."

8. Economists:
a) often disagree over conclusions from positive economic analysis.
b) debate policy.
c) help inform individuals, businesses, and the government about tradeoffs in the choices they face.
d) attempt to quantify observations about economic relationships.
e) all of the above.

9. Suppose we were interested in studying the relationship between grade point average and hours studied. Which of the following would be important to hold constant in order to clearly understand the relationship?
a) number of classes attended.
b) grade point average.
c) hours studied.
d) phases of the moon.
e) all of the above are held constant.

10. Suppose you volunteer at a local food bank and find that for every additional 100 brochures you send out seeking financial donations, the food bank sees an increase in the donations received of $1,500. If you convince the executive director of the food bank to send out 200 more brochures this year than last year, what would you predict is the change in donations?

   a) $3,000.
   b) $750.
   c) $30.
   d) $135.
   e) cannot be determined from information given.

VI. PRACTICE EXAM: ESSAY QUESTIONS

1. Consider a society that is producing two types of goods: birdhouses and pianos. Explain what happens in a society if a decision is made to produce more birdhouses.

2. Suppose you hear a commentator on the radio cite a study that says that when Vitamin A is taken daily, people are less likely to get stomach cancer. List some factors that need to be held constant in order to be able to clearly establish the relationship.

VII. ANSWER KEY: MULTIPLE CHOICE

1. Correct answer: c.

Discussion: Economics is the science of choice. More specifically, economics is about how choices are made in the face of limited or scarce resources. Economics studies not only how a country will choose to use its resources to produce goods and services from, e.g. wheat, to clothing, to toys, to computers, but how an individual will choose to use their income to the consumption of goods and services. While statements (a), (b), (d) and (e) are topics that come up in economics, the main point is that economics is a field of study that investigates choice.

2. Correct answer: e.

Discussion: Scarcity is defined as limits or constraints on the resources we have available to produce or consume goods and services. Because of scarcity, individuals, businesses, and the government confront tradeoffs in making choices. Scarcity makes it difficult to satisfy all wants and needs. Consequently, individuals and society are faced with choices. In making choices, tradeoffs must be made. For example, a choice by a student athlete to attend college may mean that playing a professional sport is given up. Thus, statements (a) and (b) are correct.

Statements (c) and (d) are not necessarily true. Limits on resources don't necessarily prevent an economy from growing but choices about how they are used might. Also, limits on resources don't necessarily lead to inefficiencies in production. But again, choices about how they are used might.

3. Correct answer: d.

Discussion: This statement does not represent the concept of scarcity because it does not reflect any sacrifice or trade-off. That is, you have decided to commit more of your limited amount of time to both activities. Thus, you are not giving up anything. Of course, you will obviously have to cut back time on other activities, (perhaps to sleeping, studying, shopping, or whatever) but such trade-offs are not expressed in the answer.

Statements a, b, and c all represent the concept of scarcity. Statement a represents the concept of scarcity because it reflects a sacrifice or tradeoff made by your parents. Their decision to put more of their savings toward college expenses means that they will have less savings to devote to life insurance. That is, while your parents have to give up some funding of life insurance, in return, they are able to increase funding for college expenses. Statement b represents the concept of scarcity because it reflects a sacrifice or tradeoff made by legislators representing the state's interests. The sacrifice is that some timber companies will be put out of business. In return, more wildlife species will be preserved. Statement c represents the concept of scarcity because it reflects a sacrifice or tradeoff made by a business. The sacrifice is that its telephone budget will be reduced. In return, the company will be able to beef up its advertising expenses for the new board game.

Note: while there is a sacrifice, there is also something earned in return. Perhaps, another way to think of sacrifice is "trade-off" whereby something must be given up in order to obtain more of something else.

4. Correct answer: e.

Discussion: Normative economics questions deal with what 'should' or 'ought' to be. They typically deal with policy issues, be it for an individual, firm, or government. Statement c deals with whether a government should fund college scholarships with lottery money. Statement d deals with whether an individual should start saving for retirement. In contrast, positive economic questions deal with what is or will be. Statements a and b are questions about what will be.

5. Correct answer: a.

Discussion: Statement a is an example of a positive economics statement because it describes and quantifies an economic relationship between health care costs and the adoption of universal health insurance. Statements b, c, d, and e are all examples of normative economics statements since they are statements of judgment about what should be done. Normative economic statements have the ring of opinion.

6. Correct answer: d.

Discussion: The elements of the economic way of thinking are not based on the need for government intervention. In fact, in many cases, the economic way of thinking proceeds under the assumption that government intervention is unnecessary.

Statements a, b, and c are all used in the economic way of thinking.

7. Correct answer: d.

Discussion: Statement d is the most accurate because it is the only statement that qualifies the relationship between the two variables, price and amount sold. For example, without the qualifier, a company may lower its price but find that its sales do not increase. This situation may arise because the company's competitors may also lower their price making it harder for the company to sell more even though it has lowered its price. The qualifier, in effect, holds fixed other variables that may be relevant to the relationship between price and amount sold. The qualifier thus makes clearer what the expected relationship is between the two variables.

Statements a, b, and c are not as accurate as statement d because none of these answers adheres to the "*ceteris paribus*" condition of holding other variables fixed that might also be important to a relationship between two variables. Statement a would be more accurate if it was qualified with a clause like "assuming that I continue to attend class regularly and take and recopy my notes." That is, even if you spend more time reading the textbook and using the study guide, if you decide at the same time, to skip class and stop taking notes, you may not see any improvement in your grade at all. Statement b would be more accurate if it was qualified with a clause like "assuming that the central bank decides not to raise interest rates." That is, a lower budget deficit may not necessarily lead to lower interest rates if something else happens in the economy to change them. Statement c would be more accurate if it was qualified with a clause like "assuming tobacco companies do not increase their advertising and/or do not lower the price they charge for a pack of cigarettes." That is, an increased tax on cigarettes may not have the desired effect of reducing the packages of cigarettes sold if tobacco producers respond by, say, lowering the price they charge for a pack of cigarettes.

8. Correct answer: e.

Discussion: Economists often disagree over conclusions from positive economic analysis. Their disagreement over conclusions from positive economic analysis often leads to difference of opinion regarding policy. Consequently, economists debate policy. Economists also help provide information to individuals, businesses, and the government about tradeoffs in the choices they face. They help to inform them by quantifying observations about economic relationships. Thus, statements a - d are all correct.

9. Correct answer: a.

Discussion: Number of classes attended is the only variable being held constant in this example. If it were not held constant, it would be difficult to know what the contribution of increased study time was to the grade point average. For example, if at the same time, a student increased study time and increased their class attendance, the grade point average may increase because both of these factors changed. To know the effect of increased study time on grade point average, therefore, class attendance must be held constant. Statements b and c are not correct because they are the variables in the relationship being described. Statement d is not correct because the phases of the moon are not relevant to the relationship between the two variables and so it doesn't matter whether it is assumed to be held constant or not. Statement e is not correct by virtue of the fact that number of classes attended is held constant, as stated in a.

10. Correct answer: a.

Discussion: The answer relies on using marginal analysis. The information in the question reveals that the change in donations received is $1,500 for every 100 additional brochures mailed out. That is, every 1 additional brochure sent out returns $15 in donations. ($1,500 donations/100 brochures = $15 donations/1 brochure). The marginal change in donations per 1 brochure is $15. So, if the food bank mails out 200 more brochures, it can expect to raise $15 per brochure X 200 brochures = $3,000.

Statements b, c, and d are not correct based on the explanation above. Statement e is not correct because there is enough information to figure out the answer.

VIII. ANSWER KEY: ESSAY QUESTIONS

1. If the society decides it wants to produce more birdhouses, then it must give up (sacrifice) the production of some pianos. Since the resources that a society has available to help produce output are scarce (limited, fixed amount) at a point in time, the only way the society can produce more birdhouses would be to cut back piano production. By cutting back piano production, the society frees up resources from producing pianos and can then allocate those resources into birdhouse production. However, if the amount of resources available to the society were to increase, then these new resources could be devoted to producing more birdhouses without having to cut back on piano production.

2. The commentator is pointing out that a study finds a relationship between two variables – a daily dose of Vitamin A and the likelihood of getting stomach cancer. Though not stated in the relationship, there may be underlying assumptions about what other factors relevant to the relationship are assumed to be held constant. For example, the relationship may assume that individuals taking a daily dose of Vitamin A are not taking any medications. The study may assume that individuals exercise three times a week. These other factors, were they to change, could affect the reported relationship between Vitamin A and stomach cancer.

We invite you to visit the book's Companion Website at:
http://www.prenhall.com/osullivan/
for further exercises and practice quizzes.

CHAPTER 2
THE KEY PRINCIPLES OF ECONOMICS

I. OVERVIEW

In this chapter, you will learn fundamental economic principles that will be used throughout this course. You will learn that decisions made by a household, business, or government generally involve an opportunity cost; choosing one option means that other options must be given up or sacrificed or foregone. You will learn about the marginal principle. The marginal principle can be used to guide decisions. It requires that the marginal benefit be compared to the marginal cost of undertaking an activity. You will learn about the principle of voluntary exchange. The principle of voluntary exchange says that when two or more people engage in voluntary exchange with each other, they are all necessarily better off. You will learn about the principle of diminishing returns. The principle of diminishing returns means that more and more effort devoted to an activity leads to smaller and smaller increases (or improvements) in the activity. Diminishing returns arise when more and more effort is exerted but there is no change in other factors which affect the activity. Lastly, you will learn about the real-nominal principle. The real-nominal principle requires that you think in "inflation-adjusted" terms. That is, you must always consider the effects of rising prices (inflation) on your income, pay raises, and interest and dividend earnings from financial investments, as well as on your debt. A true picture of the national economy also requires that you think of its performance in inflation-adjusted terms.

II. CHECK LIST

By the end of this chapter, you should be able to do the following:

- ❏ Evaluate the opportunity cost that is encountered when choosing an activity (e.g. attending a party on Saturday night, furthering your education, opening up a new factory, building more schools, cutting tax rates).
- ❏ Use the production possibilities curve to compute the opportunity cost of producing one good or bundles of goods instead of another.
- ❏ Explain why opportunity costs increase in moving either up or down the production possibilities curve.
- ❏ Use marginal analysis to decide the level at which an activity should be undertaken.
- ❏ Explain why picking an activity level where "marginal benefit" = "marginal cost" is the best choice.
- ❏ Explain why fixed costs are not relevant for marginal analysis, i.e. why it is that fixed costs do not matter in selecting an activity level.
- ❏ Explain why voluntary exchanges (or trades) between people necessarily make them better off.
- ❏ Explain the circumstances under which diminishing returns occur and under what circumstances it does not occur.
- ❏ Use the real-nominal principle to assess how well off you are based on the income you earn, any pay raises you might get, or any interest earnings you might receive from financial investments.
- ❏ Use the real-nominal principle to get a true picture of the state of the economy.
- ❏ Explain the difference between nominal and real variables.

10   Chapter 2

III. KEY TERMS

long run: A period of time long enough that a firm can change all the factors of production, meaning that a firm can modify its existing production facility or build a new one.

marginal benefit: The extra benefit resulting from a small increase in some activity.

marginal cost: The additional cost resulting from a small increase in some activity.

marginal product of labor: The change in output from one additional worker.

nominal value: The face value of an amount of money.

opportunity cost: What you sacrifice to get something.

real value: The value of an amount of money in terms of what it can buy.

short run: A period of time over which one or more factors of production is fixed; in most cases, a period of time over which a firm cannot modify an existing facility or build a new one.

external cost: A cost borne by someone other than the people directly involved in the transaction.

external benefit: A benefit experienced by someone other than the people directly involved in the transaction.

externality: The effect of a transaction on a third party.

IV. PERFORMANCE ENHANCING TIPS (PETS)

PET #1

Throughout this course, it is wise to always consider the best foregone alternative (option that is given up) when a household, firm, or government makes a decision. An understanding of what is being given up in order to have something else may alter your opinion about the proper course of action.

For example, suppose that a political candidate is proposing that household income tax rates be cut. What opportunity costs might arise if the proposal is adopted? On the surface, you might think that a tax cut is great because your take-home pay will be higher and allow you to buy more goods and services (assuming prices don't rise, remember the real-nominal principle). However, as with most decisions, there is a cost -- something that is given up. In this case, a tax cut means that the government has less money to spend. So, the government may have to cut funding for space programs, or education, or highway repair, or police protection or whatever. These are opportunity costs of the tax cut. Which one of these government programs is the "best" foregone alternative depends on your viewpoint. If you value good schools, then the cut in education would be considered the opportunity cost associated with the tax cut. As you can see, debate over the opportunity costs of the proposal to cut taxes can lead to quite a lively discussion and may mean that not everybody agrees that a tax cut is such a good thing.

PET #2

*When you see the term "marginal," you should always think of computing the **change** in a variable. Computing the change requires that you have some numeric value before the change and some numeric value after the change. The difference between the two is the change in the variable.*

For example, suppose the revenue your company earns from selling 5,000 jewelry boxes is $100,000. Furthermore, you have forecasted that if the company sells 6,000 jewelry boxes the revenue will be $108,000. What is the addition to revenue (marginal) revenue? It is $8,000 (for 1,000 more boxes). Suppose that the cost of producing 5,000 jewelry boxes is $90,000 and you forecast that the cost of producing 6,000 boxes will be $95,000. What is the addition to cost (marginal cost) associated with producing 1,000 more jewelry boxes? It is $5,000.

Now, use the marginal principle to answer whether your company would be better off by increasing production by 1,000 boxes. Since the marginal revenue (benefit to the company) is $8,000 and the marginal cost (cost to the company) is $5,000, the marginal principle dictates that production be increased since the marginal benefit exceeds the marginal cost. That is, the company will add more to its revenue than it will incur in costs by raising production. This means that the company's profits will increase.

PET #3

*The marginal cost or marginal benefit associated with **fixed** costs or fixed benefits is zero. When costs and/or benefits are fixed, the change in the costs or benefits must, by definition, be zero. This is why fixed costs and benefits are not considered when using the marginal principle to decide the best activity level.*

For example, suppose that the fixed costs of operating a factory are the rent and interest on loans (debt) that it must pay every month. Suppose these fixed costs total $3,400 per month. Consider the other monthly costs of operating a factory, including paying employees and paying for raw materials. Suppose these costs are $6,600. If the factory decides to increase production, it must hire more employees and purchase more raw materials. Suppose these costs rise to $8,900. What about rent and interest? Do they change when the company decided to produce more? No, they are fixed costs. So, what is the *marginal* cost associated with increasing production? All you have to do is compute the change in costs -- the cost of rent and interest on loans went from $3,400 to $3,400, which is a change of zero. There is no addition to fixed costs and thus no marginal cost associated with them. The costs of employees and raw materials have increased from $6,600 to $8,900 which is an increase of $2,300. The change in costs or marginal cost associated with increasing production is $0 + $2,300 = $2,300.

PET #4

*Diminishing marginal returns means that as an activity level (such as production) is **increased**, it increases but at a **decreasing** rate. Just because the term "diminishing" is used does NOT mean that an activity level (such as production) decreases or diminishes.*

For example, which table below illustrates the principle of diminishing returns?

Table A		Table B	
# of workers	Output	# of workers	Output
1	100	1	100
2	98	2	110
3	95	3	117
4	91	4	122

The correct answer is Table B. In Table B, output is increasing as more workers are hired. However, the rate at which output is increasing is decreasing. Output increases by 10 units (110-100) from hiring one additional worker, then by 7 units (117-110), and then by 5 (122-117). In Table A, output is decreasing as more workers are hired. This is not the definition of diminishing marginal returns.

PET #5

*Compare the inflation rate to the rate of change in any nominal variable to determine whether it has increased, decreased, or remained unchanged in **real** terms.*

For example, suppose your boss gives you a raise of 15% for the coming year. You may be quite happy about this until one of your economist friends points out that inflation is expected to be 18% this year. In this case, while your nominal income will grow by 15%, your real income (inflation-adjusted) will be expected to decrease by 3% (15%-18%). Maybe you should go back to your boss and ask for a bigger raise!

For another example, suppose that you invested $1,000 in the stock market at the beginning of this year. At the end of the year, your investment is now worth $1,200. What is the percent return on your investment? In nominal terms, it is 20% = [(1,200 - 1,000)/1,000] X 100. What is the percent increase in real terms? First, you'll need the inflation rate for that year. Suppose inflation was 4%. Then, in real terms, your investment has increased in value by 16% (20% - 4%).

V. PRACTICE EXAM: MULTIPLE CHOICE QUESTIONS

1. The "bowed out" shape of the production possibilities curve (PPC) arises because:
a) as we move farther inside the PPC, an economy loses increasing amounts of both goods.
b) the opportunity cost associated with a move from a point on the PPC to a point outside the PPC increases in terms of what must be given up to get there.
c) to continue to get the same increment in the production of a particular good requires that more and more of the other good be given up.
d) since resources are scarce, producing more of one good means we must produce less of another.
e) none of the above.

2. Based on the diagram below, which statement is correct?

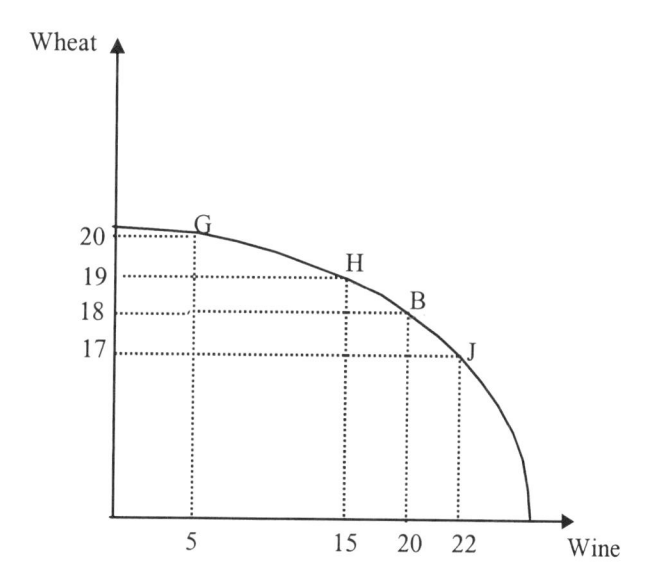

a) moving from G to H incurs an opportunity cost of 1 bushel of wheat.
b) as the economy moves along the PPC, more wheat can be obtained along with more wine.
c) the opportunity cost of moving from G to H to B increases while the opportunity cost of moving from B to H to G decreases.
d) moving from H to B incurs an opportunity cost of 5 barrels of wine.
e) moving from G to J entails no opportunity cost.

14   Chapter 2

3. Which one of the statements is true of the graph below?

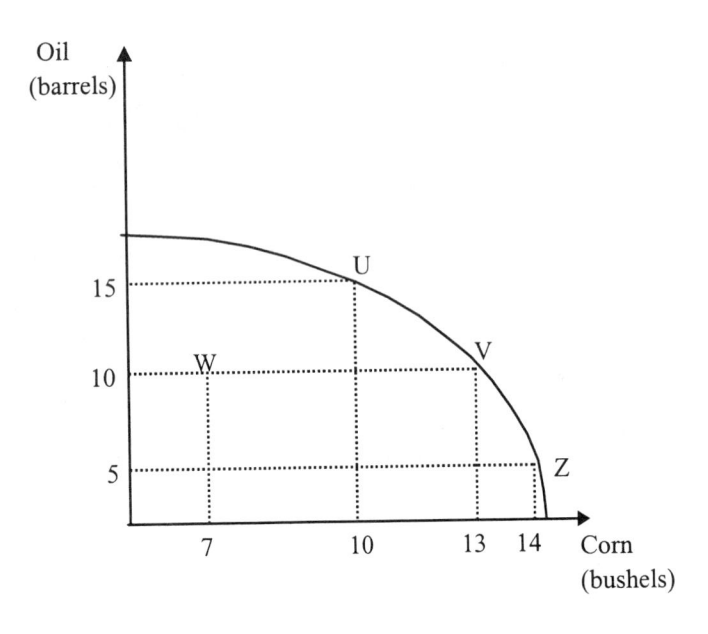

a) the opportunity cost of moving from U to V is 3 bushels of corn.
b) the opportunity cost of moving from Z to V is 5 barrels of oil.
c) the opportunity cost of moving from W to U is zero.
d) resources are not being efficiently used at point V.
e) all of the above are true.

4. You are deciding whether to stay at home and study from 3:00 p.m. - 8:00 p.m. or go to a park with friends. The park charges no admission fee. If you go to the park, which one of the following is not likely to be an opportunity cost associated with your decision?

a) your time away from studying.
b) the $1 you spent on a soda shortly after you arrived.
c) time spent eating dinner at the park.
d) cost of the gasoline used by your automobile to get to the park.
e) all of the above.

5. Which one of the following is an example of a fixed cost?
a) electricity.
b) raw materials.
c) telephone.
d) supplies.
e) rent.

6. Which one of the following would NOT be considered a factor of production (or resource) for an economy?
a) a conveyor belt.
b) a financial analyst with a B.A. degree.
c) tin.
d) a new house.
e) A computer.

7. Suppose Fred computes the marginal benefit of working one more hour as a salesclerk in an electronics store to be $7.75. However, by working one more hour, he must give up the opportunity to attend a free, one-hour workshop on how to start your own business. However, Fred believes he will learn a lot by attending the workshop. Based on this information, which one of the following statements is correct?
a) Fred should work one more hour in the electronics shop since the workshop is free.
b) Fred should not work that one more hour in the electronics shop if the implicit value of what he will learn by attending the workshop is $25.00.
c) Fred should not work that one more hour in the electronics shop if the implicit value of what he will learn by attending the workshop is $5.00.
d) Fred should work one more hour in the electronics shop if the implicit value of what he will earn by attending the workshop is $5.00.
e) (b) and (d) are correct statements.

8. Use the table below to answer the following question.

# of workers	Output
1	5
2	15
3	30
4	37
5	40
6	38

Diminishing returns occurs:
a) between the first and second worker.
b) between the second and third worker.
c) between the third and fourth worker.
d) between the fourth and fifth worker.
e) between the fifth and sixth worker.

16 Chapter 2

9. Which one of the following statements is true?

   a) diminishing returns occur when a firm can change the amount of all of the factors of production it uses.
   b) if Helena finds that the marginal benefit of eating an ice cream cone is equal to the marginal cost of eating an ice cream cone, then Helena would be better off to eat one more ice cream cone.
   c) if Jay works at a job he dislikes and is paid for his work, both he and the employer are better off.
   d) the production possibilities curve is positively sloped.
   e) none of the above statements are true.

10. Suppose that your boss just informed you that you will be receiving a raise of 8% for this coming year. Suppose further that you have heard economic forecasts that the inflation rate for this coming year will be 9%. Based on this information, you might think to yourself:

    a) "Wow, they must really like me - I'm effectively getting a 17% pay raise! I need to call home and tell mom!"
    b) "Gee, thanks for the raise but the raise isn't actually a raise at all since my real income will decline by 1%."
    c) "This isn't much of a raise but at least my real income will increase by 1%."
    d) "Well, this isn't really a raise - my real income is going to decline by 0.72%."
    e) "This isn't really a raise - my real income is going to decline by 7.2%."

11. If your salary increases from $28,000 per year to $29,400, then the percentage increase in your salary is ____%. If inflation is 6% a year, then your "real" or "purchasing power" income has changed by ____%.

    a) 5%; 11%.
    b) 14%; 8%.
    c) 5%; -1%.
    d) 50%; 45%.
    e) 5%; 1%.

12. Suppose an old high school friend calls you up and desperately pleads to borrow $1,000 from you. You've been out working for a few years and have a little bundle in savings and decide that this is a good friend who really needs your help. So, you lend them $1,000 with the promise that they pay you the $1,000 back, without interest, at the end of the year. In one year after you are paid back:

    a) In real terms, the money you will be paid back will be worth less than $1,000 if inflation was greater than 0%.
    b) In real terms, the money you will be paid back will be worth more than $1,000 if inflation was greater than 0%.
    c) In real and nominal terms, you will be paid back $1,000.
    d) In nominal terms, the money you will be paid back will be worth less than $1,000 if inflation was greater than 0%.
    e) In nominal terms, the money you will be paid back will be worth more than $1,000 if inflation was greater than 0%.

VI. PRACTICE EXAM: ESSAY QUESTIONS

1. Explain what happens when a country decides to move from one point on its production possibilities curve to another. Be sure to discuss opportunity cost and the allocation of scarce resources.

2. What advice would you give to a friend who has received two job offers both of which offer the same starting salary of $30,000 and the same benefits package? The jobs are basically the same. However, one job is located in Boston and the other job in Columbia, S.C.

VII. ANSWER KEY: MULTIPLE CHOICE QUESTIONS

1. Correct Answer: c.

Discussion: The bowed out shape of the PPC reflects increasing opportunity costs (which arise because resources are not equally-well adapted to producing one good as another). Statement c is the only one that expresses that opportunity costs are increasing, i.e. that more and more of one good must be given up in order to get back the same increment (say 1 unit) of the other good. For example, to produce 1 more motorboat may require that an economy give up producing 100 rolls of carpet; if the economy wants to produce another 1 more boat, the economy now has to give up producing 125 rolls of carpet; and if the economy wants to produce yet 1 more motorboat, the economy now has to give up producing 175 rolls of carpet.

The question asks about the bowed out shape of the PPC and so requires an answer that addresses a movement along the PPC, not to or from it. Statements a and b are incorrect because they address movements from a point not on the PPC to a point on it (or vice-versa), neither of which deals with a movement along the PPC. Statement d is incorrect because it only explains why the PPC has a negative slope, not why it has a bowed out shape. Statement e is incorrect because answer c is correct.

2. Correct answer: a.

Discussion: Opportunity cost is measured by how much is given up or sacrificed. In this case, the graph shows that in moving from G to H, the economy foregoes producing (reduces production by) 1 bushel of wheat. In return, however, the economy is able to produce 10 more barrels of wine.

Statement b is incorrect because it is not true that as the economy moves along the PPC more wheat can be obtained along with more wine. The concept of opportunity cost means that the economy can only have more wheat if it produces less wine (and vice-versa). Statement c is incorrect because increasing opportunity costs are encountered moving in both directions along the PPC. To see this, note that as the economy moves from G to H, it must give up producing 1 bushel of wheat but gets back 10 barrels of wine. As the economy moves from H to B, it must give up 1 bushel of wheat, but this time only gets back 5 barrels of wine. That is, it is more costly to produce wine because less is gotten back in return for the same 1 bushel of wheat. Thus, opportunity costs of producing more wine are increasing as the economy moves from G to H to B. If the economy moves from B to H to G, opportunity costs will also be increasing. To see this, note that as the economy moves from B to H, it must give up producing 5 barrels of wine, while it gets back 1 bushel of wheat. In moving from H to G, the economy must now give up 10 barrels of wine while still only getting back 1 bushel of wheat. This just means that producing wheat has become more costly (i.e. the opportunity cost has increased). Statement d is not correct. Opportunity cost is measured by how much is given up; in moving from H to B, the economy has gotten back (not given

18   Chapter 2

up) 5 barrels of wine. Statement e is not correct because there is an opportunity cost; the opportunity cost is 3 bushels of wheat.

3. Correct answer: c.

Discussion: Statement c is correct because at a point inside the production possibilities curve, resources are unemployed and/or not being efficiently used. This means that there are resources available to produce more of both corn and oil. That is, production in one commodity does not require sacrificing or giving up production of another commodity. Since there is no sacrifice in moving from W to U, there is no opportunity cost associated with the movement.

Statements a and b are not correct because opportunity cost is based on what is given up, not what is gained. Statement a is not correct because in moving from U to V, three bushels of corn are gained. In moving from U to V, the opportunity cost is the reduction in oil production, which in this case is five barrels of oil. Statement b is not correct because in moving from Z to V, five barrels of oil are gained. In moving from Z to V, the opportunity cost is the reduction in corn production, which in this case is one bushel of corn. Statement d is not correct because at a point on the production possibilities curve all resources are fully-employed and efficiently used. Statement e is not correct because statements a, b, and d are not true.

4. Correct answer: c.

Discussion: Statement c is correct because regardless of whether you stayed at home and studied from 3:00 p.m. - 8:00 p.m. or stayed at the park, you would have had to take time to eat dinner.

Statement a is not correct because time spent away from studying is an opportunity cost. By being at the park with friends, you give up that time for studying. Statement b is not correct because that $1 spent could have been spent on something else. Statement d is not correct because the cost of the gasoline could have been saved had you stayed home and that used money on something else. Statement e is not correct because statement c is not an example of an opportunity cost.

5. Correct answer: e.

Discussion: Rent is the only example of a cost that will not change with a firm's production level. That is, whether a firm produces 0, 1, or 1,000,000 e.g. skateboards will not change the cost of the rent the firm pays for the production facility.

Electricity, raw materials, telephone, and supplies are all examples of costs that will change with a firm's production level. The more a firm produces, the more electricity it will need to operate the factory, the more raw materials it will need to produce the product, the more telephone calls it will have to make to coordinate distribution and sales, and the more supplies (packaging, etc.) it will need in production.

6. Correct answer: d.

Discussion: A resource or factor of production is any good, service, or talent that enables a society to produce output -- other goods and services. A new house does not enable society to increase production of other goods and services.

Statements a, b, c, and e are all examples of factors of production. A conveyor belt is physical capital. It may be used by a factory in its production process. A financial analyst is both labor and human capital. The financial analyst provides physical and mental effort on the job and also brings with him or her skills acquired through formal education. Tin is a natural resource. It may be used in many different production processes -- bottling, sheeting, etc. A computer may be used in the production process of a service like banking or in manufacturing.

7. Correct answer: e.

Discussion: Statement e is correct because statements b and d are both correct. Statement b is correct because the marginal cost of not working one more hour (or of attending the workshop) is $7.75, i.e. Fred will give up $7.75 by attending the workshop. However, Fred will benefit. The marginal benefit of using that one hour to attend the workshop has a value of $25.00. In this case, the marginal benefit of attending the workshop exceeds the marginal cost of attending the workshop so Fred would be better off by attending the workshop. Statement d is also correct but for the reverse reasons. In this case, if Fred assesses the marginal benefit of the one hour of attending the workshop at $5.00, the marginal benefit exceeds the marginal cost of attending the workshop ($7.75 loss in wages from not working that one hour). Here, Fred would be better off working and not attending the workshop.

Statement a is not correct. Even though the workshop is free, it does not mean that there is no benefit to attending it. Thus, it is not correct to compare the marginal cost of attending the workshop of $7.75 to a zero benefit. Statement c is not correct. If the marginal benefit of attending the one-hour workshop is $5.00 and the marginal cost of attending it is $7.75 (loss in wages from not working that one hour), then Fred would be better off working that one hour. Here, the marginal benefit of attending the workshop is less than the marginal cost of attending the workshop. So, the workshop should not be attended. Statements b and d are both correct; however, option e allows you to pick both statements so that it is the correct answer.

8. Correct answer: c.

Discussion: Diminishing returns occurs when the addition of one more input (a worker in this example) adds less to output than the previous worker. Between the third and fourth worker, output increases by 7 units but had previously increased by 15 units (from 15 to 30). Thus, diminishing returns has set in.

Statement a is incorrect. Output has increased by 10 units from hiring one more worker but diminishing returns cannot yet be inferred until you are able to make one more comparison. Statement b is incorrect because, in this case, output has increased by 15 units from hiring one more worker (2 to 3 workers) and had previously increased by 10 units. This is an example of output increasing at an increasing rate, not a decreasing rate as is true of diminishing returns. (See PET #4). Statement d is not correct because the point at which diminishing returns has set in is where the rate of increase in output slows down; this happens between the third and fourth worker, not the fourth and fifth worker. While statement d does show that the addition to output is decreasing (it had been 7 units from the previous worker and is now 3), it is not the point at which diminishing returns has set in. Statement e is not correct because output actually *decreases* by hiring one more worker. That is, output goes from 40 units to 38 units (-2) by hiring one more worker. This is not an example of diminishing returns (see PET #4).

9. Correct answer: c.

Discussion: Statements a, b, d, and e are not true.

20   Chapter 2

Statement c is correct even though Jay dislikes the job he has. The example illustrates the principle of voluntary exchange. Jay voluntarily works at a job he dislikes, and the employer pays Jay for the work he performs for the company. Both Jay and the employer must be better off since both are engaged in trading with each other. Jay trades his time to the employer for pay (money) and the employer in turn trades money for Jay's time.

Statement a is incorrect because diminishing returns occurs because a firm CANNOT change the amount of all of the factors of production it uses. Statement b is incorrect because if Helena found the marginal benefit to eating an ice cream cone just equal to the marginal cost, then she is as well-off (or happy) as she can be. She should neither eat one more ice cream cone nor one fewer. She is eating just the right amount. Statement d is incorrect because the production possibilities curve is negatively sloped. Statement e cannot be true since statement c is true.

10. Correct answer: b.

Discussion: Since your nominal income is going to grow by 8% but prices are expected to go up by 9%, then in real terms, your income will decline by 1% (8% - 9%). (See PET #5).

Statement a is not correct. This statement assumes that you have added the two numbers. It is not correct to add the growth rate of your nominal income and the inflation rate to determine the effect on your real income. Statement c is not correct. This statement assumes that you should take the inflation rate and subtract the growth rate of the nominal variable. This is not correct; it is the other way around. Statements d and e are not correct. These statements assume that you have multiplied the numbers which is not the correct method for computing the real value of a variable.

11. Correct answer: d.

Discussion: You can calculate the percentage change in your nominal income by using the formula to calculate percentage change found in the Appendix to Chapter 1. The percentage change in your salary is calculated as [($29,400 - $28,000)/$28,000] X 100 = +5%. However, since inflation has increased by 6%, then the real or purchasing power value of your salary increase is 5% - 6% = -1%. Since the inflation rate has outpaced your salary increase, your real income has actually declined by 1%. Based on these calculations, none of the other options are correct. Do remember, however, that you must subtract the inflation rate from the increase in the nominal value to obtain the percentage change in the real value.

12. Correct answer: a.

Discussion: If you have agreed to be paid back $1,000 without interest and inflation is greater than 0%, then in real terms, your $1,000 will be worth less than $1,000. In other words, your $1,000 will not be able to buy as much as it had the year before if inflation was greater than 0%. You should note that in nominal terms, you are still getting back $1,000 but in real terms, you are getting back less than $1,000.

Statement b is incorrect. If inflation is greater than 0%, then the $1,000 you are paid back will not be able to buy as much as the year before. Thus, in real terms, the money you will be paid back is less than $1,000. Statement c is not correct. In nominal terms, you will be receiving $1,000. However, in real terms, you may be getting back more or less than $1,000 depending on whether prices have fallen (deflation) or risen (inflation). Statement d is not correct because in nominal terms, you will be getting back $1,000. Statement e is not correct because again, you will be getting back $1,000 in nominal terms. Inflation affects how much you earn in real terms, not nominal terms.

VIII. ANSWER KEY: ESSAY QUESTIONS

1. When a country moves from one point on its production possibilities curve to another, it has made a decision to produce fewer units of one good (e.g. apparel) and more of another (e.g. electronics). The country faces an opportunity cost -- the opportunity cost is that the country must cut back on production of apparel goods if it wants to produce more electronics. This is because resources are scarce. In order to produce more electronics, more resources -- land, labor, capital -- will have to be devoted to the electronics industry which means that there will be fewer resources available to produce apparel goods. That is, there will be a re-allocation of resources from the apparel industry to the electronics industry. With fewer resources available to the apparel industry, apparel production will contract; the opposite will happen in the electronics industry. While the movement along the production possibilities curve assumes that resources remain fully-employed (and efficiently used), there may be an adjustment phase (setting up new factory floors, training apparel workers to work in the electronics industry) during which some resources may become idle.

2. The advice I would give to my friend would be to consider the cost of living in Boston compared to that in Columbia, S.C. That is, I would have them consider the price of food, rent, clothing, etc. in the one city compared to the other in determining which job offer provides the higher "real" salary. Since Boston is known to be a very expensive city and Columbia is in the Southeast, where the cost of living is typically lower than in the Northeast, I would suggest to my friend that in real terms, the salary offer from the company in Columbia is better than the other offer. I would suggest to my friend that if they really want her to live in Boston, she tell the company that they will have to offer a higher nominal salary to entice her to work for them.

We invite you to visit the book's Companion Website at:
http://www.prenhall.com/osullivan/
for further exercises and practice quizzes.

CHAPTER 3
EXCHANGE AND MARKETS

I. OVERVIEW

In this chapter, you will learn what markets are. You will learn that markets exist because people find it easier and mutually beneficial to specialize in producing certain types of goods, and to exchange what they have produced with what others have produced, than to produce for all of their own needs. You will learn that specialization and exchange arise because of differences in the productivity. You will learn that specialization and exchange can increase the set and amount of goods and services that each participating party may ultimately acquire. You will learn about comparative advantage which is an application of the principle of opportunity cost. You will learn that comparative advantage can be used to determine which goods should be produced by whom and which should be exchanged. You will learn that international trade may also be based on comparative advantage and that it too, can be mutually beneficial. You will also learn about the differences between a market-based economy and a centrally-planned economy and about the role of the government in a market economy. Along the way, you will learn about the virtues and shortcomings of markets.

II. CHECK LIST

By the end of this chapter, you should be able to do the following:

- ❑ Explain why specialization and exchange can benefit all participating parties.
- ❑ Determine comparative advantage by comparing opportunity costs of production.
- ❑ Discuss the principle of voluntary exchange and what it means.
- ❑ Draw consumption and production possibilities curves and illustrate the gains from exchange.
- ❑ Explain why specialization increases the productivity of workers.
- ❑ Explain how comparative advantage can be used to understand international trade.
- ❑ Explain why governments might intervene in international trade.
- ❑ Describe some features of a market economy that makes them function better.
- ❑ Compare and contrast a centrally-planned economy to a market economy.
- ❑ Describe the virtues and shortcomings of a market economy.
- ❑ Explain the role of prices in a market economy.
- ❑ Explain the role of entrepreneurs in a market economy.
- ❑ Discuss the role of government in a market economy.
- ❑ Explain how a government may reduce uncertainty in a market economy.

III. KEY TERMS

Comparative advantage: The ability of one person or nation to produce a good at a lower opportunity cost than another person or nation.

Absolute advantage: The ability of one person or nation to produce a good at a lower absolute cost than another person or nation.

Centrally planned economy: An economy in which a government bureaucracy decides how much of each good to produce, how to produce the goods, and who gets them.

IV. PERFORMANCE ENHANCING TIPS (PETS)

PET #1

Opportunity cost calculations used to determine comparative advantage should be based on a per unit comparison.

Suppose you are given the following information:

	Country A	Country B
Wood Products	10/hour	8/hour
High-tech products	15/hour	4/hour

The information in the table tells you that Country A can produce 10 units of wood products in one hour (with its resources) and 15 units of high-tech products in one hour. Country B can produce 8 units of wood products in one hour (with its resources) and 4 units of high-tech products in one hour. How can this information be used to determine which country has a comparative advantage in wood production and which country has a comparative advantage in high-tech production?

As a side point, you may wish to note that Country A has an absolute advantage in the production of both wood and high-tech products since it can produce more per hour of either good than can Country B. But, absolute advantage does NOT determine the basis for trade.

The easiest way to compute comparative advantage is to determine what the opportunity cost of production is for each good for each country, on a per unit basis. To do this, you must first answer how much Country A must give up if it were to specialize in the production of wood. For every additional hour of effort devoted to producing wood products, Country A would give up the production of 15 units of high-tech products. (Of course, it is then able to produce 10 more units of wood products). On a per unit basis, Country A must give up 1.5 units of high-tech products for each 1 unit of wood products = (15 high-tech products/hour)/ (10 wood products/hour) = 1.5 high tech products/1 wood product. You would read this as "for Country A, the opportunity cost of 1 wood product is 1.5 high-tech products." For Country B, for every additional hour of effort devoted to producing wood products, it must give up 4 units of high tech products. (Of course, it is then able to produce 8 more units of wood products). On a per unit basis, Country B must give up 0.5 units of high-tech products for each 1 unit of wood products = (4 high-tech products/hour)/ (8 wood products/hour). You would read this as "for Country B, the opportunity cost of 1 wood product is 0.5 high-tech products." Thus, Country B has the lower opportunity cost of producing wood products since it has to give up fewer high-tech products.

Since Country B has the lower opportunity cost of wood production, it should specialize in wood production. (Wood production is "less costly" in Country B than in Country A). If this is true, then it must also be true that Country A has the lower opportunity cost of high-tech production and thus should specialize in producing high-tech goods.

Let's see if this is true using the numbers from the table above. For Country A, the opportunity cost of producing more high-tech products is that for every additional hour of producing high-tech products, it must give up producing 10 units of wood products. (Of course, it is then able to produce 15 more units of high-tech products). On a per unit basis, Country A must give up 0.67 wood products for every 1 high-tech product = (10 wood products/hour)/ (15 high-tech products per hour). You would read this as "for Country A, the opportunity cost of 1 high-tech product is 0.67 wood products." For Country B, the opportunity cost of producing more high-tech products is that for every additional hour of producing high-tech products, it must give up producing 8 units of wood products. (Of course, it is then able to produce 4 more units of high-tech products). On a per unit basis, Country B must give up 2 wood products for every one unit of high-tech products = (8 wood products/hour)/ (4 high-tech products/hour). Thus, Country A has the lower opportunity cost of producing high-tech products since it has to give up fewer wood products. (High-tech production is "less costly" in Country A than in Country B).

PET #2

The endpoints of a production possibilities curve illustrate how much of one good could be produced if all time (and resources) were devoted to the production of that good, and none to the other good. The line connecting the points illustrates the possible combinations that could be produced if some time (and resources) were devoted to the production of one good and some to the other. The slope illustrates the trade-off in production between the two goods.

Suppose over the course of one week, Jan can bake 50 loaves of bread or she can make 200 cups of coffee. That is, if Jan devotes all of her time to bread production, she can bake 50 loaves of bread and zero cups of coffee. If, instead, she devotes all of her time to coffee production, she can make 200 cups of coffee and zero loaves of bread.

A (linear or straight-line) graph illustrating Jan's production possibilities would therefore look like:

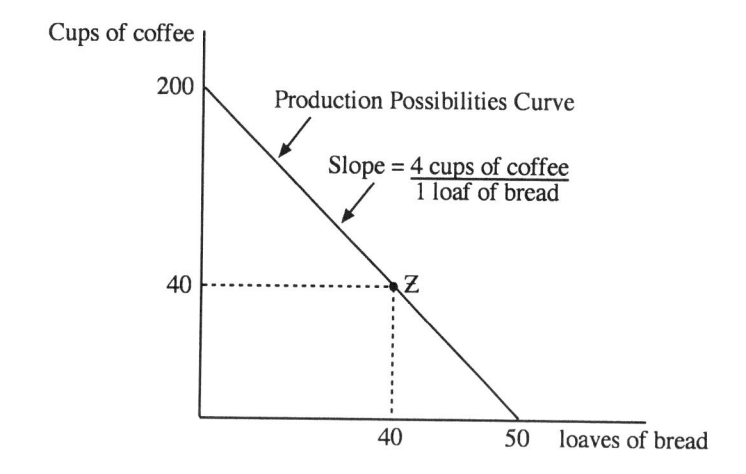

```
Cups of coffee
  |
200|\
   | \      Production Possibilities Curve
   |  \    /
   |   \  Slope = 4 cups of coffee
   |    \         1 loaf of bread
   |     \  /
 40|------ Z
   |     : \
   |     :  \
   |_____:_____
        40   50   loaves of bread
```

The slope of the line shows how many more cups of coffee Jan could produce if she cut back production of bread by one loaf. In this case, the slope is 4 cups of coffee/1 loaf of bread (200/50) which shows that for every four more cups of coffee Jan wants to produce, she must give up producing one loaf of bread. Alternatively, we could say that Jan will be able to produce one more loaf of bread for every four cups of coffee she is willing to cut back the production of.

All points between the endpoints illustrate combinations of the two goods that Jan could produce in a given day. For example, suppose Jan cuts back bread production by 10 loaves, from fifty to forty, she would now have the time to produce 40 cups of coffee (based on the trade-off) instead of zero. Thus, one combination of goods Jan could produce is 40 loaves of bread and 40 cups of coffee. This is illustrated as point Z on the production possibilities curve.

PET #3

The consumption possibilities curve will have an endpoint based on the good the individual is more capable of producing (more productive at) and will be above the production possibilities curve. The slope of the consumption possibilities curve will depend on the rate of exchange in goods between one individual and another.

Let's continue with the example from PET #2. Suppose another individual, Alex, can produce 25 loaves of bread in one day and 500 cups of coffee in one day. A calculation of comparative advantage shows that Jan is more productive in baking bread (since the opportunity cost to her is four cups of coffee per loaf of bread) and that Alex is more productive in making cups of coffee (since the opportunity cost to him of making one *loaf of bread* is twenty cups of coffee). Based on comparative advantage, Jan will specialize in making bread (and thus no coffee) and Alex will specialize in making coffee (and thus no bread). So, Jan will produce 50 loaves of bread per day and Alex will produce 500 cups of coffee per day. Let's say Jan is willing to trade 10 loaves of bread with Alex. This time, instead of getting back 40 cups of coffee (as in PET #2 where Jan does not exchange), Alex may be willing to give Jan, e.g. 100 cups of coffee. Thus, another point on Jan's consumption possibilities curve is point G which is a combination of goods better than had she not exchanged with Alex. So, Jan's consumption possibilities curve is above her production possibilities curve (except at the end point).

26 Chapter 3

The graph below illustrates the consumption possibilities curve for Jan based on Alex' willingness to trade 100 cups of coffee for 1 loaf of bread.

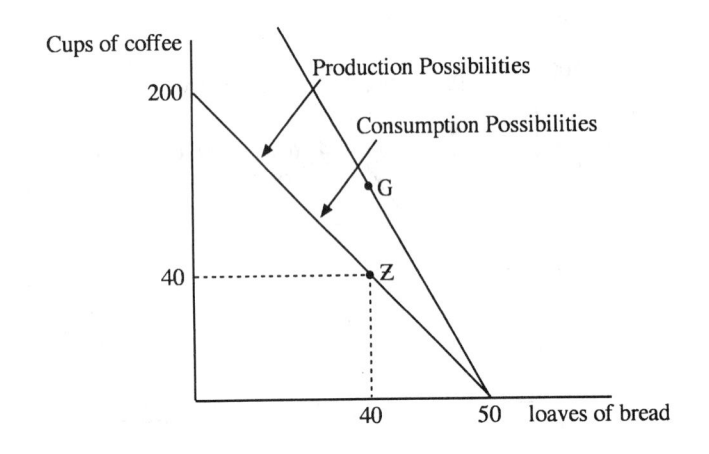

V. PRACTICE EXAM: MULTIPLE CHOICE QUESTIONS

1. Use the information below to determine which answer is correct.

	Lena	J. Martin
Brownies produced per week	4	5
Pictures painted per week	2	10

a) the opportunity cost of one picture for Lena is 1/2 brownies.
b) the opportunity cost of one picture for J. Martin is 2 brownies.
c) Lena has a comparative advantage in brownies production.
d) Lena's opportunity cost of brownies is greater than J. Martin's.
e) (c) and (d).

2. Using the information from question (1), which one of the following statements is correct?
a) Lena will specialize in brownies.
b) J. Martin will specialize in brownies.
c) Lena will specialize in painting pictures.
d) J. Martin will specialize in painting pictures.
e) (a) and (d).

3. Use the table below to answer the following question.

	Country A	Country B
Toys	50 per day	20 per day
Ships	2 per day	1 per day

Which country has the comparative advantage in producing toys and which country has the comparative advantage in producing ships?

a) Country A has the comparative advantage in producing both toys and ships.
b) Country B has the comparative advantage in producing both toys and ships.
c) Country A has the comparative advantage in producing toys and Country B has the comparative advantage in producing ships.
d) Country B has the comparative advantage in producing toys and Country A has the comparative advantage in producing ships.
e) need information on exchange rates to answer the question.

4. Using the information below to complete the following question. Country A's production possibilities curve is represented by graph ___ and Country B's production possibilities curve is represented by graph ___.

	Country A	Country B
Autos	400 per day	500 per day
Airplanes	10 per day	5 per day

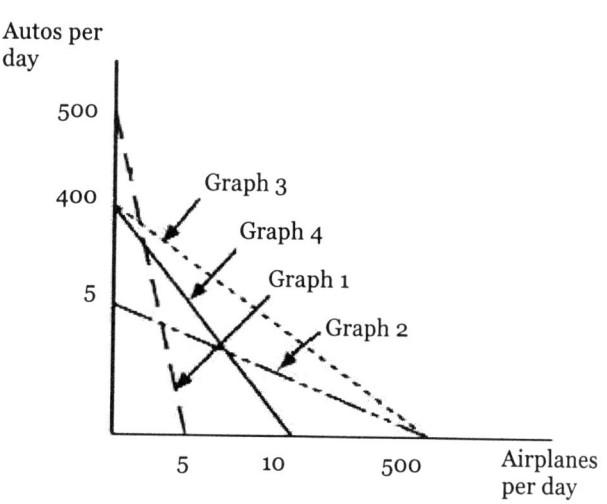

a) Graph 4; Graph 1.
b) Graph 2; Graph 1.
c) Graph 3; Graph 4.
d) Graph 4; Graph 3.
e) Graph 1; Graph 4.

28 Chapter 3

5. Which one of the following statements is true?
a) an individual can have an absolute advantage in the production of both goods yet still be made better off by exchanging with an individual who does not have an absolute advantage in either.
b) the consumption possibilities curve will be above the production possibilities curve in the case where exchange makes individuals better off.
c) specialization and exchange result from differences in productivity.
d) Adam Smith claimed that specialization would increase productivity through the division of labor.
e) all of the above.

6. Which one of the following statements is NOT true?
a) repetition leads to increases in productivity.
b) specialization leads to time-savings which enhances the productivity of a worker.
c) specialization can foster innovation.
d) insurance makes starting up new ventures by entrepreneurs less likely.
e) contracts make markets work better.

7. Which one of the following characterizes a market economy?
a) people make decisions regarding production and consumption.
b) competition keeps prices lower than would otherwise be.
c) decisions regarding production and consumption are guided by prices in the market.
d) people act in their own interest.
e) all of the above.

8. In a centrally-planned economy:
a) entrepreneurs enter markets where they observe profits being earned.
b) an increase in the price of a good indicates that it is now more scarce.
c) the planning authority (government) decides what production techniques will be used.
d) the 'invisible hand' is at work.
e) losses in an industry will cause firms to exit from it.

9. A government's role in a market economy is to:
a) help overcome market failures.
b) establish rules (laws) of exchange.
c) enforce and protect property rights.
d) reduce economic uncertainty.
e) all of the above.

10. An example of rules of exchange is:
a) enforcement of laws.
b) product liability laws.
c) ads warning about potentially dangerous products.
d) patent laws.
e) all of the above.

VI. PRACTICE EXAM: ESSAY QUESTIONS

1. Use the information below to explain how international trade between Lithuania and Italy may alter the consumption possibilities of the Lithuania compared to when it is 'self-sufficient.' Discuss what might happen on the production side when international trade arises. What might the government do?

	Ore	Wine
Lithuania	2 tons/day	50 bottles/day
Italy	4 tons/day	60 bottles/day

2. Discuss how a market economy works, the importance of rules of exchange and the potential effects of economic uncertainty and how they can be overcome.

VII. ANSWER KEY: MULTIPLE CHOICE QUESTIONS

1. Correct answer: c.

Discussion: For Lena, the opportunity cost of producing one picture is the two brownies that must be given up (4 brownies/2 pictures) = (2 brownies/1 picture). For J. Martin, the opportunity cost of producing one picture is 1/2 brownie (5 brownies/10 pictures) = (1/2 brownie/1 picture). Since Lena must give up more brownies to produce one picture, the opportunity cost of producing pictures is higher for Lena than it is for J. Martin. This also means that for Lena, the opportunity cost of producing one brownie must be lower than it is for J. Martin. To see this, invert the ratios above. From this you'll see that so that for Lena, the opportunity cost of one brownie is 1/2 picture and for J. Martin, the opportunity cost of one brownie is two pictures. Since the opportunity cost of brownie production is lower for Lena than for J. Martin, Lena has a comparative advantage in brownie production. Statements a and b are wrong since these statements have the numbers reversed for Lena and J. Martin. Statement d is wrong since Lena's opportunity cost of pictures, not brownies, is greater than J. Martin's.

2. Correct answer: e.

Discussion: Since Lena has a comparative advantage in making brownies (see answer 1, above) and J. Martin has a comparative advantage in painting pictures, Lena will specialize in baking brownies and J. Martin in painting pictures. None of the other statements are correct.

30   Chapter 3

3. Correct answer: c.

Discussion: Country A must give up 50 toys to produce 2 ships. On a per unit basis, Country A must give up 25 toys to produce 1 ship. On the other hand, Country B must give up 20 toys to produce 1 ship. Since Country B has to give up fewer toys to produce 1 ship, Country B incurs a smaller opportunity cost of building one more ship. That is, it is less costly to produce a ship in Country B than in country A. So, Country B should produce ships, which means Country A should produce toys. The two countries will be able to acquire more of both goods by trading or exchanging toys for ships and vice-versa.

Statement a is not correct. It would be correct if the question had been "which country has an absolute advantage in toy production and which in ship production?" The table shows that Country A can produce more toys and more ships per day than can Country B. However, this is not the concept of comparative advantage. Statement b is not correct for similar reasons just mentioned. Statement d is not correct because it is the other way around -- Country A has a comparative advantage in toy production and Country B in ship building. Statement e is not correct because comparative advantage can be computed using the table of numbers given.

4. Correct answer: a.

Discussion: Graph 4 represents Country A's production possibilities since it illustrates that Country A can produce 400 autos per day if it produces no airplanes and 10 airplanes per day if it produces no autos. Graph 1 represents Country B's production possibilities since it illustrates that Country B can produce 500 autos per day if it produces no airplanes and 5 airplanes per day if it produces no autos.

5. Correct answer: e.

Discussion: All of the statements are true. It is especially important that you remember that statement a is true since many students tend to think that absolute advantage is the basis for deciding who produces what good.

6. Correct answer: d.

Discussion: Statement d is not true. Insurance helps to reduce the uncertainty associated with new business ventures and therefore makes it more likely that an entrepreneur may be willing to start up a venture.

7. Correct answer: e.

Discussion: A market economy functions largely through the actions of self-interested (rational) consumers and producers with prices providing information as to relative value of goods and services. In a market economy, the government plays much less of a role in determining what gets produced, how it gets produced, and who gets to buy it, and at what price. A market economy is also characterized by competition between businesses and one of the benefits of competition is that it helps keep prices down. A market economy is the opposite of a centrally-planned economy.

8. Correct answer: c.

Discussion: A centrally-planned economy requires a planning authority to make decisions regarding not only what production techniques to use (as answer c indicates), but what goods are produced and at what price they will be sold.

Statement a characterizes a market economy since entrepreneurs play a key role in determining what gets produced and how. In a market economy, entrepreneurs are motivated to produce by the opportunity to profit from their ventures. Statement b also characterizes a market economy where prices provide information about the relativity scarcity of a good. An increase in the price of a good provides information that it is in greater demand and/or lesser supply. Statement d offers a term introduced by Adam Smith that explains how a market economy works. There is no central planning authority but the outcomes are as if there is an 'invisible hand' guiding the outcomes. Statement e is also characteristic of a market economy. While profits motivate entry into an industry, losses can also cause entrepreneurs to exit the industry, as well.

9. Correct answer: e.

Discussion: Statements a – d are all true of a government's role in a market economy.

10. Correct answer: e.

Discussion: Statements a – d all provide examples of rules of exchange. Rules of exchange ensure that both parties to a transaction (buyers and sellers) are treated 'fairly' and are protected from abuses by the other. In a sense, rules of exchange can provide a basis for trust between parties engaged in exchange.

VIII. ANSWER KEY: ESSAY QUESTIONS

1. The information in the table reveals that the opportunity cost to Lithuania for 1 ton of ore per day is 25 bottles of wine per day. That is, Lithuania must give up producing 25 bottles of wine in order to produce 1 ton of ore. By contrast, the opportunity cost to Italy for 1 ton of ore per day is 15 bottles of wine. If Italy gives up producing 15 bottles of wine per day, she will be able to produce 1 ton of ore. The opportunity cost calculations show that it is less 'costly' for Italy to produce ore. This necessarily means that it is less costly for Lithuania to produce wine. Let's see if the numbers confirm this. For Lithuania to produce one bottle of wine, it must give up producing 1/25th ton of ore. For Italy, the opportunity cost of producing one bottle of wine is 1/15th ton of ore. Since 1/25th is less than 1/15th, the opportunity cost of producing wine in Lithuania is less than it is in Italy.

The production possibilities curve below illustrates the situation for Lithuania prior to engaging in exchange. Any point on the curve is also a consumption possibilities for Lithuania were she not to engage in trade.

32   Chapter 3

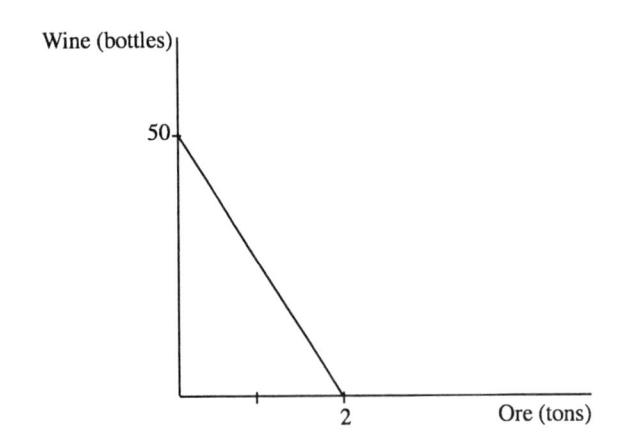

```
Wine (bottles)

50 |\
   | \
   |  \
   |   \
   |    \
   |_____
         2      Ore (tons)
```

However, based on Lithuania's comparative advantage in wine production, Lithuania could devote all of its resources to producing wine (and Italy to ore). That is, Lithuania could specialize in wine production and Italy in ore production. Then, Lithuania and Italy could trade or 'exchange' with each other. Lithuania could exchange some bottles of wine for ore. The consumption possibilities for Lithuania will now be greater than were she to remain self-sufficient.

When Lithuania begins to trade with Italy, resources that were used in ore production will become idle. For example, workers that were producing ore in Lithuania may lose their jobs until they can be trained to work in the wine-making industry. The government may pay for programs that promote re-training of the workers. Alternatively, the government may restrict trade with Italy so that workers in the ore industry are 'protected' from job losses.

2. A market economy works when consumers and producers conduct transactions with each other to satisfy their mutual interests and there is little government involvement in the decisions regarding consumption and production. In a market economy, prices and relatedly, profits, provide information as to the relative scarcity of goods. In a market economy, an increase in the price of a good reflects that it is in greater demand or lesser supply. That is, it is relatively more scarce. The increase in the price of a good leads to higher profits. Higher profits prompt entrepreneurs to enter the industry. Their entry increases the availability of the good and thus relieves its relative scarcity. The opposite happens when prices decrease.

In a market economy, producers and consumers interact with each other within the rules of exchange. These rules include things like no stealing, paying for what you purchased, producing a good that is free of defects, being able to keep what you purchased, etc. These rules of exchange provide a basis for trust between consumers and producers and thereby increase the willingness to exchange. Exchange benefits all parties. To see why this is so, imagine a world with no Food and Drug Administration. That is, there is no agency to oversee the sale of anything from drugs to meat products. In this world, consider a consumer who does not trust the quality of meat sold at the local grocery store. Such a consumer may then forego purchasing any meat products even if he desired them. If there are rules and regulations that mandate the meat products pass a quality standard, then the rules and regulations can provide a basis for trust between the consumer and the grocery store. Thus, the consumer may now be willing to purchase meat products and satisfy his desire for a nice, juicy steak! So, rules of exchange benefit the consumer. They benefit the producer as well. With trust, more consumers enter the market, willing to purchase meat at the grocery store. The producer (grocery store) sees its revenue and profits rise. Thus, the grocery store benefits, too. The example illustrates how important rules of exchange can be in a market economy. Rules of exchange, thus, can help enhance trust and reduce uncertainty regarding product quality. There are other types of uncertainty that can impede transactions in a market economy. For entrepreneurs, uncertainty regarding the financial outcome of business ventures may cause them to be less willing to start up new ones. If the government can provide a safety net (perhaps through tax breaks, protection under bankruptcy proceedings, etc), more new businesses may be started up since entrepreneurs may view it as less risky to do so. Your book discusses several other safety net programs that reduce uncertainty in the face of natural disasters, accidents, or unforeseen hardship.

We invite you to visit the book's Companion Website at:
http://www.prenhall.com/osullivan/
for further exercises and practice quizzes.

CHAPTER 4
SUPPLY, DEMAND, AND MARKET EQUILIBRIUM

I. OVERVIEW

In this chapter, you will learn about two basic economic constructs: demand and supply. These two constructs can be used to answer questions like: what might happen to housing prices in a subdivision if a new mall is built near the subdivision? What might happen to the price of a share of a health services company when the government revamps the health care system? What might happen to the price of bread when former Soviet-block countries begin to trade with the U.S? What might happen to the price of tea when the price of coffee rises? Not only can demand and supply be used to guide your thinking about what will happen to prices, it can also be used to guide your thinking about whether more or less will be bought and sold. In this chapter, you will learn how to use graphs of demand and supply to determine what happens to a market price and the quantity bought and sold. Thus, in this chapter it is imperative that you familiarize yourself with shifts of a curve versus movements along a curve (see Chapter 1 of Practicum).

II. CHECKLIST

By the end of this chapter, you should be able to do the following:

- Explain the Law of Demand and the Law of Supply (for both price increases and price decreases).
- Understand what will cause a movement along a demand or supply curve and what will cause the curves to shift.
- Explain what happens to equilibrium price and equilibrium quantity when:
- demand increases (shifts right)
- demand decreases (shifts left)
- supply increases (shifts right)
- supply decreases (shifts left)
- List factors that will cause demand to shift (and in which direction).
- List factors that will cause supply to shift (and in which direction).
- Explain what happens to price, quantity demanded and quantity supplied when there is an excess demand and use a graph in your explanation.
- Explain what happens to price, quantity demanded and quantity supplied when there is an excess supply and use a graph in your explanation.
- Define a normal and inferior good and represent their response, using a demand curve, to an increase in income and to a decrease in income.

- ❏ Explain whether or not you can determine for certain what happens to equilibrium price and equilibrium quantity when demand and/or supply both shift.
- ❏ Infer whether demand or supply shifted and in which direction by having information on the direction in which the equilibrium price and quantity moved.

III. KEY TERMS

perfectly competitive market: A market with a very large number of firms, each of which produces the same standardized product in amounts so small that no individual firm can affect the market price.

demand schedule: A table of numbers that shows the relationship between price and quantity demanded by a consumer, ceteris paribus (everything else held fixed).

individual demand curve: A curve that shows the relationship between price and quantity demanded by an individual consumer, ceteris paribus (everything else held fixed).

quantity demanded: The amount of a good an individual consumer or consumers as a group are willing to buy

law of demand: The higher the price, the smaller the quantity demanded, ceteris paribus (everything else held fixed).

change in quantity demanded: A change in the amount of a good demanded resulting from a change in the price of the good; represented graphically by movement along the demand curve.

substitution effect: The change in consumption resulting from a change in the price of one good relative to the price of another good.

income effect: The change in consumption resulting from a change in the consumer's real income.

market demand curve: A curve showing the relationship between price and quantity demanded by all consumers together, ceteris paribus (everything else held fixed).

supply schedule: A table of numbers that shows the relationship between price and quantity supplied, ceteris paribus (everything else held fixed).

quantity supplied: The amount of a good an individual firm or firms as a group are willing to sell.

change in quantity supplied: A change in the quantity supplied resulting from a change in the price of the good; represented graphically by movement along the supply curve.

market supply curve: A curve showing the relationship between price and quantity supplied by all producers together, ceteris paribus (everything else held fixed).

market equilibrium: A situation in which the quantity of a product demanded equals the quantity supplied, so there is no pressure to change the price.

excess demand: A situation in which, at the prevailing price, consumers are willing to buy more than producers are willing to sell.

excess supply: A situation in which, at the prevailing price, producers are willing to sell more than consumers are willing to buy.

change in demand: A change in the amount of a good demanded resulting from a change in something other than the price of the good; represented graphically by a shift of the demand curve.

normal good: A good for which an increase in income increases demand.

substitutes: Two goods that are related in such a way that an increase in the price of one good increases the demand for the other good.

complements: Two goods that are related in such a way that an increase in the price of one good decreases the demand for the other good.

inferior good: A good for which an increase in income decreases demand.

change in supply: A change in the amount of a good supplied resulting from a change in something other than the price of the good; represented graphically by a shift of the supply curve.

IV. PERFORMANCE ENHANCING TIPS (PETS)

PET #1

Since price is a variable on the axis of a graph of the demand and supply of a particular good, a change in the price will NOT cause the demand or supply curve for that good to shift but will instead be represented by a movement along the demand and supply curves.

PET #2

When the price of good X rises (falls), the quantity demanded falls (rises). Do NOT say that the demand falls (rises) since this means the whole curve shifts left (right).

For example, suppose you read on the exam a statement that says, "What happens in the market for peanut butter when the price of peanut butter falls?" One of the test options might be "the demand for peanut butter increases." This is not the correct answer. A statement like "the demand for peanut butter increases" would be represented by shifting the whole demand curve out to the right. However, since the price of peanut butter has fallen and is a variable on the axis for which the demand and supply of peanut butter are drawn, the decline in the price of peanut butter will be represented by moving along the demand curve. As the price of peanut butter falls, the quantity of peanut butter demanded increases. This would be the correct answer.

PET #3

When the price of good X rises (falls), the quantity supplied rises (falls). Do NOT say that the supply rises (falls) since this means the whole supply curve shifts right (left).

For example, suppose you read on the exam a statement that says, "What happens in the market for jelly when the price of jelly falls?" One of the test options might be "the supply of jelly decreases." This is not the correct answer. A statement like "the supply of jelly decreases" would be represented by shifting the whole supply curve to the left. However, since the price of jelly has fallen and is a variable on the axis for which the demand and supply of jelly are drawn, the decline in the price of jelly will be represented by moving along the supply curve. As the price of jelly falls, the quantity of jelly supplied decreases. This would be the correct answer.

PET #4

A rightward shift in the demand curve can be expressed in the following ways:

a. at every price, the quantity demanded that buyers want is now higher.
b. at every quantity demanded, the price buyers would be willing to pay is now higher.

To see this, look at the two graphs below. Demand curve a corresponds to statement a because at every price, the quantity demand is now higher. Demand curve b corresponds to statement b because at every quantity demanded, the price buyers would be willing to pay is now higher. In both cases, the demand curve is further to the right after the shift than before.

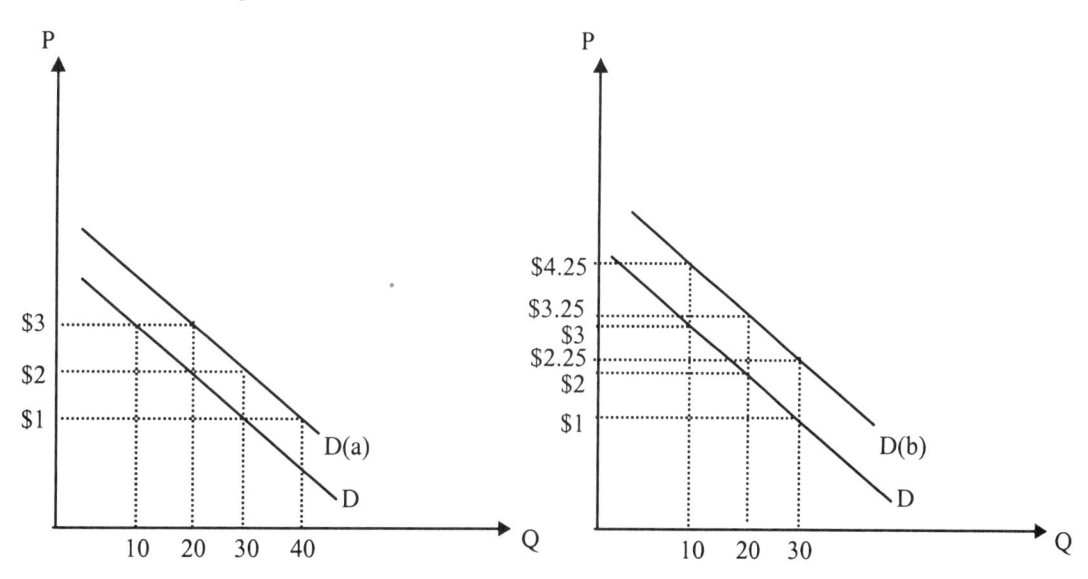

You should be able to re-write statements (a) and (b) for a leftward shift in demand.

PET #5

A rightward shift in the supply curve can be expressed in the following ways:

a. at every price, the quantity that producers are willing to supply is now higher.
b. at every quantity supplied, the price at which producers would be willing to sell is now lower.

38 Chapter 4

To see this, look at the two graphs below. Supply curve a corresponds to statement a and supply curve b corresponds to statement b. In both cases, the supply curve is further to the right after the shift than before.

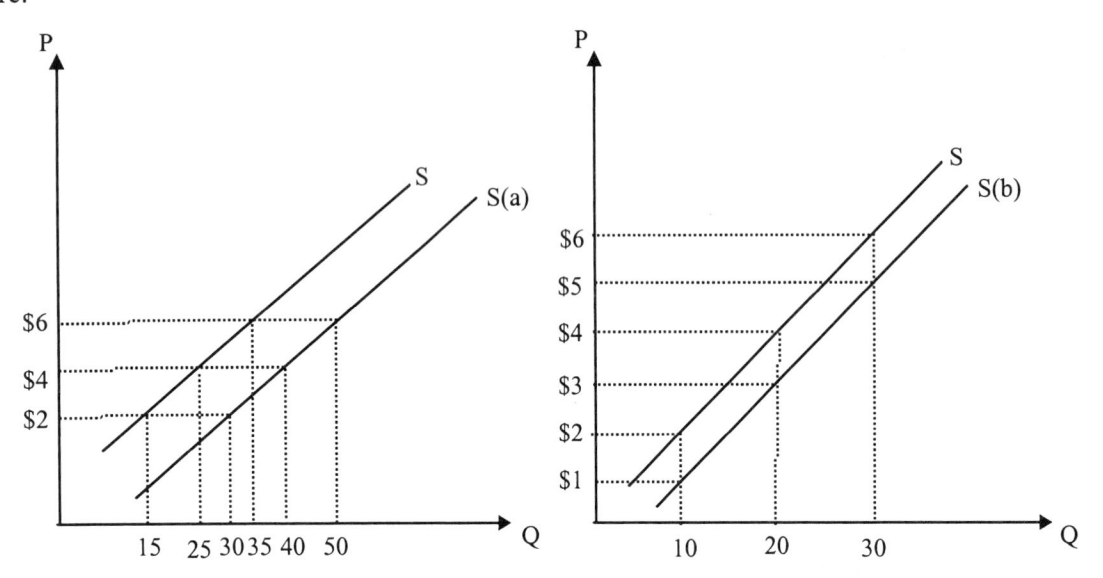

You should be able to re-write statements a and b for a leftward shift in supply.

PET #6

Factors other than a change in the price of good X may cause the demand and/or supply curves to shift to the right or left. These factors can be remembered with the simple mnemonic: P.I.N.T.E.O.

	For Demand	**For Supply**
P -	prices of related goods	prices of related goods
I -	income	input prices
N -	number of buyers (population)	number of producers
T -	tastes	technology
E -	expectations	expectations
O -	other (advertising, fads, etc.)	other (weather, strikes, taxes on producers, etc.)

While this mnemonic should help you if basic logic fails you during an exam (perhaps due to exam-induced stress), you should not simply memorize these lists. They should make sense to you. So, for example, if there is a technological improvement in producing computer chips, it should make sense that the technological improvement makes production of chips more efficient and less costly which you would represent by shifting the supply curve for computer chips to the right. That is, supply increases. Likewise, it should make sense to you than when the price of peanut butter goes up, the demand for jelly (a complement) will decrease which you would represent by shifting the demand curve for jelly to the left. You should work through different examples of each to ensure that your logic is correct.

PET #7

When you are asked to consider the effects of a shift in demand together with a shift in supply, you should first consider the directional effects on price and quantity of each shift individually. Then, you should assess whether the combined shifts move price in the opposite or the same direction and whether the combined shifts move quantity in the opposite or same direction. If the shifts move price (or quantity) in opposite directions, you will be unable to determine (without further information) the ultimate effect on price (or quantity).

To see why this is so, look at the table below and read the discussion following it. You may want to draw a graph of each shift listed below to assure yourself that the table is correct.

Shift	Effect on Price	Effect on Quantity
Demand increases (shifts right)	Price rises	Quantity rises
Demand decreases (shifts left)	Price falls	Quantity falls
Supply increases (shifts right)	Price falls	Quantity rises
Supply decreases (shifts left)	Price rises	Quantity falls

Suppose you are given a test question that asks what happens in the market for bicycles when rollerblading becomes the rage and when the price of aluminum used in making bicycles increases.

First, you must categorize the rollerblading rage as one of the four shift factors above and the increased price of aluminum as one of the four shift factors above. The rollerblading rage would be categorized as a leftward shift in the demand for bicycles and the increased price of aluminum as a leftward shift in the supply of bicycles. Since rollerblading and bicycling are substitutes, the increased rollerblading rage might decrease the demand for bicycles (leftward shift) which is to say that at every price, the quantity of bicycles demanded would now be lower. Since aluminum is an input into bicycles, the increased price of aluminum makes bicycle production more costly which is to say that at every quantity supplied, the price that producers would be willing to accept would be higher (to cover their costs). That is, the supply of bicycles decreases (shifts left).

Now, the decrease in demand for bicycles will lower both the equilibrium price and quantity of bicycles. The decrease in the supply of bicycles will raise the equilibrium price and lower the equilibrium quantity of bicycles. In this case, the two shifts together move price in the opposite direction but have the same directional effect on the equilibrium quantity. Therefore, you can only answer for sure what happens to the equilibrium quantity. (It falls). If you knew the magnitudes of the shifts in demand and supply, you would be able to answer what happens to the equilibrium price.

PET #8

Maximum prices (price ceilings) that are set below the equilibrium price create an excess demand where quantity demanded exceeds quantity supplied. A price ceiling set above the equilibrium price is ineffective.

To see this, compare the two graphs below. Graph A illustrates a maximum price (or price ceiling) set below the equilibrium price and graph B a price ceiling set above the equilibrium price. A maximum price is typically a government-controlled price above which the equilibrium price may not rise.

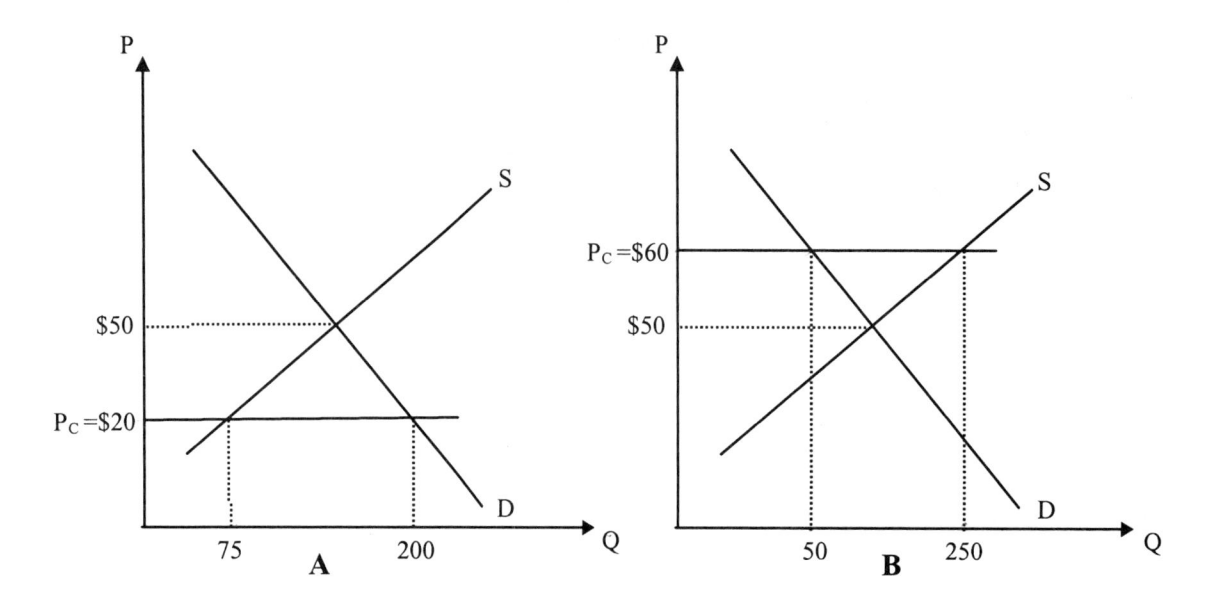

In Graph A, at a price of $20, the quantity demanded is 200 units and the quantity supplied is 75 units. Thus, there is an excess demand (or shortage) of 125 units. If the maximum price was removed, the price would rise to $50 and the excess demand would be eliminated as quantity demanded would decline and quantity supplied would increase (movements along the curves).

In Graph B, at a maximum price (or price ceiling) of $60, the quantity demanded is 50 units and the quantity supplied is 250 units. However, the equilibrium (or market-determined) price is $50. Thus, there is no tendency for the price to rise above the imposed price of $60 and so the price ceiling, in this case, is not effective.

PET #9

Minimum prices (price floors or price supports) that are set above the equilibrium price create an excess supply (or surplus) where quantity supplied exceeds quantity demanded. A price floor set below the equilibrium price is ineffective.

To see this, compare the two graphs below. Graph A illustrates a minimum price (or price floor) set above the equilibrium price and graph B a minimum price set below the equilibrium price. A minimum price is typically a government-controlled price below which the equilibrium price may not fall.

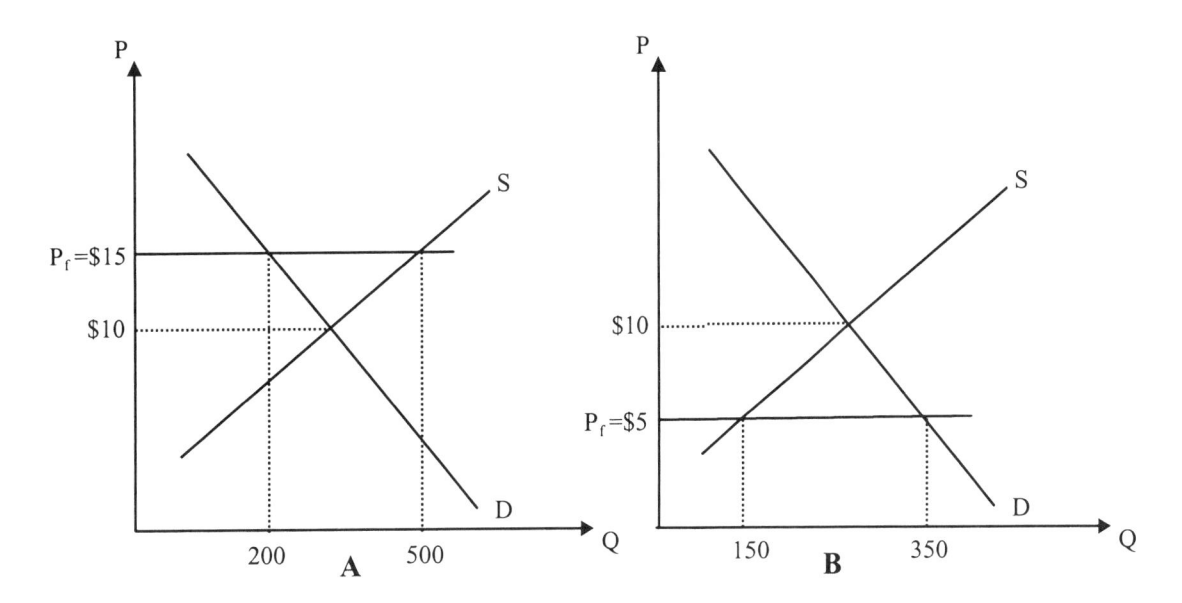

In Graph A, at a minimum price of $15, the quantity demanded is 200 units and the quantity supplied is 500 units. Thus, there is an excess supply (or surplus) of 300 units. If the minimum price was removed, the price would fall to $10 and the excess supply would be eliminated as quantity demanded would rise and quantity supplied would decrease (movements along the curves).

In Graph B, at a minimum price of $5, the quantity demanded is 350 units and the quantity supplied is 150 units. However, the equilibrium (or market-determined) price is $10. Thus, there is no tendency for the price to fall below $10 and so the minimum price of $5 is not effective.

V. PRACTICE EXAM: MULTIPLE CHOICE QUESTIONS

1. Which one of the following statements is correct about the Law of Demand?
a) as the price of oranges decreases, the demand for oranges increases.
b) as the price of oranges increases, the demand for oranges increases.
c) as the price of oranges decreases, the quantity of oranges demanded increases.
d) as the price of oranges increases, the quantity of oranges demanded increases.
e) as the price of oranges decreases, the demand for oranges shifts left.

2. A decrease in the demand for product X will:
a) cause the equilibrium price of product X to rise.
b) cause the equilibrium price of product X to fall.
c) cause the equilibrium quantity of product X to rise.
d) cause the equilibrium quantity of product X to fall.
e) (b) and (d).

42   Chapter 4

3. Consider the market for flavored mineral water. If the price of soda (a substitute for flavored mineral water) increases, which one of the following might be an outcome?
a) the demand for soda will decrease.
b) the demand for mineral water will increase (shift right).
c) the price of mineral water will fall.
d) the equilibrium quantity of mineral water will fall.
e) (b) and (c).

4. Which one of the following statements is correct about the Law of Supply?
a) as the price of dog bones decreases, the supply of dog bones increases.
b) as the price of dog bones increases, the supply of dog bones increases.
c) as the price of dog bones decreases, the quantity of dog bones supplied decreases.
d) as the price of dog bones increases, the quantity of dog bones supplied decreases.
e) as the price of dog bones increases, the supply of dog bones shifts right.

5. Consider the market for mattresses. If the price of foam used in making mattresses declines, which one of the following might be an outcome?
a) the supply of mattresses will increase (shift right).
b) the demand for mattresses will increase.
c) the price of mattresses will rise.
d) there will be a shortage of mattresses.
e) (a) and (b).

6. Which one of the following would NOT cause the supply of bananas to decrease?
a) a technological advance in banana production.
b) a decrease in the number of producers of bananas.
c) an increase in the price of a fertilizer used in growing bananas.
d) a severe rain shortage.
e) a tax placed on banana producers.

7. Which one of the following would NOT cause the demand for walking shoes to increase?
a) an advertising campaign that says walking is good for your health.
b) an increase in income.
c) a decrease in the price of rubber used in producing walking shoes.
d) an increased preference for walking rather than running.
e) all of the above will cause the demand for walking shoes to increase.

8. Consider the market for tulips depicted below.

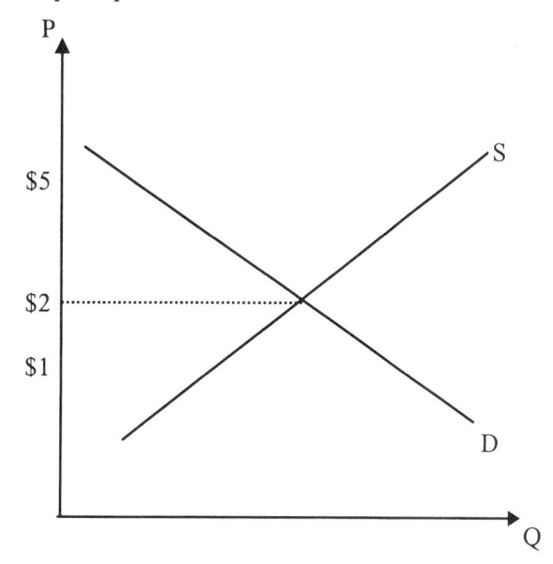

Which one of the following statements is correct based on the graph above?

a) if the price of tulips declines from $5 to $2, the demand for tulips will increase.
b) at a price of $1, there would be an excess demand for tulips.
c) at a price of $5, the quantity of tulips demanded exceeds the quantity supplied.
d) if the price of tulips increases from $1 to $2, the quantity of tulips demanded would increase.
e) none of the above.

9. Consider the market for chocolate candy. What is the effect on the equilibrium price and equilibrium quantity of a decrease in demand for and an increase in the supply of chocolate candy?
a) equilibrium price rises; equilibrium quantity falls.
b) equilibrium price falls; equilibrium quantity rises.
c) equilibrium price = ?; equilibrium quantity falls.
d) equilibrium price rises; equilibrium quantity rises.
e) equilibrium price falls; equilibrium quantity = ?.

10. Use the graph below to answer the following question.

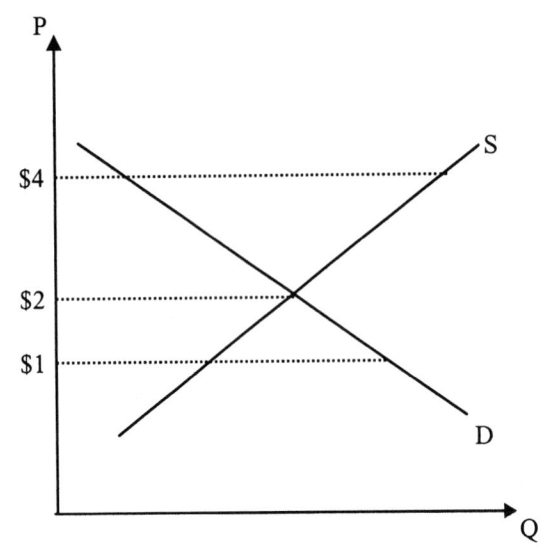

Which one of the following statements is true about the graph?

a) there is an excess demand at a price of $4.
b) there is an excess supply at a price of $4.
c) at a current price of $1, there is pressure for the equilibrium price to fall.
d) if the price fell from $4 to $2, quantity supplied would increase.
e) if the price fell from $4 to $2, demand would shift right.

11. Pretend that you are an economic detective and are given the following clues about the market for wine: the price of wine rose and the equilibrium quantity of wine declined. In writing up your investigative report, which one of the following would you conclude might be responsible for the outcome?

a) a decrease in the supply of wine.
b) a decrease in the demand for wine.
c) an increase in the demand for wine.
d) an increase in the supply of wine.
e) a decrease in the demand for wine and an increase in the supply of wine.

12. Suppose you hear reported in the news that the price of greeting cards declined at the same time the equilibrium quantity of greeting cards increased. Which one of the following would most likely be responsible?

a) a decrease in the price of paper used to make greeting cards.
b) a decrease in the demand for greeting cards.
c) a decrease in supply and an increase in demand for greeting cards.
d) an effective advertising campaign by the greeting card industry.
e) a decrease in the supply of greeting cards.

13. The U.S. imports a lot of cars from Japan. Suppose that the price of steel that Japan uses in making cars declines. What effect might this have in the U.S. market for cars?
a) the supply of Japanese-made cars to the U.S. will decrease.
b) the price of Japanese-made cars sold in the U.S. will decrease.
c) the price of Japanese-made cars sold in the U.S. will increase.
d) the demand for Japanese-made cars will increase.
e) the quantity of Japanese-made cars sold in the U.S. will decrease.

14. Which one of the following statements would be true of an increase in demand for cameras?
a) equilibrium price rises and the supply of cameras increases.
b) equilibrium price rises and the supply of cameras decreases.
c) equilibrium price falls and the quantity of cameras supplied decreases.
d) equilibrium price rises and the quantity of cameras supplied increases.
e) equilibrium price falls and the supply of cameras falls.

15. Suppose you are given the following information about tattoos. (1) the Center for Disease Control reports that tattoos can cause liver and kidney problems; and (2) the price of dye used in tattooing has increased. Given this information, what can you say about the equilibrium price and quantity of tattoos?
a) equilibrium price will fall.
b) equilibrium price will rise and equilibrium quantity will fall.
c) equilibrium price will fall and equilibrium quantity will fall.
d) equilibrium quantity will fall.
e) equilibrium price will rise and effects on equilibrium quantity are uncertain.

16. Suppose income declines. What will be the effects on the equilibrium price and quantity of an inferior good like macaroni and cheese?
a) demand will increase and the price of macaroni and cheese will increase.
b) demand will decrease and the price of macaroni and cheese will decrease.
c) demand will increase and the price of macaroni and cheese will decrease.
d) demand will decrease and the price of macaroni and cheese will increase.
e) uncertain price effects.

VI. PRACTICE EXAM: ESSAY QUESTIONS

1. Consider the market for athletic wear. Describe what happens to demand, supply, quantity demanded, quantity supplied, equilibrium price and equilibrium quantity when the price of spandex used in making athletic wear rises and at the same time a fitness craze sweeps the country, thanks in part, to Richard Simmons. Do not simply draw graphs. Write in complete sentences as you describe what happens.

2. Consider the market for American-made cheese. Suppose that the current equilibrium price is $1 per pound. Suppose that the French develop a preference for American-made cheese. Describe what would be true in the market if after this development, the price remained at $1. Would this be an equilibrium price? Why or why not? What would eventually happen in the market for American-made cheese?

VII. ANSWER KEY: MULTIPLE CHOICE QUESTIONS

1. Correct Answer: c.

Discussion: The law of demand expresses an inverse or negative relationship between the price of a good and the quantity demanded (holding other factors constant). Thus, when the price of X rises, the quantity of X demanded falls and when the price of X falls, the quantity of X demanded rises.

Statement a is incorrect because demand does not increase (which would be represented by the demand curve shifting right). The law of demand is about a movement along a demand curve, not a shift in the curve. Statement b and e are incorrect for similar reasons. Statement d is incorrect because it infers a positive relationship between price and quantity demanded.

2. Correct answer: e.

Discussion: A decrease in demand is represented by a leftward shift of the demand curve (which you may want to draw out using a demand and supply graph with price on the vertical axis and quantity on the horizontal axis). A decrease in demand has the result of lowering the equilibrium price of a product and reducing the equilibrium quantity. Thus, statement e is correct since statements b and d are correct.

Statement a is not correct because a decrease in demand causes the equilibrium price to fall, not to rise. Statement c is not correct because a decrease in demand causes the equilibrium quantity to fall, not to rise.

3. Correct answer: b.

Discussion: Since mineral water and soda are substitutes, when the price of soda rises, consumers may switch to buying mineral water instead. Thus, the demand for mineral water increases, represented by a rightward shift in demand.

Statement a is incorrect because the price of soda is not a shift factor in the market for soda; a fall in the price of soda causes a movement along the demand curve for soda and thus causes the quantity of soda demanded (not the Demand) to decrease.

Statement c is not correct because when the demand for mineral water increases, the price of mineral water will rise. Statement d is not correct because when the demand for mineral water increases, the equilibrium quantity will rise. Statement e is not correct because statement a is not correct.

4. Correct answer: c.

Discussion: The Law of Supply states that there is a positive relationship between the price of X and the quantity of X supplied, holding other factors constant. This means that when the price of X increases, the quantity of X supplied increases and when the price of X decreases, the quantity of X supplied decreases. Statement c describes a positive relationship between the price of dog bones and the quantity of dog bones supplied.

Statements a, b and e are incorrect because a change in the price of dog bones will not cause the supply curve to shift in either direction but rather cause a movement along the supply curve (quantity supplied changes). Statement d is not correct because there is a positive relationship between the price and quantity supplied, not a negative relationship as implied in statement d.

5. Correct answer: a.

Discussion: Foam is an input into mattresses. When the price of foam decreases, it makes mattress production less costly. This would be represented by shifting the supply of mattresses to the right, i.e. supply increasing.

Statement b is not correct because the price of foam will not shift the demand for mattresses. What will happen, however, is that as the supply of mattresses increases, which will cause the price of mattresses to fall, the quantity of mattresses demanded will rise in response. Thus, b would have been correct if it had said "quantity demanded." Statement c is not correct because an increase in the supply of mattresses caused by the decrease in the price of foam will decrease the price of mattresses. Statement d is not correct because there is no reason given to think a shortage would occur. Statement e is not correct because statement b is not correct.

6. Correct answer: a.

Discussion: A technological advance in banana production would increase the supply of bananas, not decrease it.

Statements b, c, d, and e are all factors that would cause the supply of bananas to decrease. A decrease in the number of producers would obviously reduce the supply of bananas. An increase in the price of fertilizer raises the cost of producing bananas and would be represented by a leftward shift in supply, i.e. supply decreases. A severe rain shortage would obviously reduce the banana crop and thus decrease the supply of bananas. A tax on banana growers has the effect of raising the cost of doing business. This acts just like an increase in the price of fertilizer, i.e. the supply of bananas would shift left (decrease).

7. Correct answer: c.

Discussion: A decrease in the price of rubber used in producing walking shoes will lower the cost of producing walking shoes and cause the supply of walking shoes to increase, not the demand. However, quantity demanded would rise since the lower cost of production would translate to a lower price of walking shoes, which would raise the quantity of walking shoes demanded (movement along the demand curve).

Statements a, b, and d would lead to an increase in the demand for walking shoes. However, it may be worth noting that if walking shoes are considered inferior goods, then an increase in income would actually reduce the demand for walking shoes. Statement e is not correct because statement c should have been selected.

8. Correct answer: b.

Discussion: A price of $1 is below the equilibrium price of $2. As the price declines from $2 to $1, two things happen. First, quantity demanded increases based on the Law of Demand. Second, quantity supplied decreases based on the Law of Supply. Since quantity demanded has increased and quantity supplied has decreased, an excess demand (or shortage) is created at the $1 price. So, statement b is correct.

Statement a is not correct because it confuses what happens to quantity demanded with demand. A drop in the price of tulips will increase the quantity demanded, not demand. In other words, a decrease in the price of tulips will not shift the demand curve rightward. Statement c is not correct because at a price of $5, the quantity of tulips supplied will be greater than the quantity demanded. This happens because as the price of tulips rises, the quantity of tulips supplied increases (using the Law of Supply). Also, as the price of tulips rises, the quantity of tulips demanded decreases (using the Law of Demand). Thus, at a price of $5, which is above the equilibrium price, an excess supply will be created. Statement d is not correct, because as the price of tulips increases from $1 to $2 (or increases in general), the quantity of tulips demanded would decline, not increase. Statement e is not correct because statement b is a correct statement.

9. Correct answer: e.

Discussion: A decrease in demand for chocolate candy will lower the equilibrium price and lower the equilibrium quantity. An increase in the supply of chocolate candy will lower the equilibrium price and raise the equilibrium quantity. You can see these two cases by drawing graphs of them, separately. Since the demand and supply shift only push the price in the same direction, price will decline for sure. However, the demand and supply shifts push the equilibrium quantity in opposite directions so the effect is not known for certain.

10. Correct answer: b.

At a price of $4, the quantity supplied exceeds the quantity demanded which is the case of an excess supply or surplus. Just take the price of $4 and draw a line over to the demand and supply curves and then drop those points down to the quantity axis. You will see that the quantity supplied exceeds the quantity demanded.

Discussion: Statement a is not correct because there is not an excess demand (or shortage) but rather an excess supply (or surplus). Statement c is not correct because there would be pressure for the price to rise to the equilibrium price of $2. In fact, at a price of $1, there is a shortage. Statement d is not correct because if the price fell from $4 to $2, the quantity supplied would decrease. Statement e is not correct because if the price fell from $4 to $2, the quantity demanded would increase (not demand).

11. Correct answer: a.

Discussion: A decrease in the supply of wine is represented by shifting the supply curve to the left. A leftward shift in supply raises the equilibrium price and reduces the equilibrium quantity. You can see this by drawing a graph where supply shifts to the left and sketching out what happens to the equilibrium price and quantity.

Statement b is not correct because a decrease in demand would reduce the equilibrium price and reduce the equilibrium quantity. Statement c is not correct because an increase in demand would raise the equilibrium price and raise the equilibrium quantity. Statement d is not correct because an increase in supply would lower the equilibrium price and raise the equilibrium quantity. Statement e is not correct because the effects of these two shifts will have an uncertain effect on price but lower the equilibrium quantity for certain

12. Correct answer: a.

Discussion: A rightward shift in supply is a shift that will cause the price of a good to decline and the equilibrium quantity to rise. Thus, for the greeting card industry, there must have been an increase in supply. In this case, a decrease in the price of paper, which is an input into greeting cards, is the shift factor or cause for the increase in supply, and consequently for the decrease in equilibrium price and rise in equilibrium quantity.

Statement b is not correct because a decrease in demand for greeting cards (represented by a leftward shift in demand) will cause both the equilibrium price and equilibrium quantity to decline. Statement c is not correct because a decrease in supply and an increase in demand for greeting cards will raise the price of greeting cards and have uncertain effects on the equilibrium quantity. (See PET #7 for review). Statement d is not correct because an advertising campaign that is effective will increase the demand for greeting cards (represented by a rightward shift of demand) and thus raise the equilibrium price and quantity of greeting cards. Statement e is not correct because a decrease in the supply of greeting cards (represented by a leftward shift in supply) will cause the equilibrium price of greeting cards to rise and the equilibrium quantity to decline.

13. Correct answer: b.

Discussion: A decrease in the price of steel reduces the cost of manufacturing cars and thus increases the supply of Japanese-made cars. The increase in supply of Japanese-made cars will lower the price that American buyers pay for the cars. You can see this by drawing a graph where supply shifts to the right along the demand curve.

Statement a is not correct because the supply will increase, not decrease. Statement c is not correct because the price will decrease, not increase. Statement d is not correct because the event will not cause demand to shift; quantity demanded will however rise. Statement e is not correct because the quantity of cars sold in the U.S. will increase, not decrease.

14. Correct answer: d.

Discussion: An increase in the demand for cameras would be represented by shifting the demand curve to the right. The increase in demand raises the equilibrium price and quantity. As the equilibrium price rises, there is a movement along the supply curve which shows that the quantity supplied increases. You may wish to draw a graph to see this.

Statement a is not correct because the supply curve for cameras does not shift to the right; the quantity of cameras supplied increases. Statement b is not correct because the supply curve does not shift. Statement c is not correct because the equilibrium price rises, not falls, and the quantity of cameras increases not decreases. Statement e is not correct because the price of cameras rises and because the supply curve does not shift.

15. Correct answer: d.

Discussion: The report by the Center for Disease Control noting the health hazards associated with getting a tattoo should cause the demand for tattoos to decline. By itself, the decline in demand (represented by a leftward shift in demand) will cause the equilibrium price of tattoos to decline and the equilibrium quantity to decline, too. The effect of a rise in the price of dye used in tattooing causes the supply of tattoos to decline. This is represented by a leftward shift in the supply of tattoos. By itself, the reduction in supply of tattoos will raise the equilibrium price of tattoos and reduced the equilibrium quantity. When these two events are combined, you can see that the directional effects of the two events is the same on equilibrium quantity (it declines) but not on the equilibrium price. Therefore, without further information, you can only say that the equilibrium quantity of tattoos has fallen. Thus, statement d is correct and none of the other options can be correct.

16. Correct answer: a.

Discussion: An inferior good is a good for which demand increases when income decreases. Thus, a decline in income will have the effect of increasing the demand for macaroni and cheese. This would be represented by a rightward shift in demand. The increase in demand will have the effect of raising the equilibrium price of macaroni and cheese and increase the equilibrium quantity. Thus, statement a is correct.

Statements b and d are not correct since a decrease in income will increase the demand for an inferior good like macaroni and cheese. Statement c is not correct because while demand increases, the price of macaroni and cheese will increase, not decrease. Statement e is not correct since the directional effect on price is certain.

VIII. ANSWER KEY: ESSAY QUESTIONS

1. I will analyze the two events of an increase in the price of spandex and the fitness craze separately for their effect on the equilibrium price and quantity of athletic wear. Then, I will consider the combined effect of the two events on price and quantity. First, the increase in the price of spandex used in making athletic wear is an increase in an input price. As such, the increased input price raises the cost of producing athletic wear at every quantity supplied. This can be represented by shifting the supply curve of athletic wear to the left. The shift reflects that at every quantity supplied, the price that producers would be willing to accept in order to produce various amounts of athletic wear is now higher. By itself, this raises the equilibrium price of athletic wear and lowers the equilibrium quantity. (Notice that the price increase caused by supply shifting left will cause a movement along the demand curve which means that the quantity of athletic wear demanded will decrease). The fitness craze spawned in part by Richard Simmons will increase the demand for athletic wear. That is, at every price, the quantity demanded will now be higher than before. An increase in demand is represented by shifting the demand curve for athletic wear to the right. By itself, the rightward shift raises the price of athletic wear and increases the equilibrium quantity. (Notice that the price increase caused by demand shifting right will cause a movement along the supply curve which means that the quantity of athletic wear supplied will increase).

When the effects of the shifts in demand and supply are combined, we know for certain that the equilibrium price will increase since both events cause price to increase. However, we do not know for sure what the effect is on the equilibrium quantity since in the first case, the equilibrium quantity declines but in the second case, the equilibrium quantity rises.

2. An increased preference by the French for American-made cheese would mean that there would be an increase in the demand for American-made cheese. This would be represented by shifting the demand curve for American-made cheese to the right, as the graph below shows. At every price, the quantity demanded is now higher (or at every quantity, the price that buyers would be willing to pay is now higher). If the price remained at $1 (rather than rising as it should), there would be a shortage of American-made cheese. That is, if the price remained at $1, the new quantity demanded would now exceed the quantity supplied at a price of $1. This would not be an equilibrium price any more. The shortage should not persist for too long because the shortage creates upward pressure on the price of cheese. Eventually, the price of cheese will rise to a new equilibrium price which is above $1. As the price rises, two things happen to eliminate the shortage. (1) As the price rises, the quantity supplied increases as the arrows along the supply curve indicate (Law of Supply; movement along supply curve); this helps eliminate the shortage. (2) As the price rises, the quantity demanded decreases as the arrows along the demand curve indicate (Law of Demand; movement along demand curve); this too helps eliminate the shortage. Eventually, a new equilibrium price will be reached where the new quantity supplied is equal to the new quantity demanded.

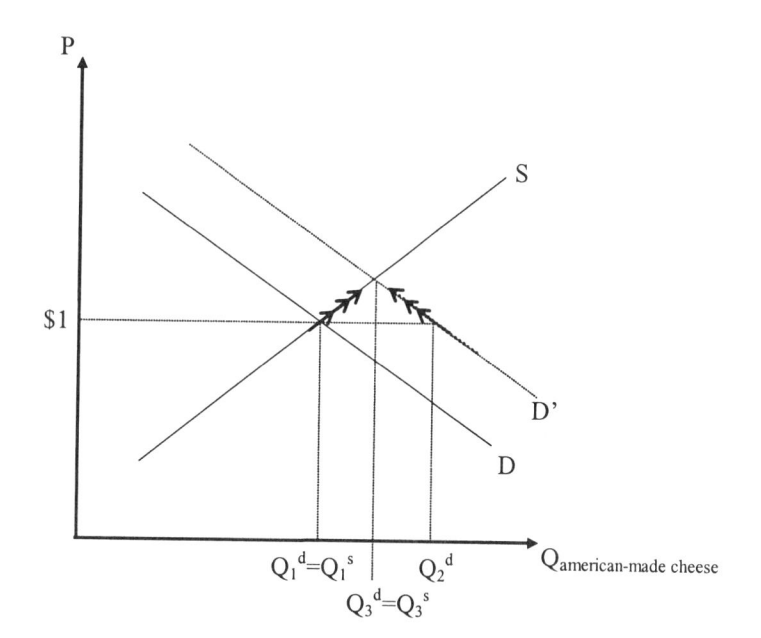

We invite you to visit the book's Companion Website at:
http://www.prenhall.com/osullivan/
for further exercises and practice quizzes.

CHAPTER 5
MEASURING A NATION'S PRODUCTION AND INCOME

I. OVERVIEW

In this chapter, you will learn about Gross Domestic Product (GDP) -- a measure of a nation's total production. You will also learn about national income -- a measure of a nation's total income. You will see, through the circular flow diagram, that a nation's production and its income are related. You will learn about the way GDP is measured and the basic categories that the government defines in calculating GDP. You will learn about the way national income is measured and what constitutes it. You will learn about the difference between nominal and real GDP by revisiting the real-nominal principle. Along the way, you will also learn about the GDP deflator, which is one price index that tracks inflation. You will also learn about fluctuations in GDP, sometimes referred to as the business cycle. Finally, you will consider whether GDP is a good measure of a nation's welfare. And, you will learn about some problems with obtaining an accurate measure of a nation's production.

II. CHECKLIST

By the end of this chapter, you should be able to:

- Explain the study of macroeconomics.
- Define 'recession' and 'inflation'.
- Explain why production and income are flip sides of the same coin.
- Describe the circular flow diagram and how it illustrates the relationship between production and income.
- Define gross domestic product (GDP).
- Explain why intermediate goods are not included in GDP.
- Explain the difference between nominal and real GDP.
- Define economic growth.
- Give two reasons why nominal GDP can change.
- Describe the four main categories of purchasers of GDP.
- Discuss the subcategories of consumption expenditures, private investment expenditures, government expenditures, and net exports.
- Define depreciation.
- Discuss the distinction between "investment" to economists and "investment" in common parlance.
- Define transfer payments and explain why they are not considered a government purchase of GDP.
- Explain why imports are subtracted from purchases of GDP and exports are added to purchases of GDP.
- Define a trade deficit and explain how it relates to foreigners' purchases of U.S. assets.
- Use the GDP equation.
- Explain the relationship between GDP and GNP.
- Define personal income and personal disposable income.

Measuring a Nation's Production and Income 53

- ❑ Define value added.
- ❑ Define and be able to calculate the GDP deflator.
- ❑ Explain the difference between real and nominal GDP and which measure is used for assessing economic growth.
- ❑ Discuss terminology related to economic fluctuations (the business cycle) and discuss characteristics of the business cycle in the United States.
- ❑ Explain the limitations of GDP (what it does not measure) and explain whether or not these limitations lead to an over or underestimate of GDP.

III. KEY TERMS

macroeconomics: The branch of economics that looks at a nation's economy as a whole.

recession: Commonly defined as six consecutive months of negative economic growth.

Product markets: The markets in which goods and services are traded.

Factor markets: The markets in which labor and capital are traded.

Gross domestic product (GDP): The total market value of all the final goods and services produced within an economy in a given year.

Intermediate goods: Goods used in the production process that are not final goods or services.

Nominal GDP: The value of GDP in current dollars

Real GDP: A measure of GDP that controls for changes in prices.

Economic growth: Sustained increases in the real production of an economy over a period of time.

Private investment expenditures: Purchases of newly produced goods and services by firms.

Services: Reflect work done in which people play a prominent role in delivery, ranging from haircutting to health care.

Nondurable goods: Goods that last for short periods of time, such as food.

Durable goods: Goods that last for a long period of time, such as household appliances.

Consumption expenditures: Purchases of newly produced goods and services by households

Net investment: Gross investment minus depreciation.

Depreciation: The wear and tear of capital as it is used in production.

Gross investment: Actual investment purchases.

Transfer payments: Payments to individuals from governments that do not correspond to the production of goods and services.

Government purchases: Purchases of newly produced goods and services by all levels of government.

Net exports: Exports minus imports.

Exports: Goods produced in the home country (for example, the United States) and sold in another country.

Imports: A good produced in a foreign country and purchased by residents of the home country (for example, the United States).

Trade surplus: The excess of exports over imports.

Trade deficit: The excess of imports over exports.

National income: Net national product less indirect taxes.

54 Chapter 5

Gross national product (GNP): GDP plus net income earned abroad.

Indirect taxes: Sales and excise taxes.

Net national product (NNP): GNP less depreciation.

Personal disposable income: Personal income after taxes.

Personal income: Income (including transfer payments) received by households.

Value added: The sum of all the income (wages, interest, profits, rent) generated by an organization.

GDP deflator: An index that measures how the price of goods included in GDP changes over time.

Chain index: A method for calculating changes in prices that uses base years from neighboring years.

Expansion: The period after a trough in the business cycle during which the economy recovers

Trough: The time at which output stops falling in a recession.

Peak: The time at which a recession begins.

Depression: The common name for a severe recession.

IV. PERFORMANCE ENHANCING TIPS (PETS)

PET #1

Nominal GDP may increase because of an increase in the price level and/or because of an increase in output (production). Real GDP may increase because of an increase in output (production).

Nominal GDP is the "market value" or "current-dollar" (today's prices) measure of the amount of output an economy in total produced over a given time period (usually a year). If prices rise, without any increase in the amount of output produced, nominal GDP will increase. Such an increase, however, should in no way be construed as economic growth since output did not grow at all.

To make an analogy, suppose you are the financial analyst for a particular firm and you observe that its revenue has increased. The firm's revenue may have increased either because (1) the price at which the firm sells its output has increased; (2) the firm sold more output (while there was no increase in price); or (3) some combination of the two.

The same is true of nominal GDP. However, economic analysts and policymakers are interested in what has happened to output exclusively. This is because an increase in output typically means that more people were employed and/or that labor was more productive and this is good news for the economy. Nominal GDP unfortunately isn't an accurate picture of what has happened to output because a change in nominal GDP is influenced by what has happened to prices as well as production. Real GDP, which takes out the effects of price changes on nominal GDP, gives a more accurate picture of what has happened to production.

PET #2

Economic growth is measured by the percentage change in real GDP, not by the percentage change in nominal GDP.

Suppose you calculate the growth rate of real GDP to be 3.2% and the growth rate of nominal GDP to be 6%. Which measure is appropriate to evaluate economic growth and what can you infer about inflation?

The appropriate measure of economic growth is the rate of change in real GDP. In this case, we would say that the economy grew by 3.2%. Since nominal GDP increased by 6%, we could infer that the inflation rate was roughly 2.8% (= 6% - 3.2%). We should not say that the economy grew by 6%.

PET #3

The expenditure approach to measuring U.S. GDP is to sum up the purchases, whether purchases of U.S. or foreign-produced goods and services, by U.S. consumers (or "households"), businesses and the government, add expenditures by foreign residents on goods and services produced in the U.S (exports of the U.S.) and to subtract expenditures by U.S. consumers, businesses, and the government on foreign-produced goods and services (imports of the U.S.).

Your professor may write it as:

GDP = C + I + G + EX - IM

where:

C = consumption expenditures by households on goods and services whether produced domestically or abroad.

I = gross investment expenditures by firms. This is primarily spending on plant and equipment, whether produced domestically or abroad.

G = government expenditures on goods and services, whether produced domestically or abroad.

EX = exports.

IM = imports.

PET #4

An increase in businesses' inventories reflects production that took place in the current year and should be added to GDP, even though the output was not purchased. A decrease in businesses' inventories reflects purchases of output that was produced in a prior year and should be subtracted from GDP.

PET #5

Net investment that is positive is the addition to a nation's stock of capital above and beyond its current level. Net investment that is zero means that a nation's stock of capital is neither increasing nor decreasing beyond its current level. Net investment that is negative means that a nation is not investing enough to replace capital that is being worn out.

To illustrate the difference between gross investment and net investment, consider the stock of shoes that you currently have. Suppose you have 10 pairs of shoes. Over the course of the year, 3 of the pairs wear out (depreciate) and are no longer any good. If you buy 7 more pairs of shoes that year, your gross investment in shoes is 7 pairs. However, because you are replacing 3 pairs that have worn out, your net investment in shoes is 4 pairs. That is, at the end of the year, you will now have 14 pairs of shoes. You have, on net, added 4 (7-3) pairs to the stock of 10 pairs of shoes that you started out with.

Suppose instead that you bought 3 pairs of shoes that year. While three pairs would be your gross investment, your net investment would be zero. You have only replaced what you have worn out. Thus, you are no better off at the end of the year since your stock of shoes remains at 10 pairs.

Now, suppose that you bought 1 pair of shoes that year. While three pairs would be your gross investment, your net investment would be -2 (1-3). You have not invested enough to replace the 3 pairs of shoes worn out. Thus, your stock of shoes will decline from 10 pairs to 8 pairs.

The same is true for a country. A country whose net investment is zero will not be adding to its capital stock; a country that is not replacing its worn out capital will see its capital stock shrink. As you will see in later chapters, this can have implications for the rate of growth an economy will be able to achieve.

PET #6

Government purchases included in GDP are government spending on goods and services for which there was productive effort. Thus, government spending on transfer payments (e.g. social security, unemployment compensation) and interest on the national debt are not part of the government purchases included in GDP.

While your textbook makes this PET quite clear, it is worth repeating.

PET #7

A country that runs a trade deficit (the value of imports is greater than the value of exports) is on net borrowing from foreigners. A country that runs a trade surplus (the value of exports is greater than the value of imports) is on net lending to foreigners.

For example, suppose the U.S. has a trade deficit of $100 billion. This means that the U.S. is not earning enough foreign currency on its exports to cover payments in foreign currency on its imports. Where can the U.S. get the extra $100 billion in foreign currency to cover the trade deficit? The U.S. must borrow the funds from foreigners (i.e. foreigners lend foreign currency to the U.S). Since residents of the U.S. can also lend to foreigners, we say that the trade deficit implies that the U.S. is borrowing $100 billion more from foreigners than it is lending to them. In other words, on net the U.S. is borrowing from foreigners.

Another way of saying that the U.S. is on net borrowing from foreigners is to say that foreigners are on net lending to the U.S. They are lending to the U.S. by taking their savings and using them to buy U.S. assets (e.g. U.S. stocks and bonds). As an analogy, if you buy a bond from a company, you are in effect, lending your savings to the company and the company is borrowing from you.

The reverse holds true for a country with a trade surplus.

V. PRACTICE EXAM: MULTIPLE CHOICE QUESTIONS

1. Which one of the following would NOT be considered a macroeconomic issue?
a) inflation.
b) economic growth.
c) international trade.
d) national unemployment.
e) consumer behavior.

2. The output of an economy is called:
a) market goods.
b) gross domestic product.
c) national volume.
d) the net balance.
e) national product.

3. GDP is the total market value of:
a) all final goods and services sold in an economy in a given year.
b) all goods and services purchased by households in a given year.
c) all final goods and services produced within an economy since 1900.
d) all final goods and services produced within the borders of a country in a given year.
e) intermediate and final goods produced in a given year.

4. Which one of the following would NOT be included in current GDP?
a) the purchase of a new jet ski.
b) services rendered by a financial planner.
c) a trip to Hilton Head.
d) the purchase of a two-year old used set of Ping golf clubs.
e) the purchase of flour by a househusband or housewife.

5. The most common measure of economic growth is:
a) changes in real GDP because only changes in output are measured.
b) changes in nominal GDP because it considers changes in both output and prices.
c) changes in the consumer price index because it measures changes in the income of a typical family of four.
d) changes in the chain-type price index because it measures the ability of the economy to respond to higher costs of production.
e) changes in labor productivity since it measures whether workers' standard of living is changing.

6. Which one of the following defines a "recession"?
a) a one-month decline in real GDP.
b) a protracted period of low economic growth.
c) a decline in real GDP that lasts for six consecutive months or longer.
d) a growth rate of real GDP that is negative.
e) the movement of real GDP from trough to peak.

58   Chapter 5

7. Which one of the following would NOT be considered a component of GDP?
   a) spending by a household on a used television set.
   b) spending by the government on social security benefits.
   c) a decline in the level of businesses' inventories over last year.
   d) spending by a firm on a foreign-made piece of equipment.
   e) none of the above.

8. Which one of the following sectors purchases the largest share of GDP?
   a) consumers.
   b) firms.
   c) the government.
   d) foreigners.
   e) proprietors.

9. Which one of the following statements is true?
   a) durable goods are those that last for a short period of time.
   b) an example of a non-durable good is a dishwasher.
   c) services are the fastest growing component of consumption spending.
   d) net investment = gross investment + depreciation.
   e) an example of investment in economics would be the purchase of a stock.

10. Which one of the following would give a correct measure of GDP?
    Let C = consumption expenditures, I = gross investment expenditures, G = government expenditures, EX = exports, and IM = imports.
    a) GDP = C + I + G + EX + IM.
    b) GDP = C + I + G + EX - IM.
    c) GDP = C + I + G.
    d) GDP = C + I + G - EX - IM.
    e) GDP = C + I - G + EX + IM.

11. If the U.S. runs a trade surplus,
    a) U.S. exports are greater than U.S. imports.
    b) U.S. imports are greater than U.S. exports.
    c) the U.S. is a net lender to foreign countries.
    d) U.S. sales of assets to foreigners are greater than U.S. purchases of assets from foreigners.
    e) (a) and (c).

12. Which one of the following statements is true?
a) an economic expansion is defined to occur after the trough of a business cycle.
b) a severe recession is termed a 'depression.'
c) the trough of a business cycle is when output stops falling.
d) a recession is defined as six consecutive months or more of a decline in real GDP.
e) all of the above are true.

13. Which one of the following statements is true?
a) GDP calculations include the value of services performed by a homemaker such as cleaning or cooking.
b) under the table transactions lead to an overestimate of GDP.
c) personal income is the sum of all payments made to households minus taxes they paid to the government.
d) manufactured goods are the fasted growing component of consumption expenditures.
e) the GDP deflator is calculated as (nominal GDP divided by real GDP) x 100.

14. Which one of the following would NOT be included in U.S. GNP?
a) income earned by a U.S. citizen working in Japan.
b) profits earned by a Canadian factory operating in the U.S..
c) earnings on a foreign investment by a U.S. citizen.
d) profits earned by a U.S. corporation located in Brazil.
e) none of the above.

15. Which one of the following statements is true?
a) GDP is a good measure of how happy a society is.
b) an improved system of capturing tax evaders would raise the estimate of GDP.
c) the value of leisure time is included in GDP.
d) the National Bureau of Economic Research is responsible for predicting when the United States will go into a recession.
e) all of the above are true.

VI. PRACTICE EXAM: ESSAY QUESTIONS

1. Suppose you are an economic advisor to a tiny island country that produces only volleyballs. As part of your job, you must help the president of the island prepare the "State of the Island" address. In the first quarter of 2001, you find that island produced a market value (or current dollar value) of $1,000,000 volleyballs. In the second quarter of 2001, the island produced a market value of $1,200,000 of volleyballs. Furthermore, your statistics tell you that annual inflation (based on the GDP deflator) for the tiny island country from the first quarter to the second quarter of 2001 was 80%. What would you tell your president to report in her "State of the Island" address?

60   Chapter 5

2. Discuss the four components of spending on GDP and explain why intermediate goods purchased by businesses are not included in GDP.

VII. ANSWER KEY: MULTIPLE CHOICE QUESTIONS

1. Correct answer: e.

Discussion: Consumer behavior is an issue studied in microeconomics. Statements a-d are all macroeconomic issues.

2. Correct answer: b.

Discussion: No discussion necessary.

3. Correct answer: d.

Discussion: GDP is the total market value of all final goods and services produced within the borders of a country in a given year. The terms that are bolded in the sentence are important to the definition.

Statement a is not correct because GDP is a measure of what is produced, not what is sold, in a given year. There may be goods sold in a given year, that were produced in a prior year. These goods would be "used goods" and should not be part of current year GDP. Statement b is not correct because GDP is the purchase of final (for end use) goods and services. Households and businesses purchase goods and services for end use. For example, a business may purchase a computer for its use. Statement c is not correct because GDP is the value of what is produced in a particular (or given) year. It is not the sum of the value of production since the turn of the century. Statement e is not correct because GDP does not include the market value of intermediate goods (such as plastics used in auto production or wood used in furniture).

4. Correct answer: d.

Discussion: GDP is a measure of the value of goods and services produced in a given year. Since the golf clubs are used, they were produced two years ago and hence should not be included in current GDP.

Statements a, b, c, and e are all examples of either goods or services purchased for "end use." In other words, they are "final" goods or services.

5. Correct answer: a.

Discussion: Economic growth is measured as the percentage change in real GDP, typically reported on an annualized basis. Real GDP takes out the effects of price changes on nominal GDP. (See PET #1 of this chapter for review).

Statement b is not correct because nominal GDP is influenced by not only changes in output (production) but changes in prices as well. Changes in prices do not reflect economic growth and so should not be considered. This last sentence also means that statements c and d are not correct. Statement e is not correct although labor productivity and economic growth are related.

6. Correct answer: c.

Discussion: A recession is a decline in real GDP that lasts for six months or longer. This also means that economic growth would be negative for two quarters.

Statement a is not correct because decline in real GDP must last at least six months, not just one month. Statement b is not correct. Low (but positive) economic growth does not define a recession. Statement d is not correct because it needs a qualifier on how many quarters there was negative growth. For example, a one-quarter negative growth rate would not constitute a recession. Statement e is not correct because a movement from trough to peak would define an economic expansion.

7. Correct answer: e.

Discussion: Only spending for goods and services produced domestically, this year, is a component of GDP. Spending on a used television set constitutes spending this year on a prior year's production. Spending by the government on social security benefits is spending on a good or service for which there is no underlying productive effort and thus does not constitute spending on this year's GDP. A decline in businesses' inventories over last year means that businesses sold goods this year that were produced in a prior year. (Likewise, an addition to businesses' inventories means that there were goods produced this year that did not get sold this year -- an addition to inventories that is included in GDP). Spending by a firm (or individual) on a foreign-made good or service (imports) constitutes spending on good or service not produced in the domestic (home) country. Thus, such spending does not reflect spending on domestically-produced GDP.

8. Correct answer: a.

Discussion: Consumers are, by far, the largest spending sector in the U.S. economy. The government is a larger spending sector than are firms.

9. Correct answer: c.

Discussion: Services are the fastest growing component of consumption spending. This is partly driven by demographic changes.

Statement a is not correct; durable goods are goods that last a long time. Statement b is not correct. In fact, a dishwasher is an example of a durable good. Most households will keep a new dishwasher at least three years. Statement d is not correct. Net investment = gross investment minus depreciation. Statement e is not correct. In economics, investment is defined as the purchase of plant, machinery, and equipment. Investment in economics, is not "financial investment."

10. Correct answer: b.

Discussion: Remember that GDP is the total dollar value of the goods and services an economy produces in a given year. That production is purchased by consumers, businesses, the government and foreigners. Thus, it must be a truism that the total dollar value of production equals the total dollar value of spending on that production. However, since consumers, businesses, and the government can also purchase foreign-made goods and services (termed "imports"), we must subtract these out of C, I and G in order to have a measure of spending by consumers, businesses, and the government on only domestically-produced goods and services (which constitute GDP). We add spending by foreigners on domestically-produced goods and services (termed "exports") to spending by the other sectors of the economy to arrive at the total amount of spending for the goods and services our economy has produced in a given year.

11. Correct answer: e.

Discussion: A trade surplus is defined as an excess of exports over imports. Thus, statement a is correct and means that the U.S. is selling more goods and services to foreigners than it is in total purchasing from foreign countries. Alternatively, this means that foreigners are purchasing more goods and services from the U.S. than they are selling to us. This means that through trade, foreigners are not earning enough dollars on their sales of goods and services to the U.S. to pay for their purchases of goods and services from the U.S. The way in which foreign countries can finance their trade deficits is for them to borrow dollars from the U.S. In other words, the U.S. (the trade surplus country in this example) is on net lending dollars to foreign countries. Thus, statements a and c are correct.

Statement b is not correct; it would imply a trade deficit. Statement d is not correct. Statement d is a way of saying that the U.S. would be on net borrowing from foreign countries (i.e. issuing bonds, etc. -- assets -- that foreigners are in turn, buying). If foreigners were buying U.S. assets, they would be in effect lending to the U.S. (This would imply that the U.S. had a trade deficit).

You may wish to review PET #7 of this chapter.

12. Correct answer: e.

Discussion: No discussion necessary.

13. Correct answer: e.

Discussion: Statement e is correct. For example, if nominal GDP in the year 2000 was $8 trillion dollars and in GDP increased on average by about 6.7%.

Statement a is not correct. GDP calculations do not consider the value of services provided by a homemaker. If the value of services (such as laundry service, cleaning service, chauffeur, etc.) provided by homemakers were considered, the GDP figures would be higher. In fact, it is estimated that a homemaker's services should be valued at roughly $40,000. Statement b is not correct because under the table transactions are unrecorded. They escape government calculations and hence government statistics. It is believed that if the value of these transactions were recorded they would add an additional 7% to GDP (since they do constitute production of a good or service). Statement c is not correct; personal disposable income is personal income minus taxes paid. Personal income is all payments earned by households prior to paying taxes. Statement d is not correct because services, not manufactured goods, are the fastest growing component of consumption expenditures.

14. Correct answer: b.

Discussion: Statement b is the correct answer because GNP is a measure of the income earned by U.S. citizens and businesses regardless of where the income or earnings are derived. Profits earned by a Canadian factory are thus obviously not earnings of a U.S. citizen or business. Hence, they would not be included in U.S. GNP. The earnings of a Canadian factory operating in the United States would be included in U.S. GDP since GDP is a measure of income earned within the borders of a country regardless of the nationality of the citizen or business.

Statements a, c, and d are all examples of income or earnings that would be included in U.S. GNP since the entity to which the income or earnings accrue are U.S. citizens or businesses.

15. Correct answer: b.

Discussion: Statement b is true. Illegal economic transactions that take place in an economy escape statistics prepared by the government on the economy. Consequently, GDP is likely to be underestimated. If a system were devised to capture tax evaders and the dollar value of transactions they engaged in, the estimate of GDP would increase.

Statement a is not true. GDP does not measure 'well-being' or 'welfare.' It is a measure of how much production and income was generated by an economy. Statement c is not true. Leisure time is not an activity that generates production (output) or income. While it may improve a society's well-being, it does not translate into higher GDP. Statement d is not true because the National Bureau of Economic Research (NBER) does not make predictions about when the economy will enter recession (or even by how much). The NBER is responsible for deciding whether the economy was in a recession. It looks at data from the past in making its assessment. Statement e cannot be true since statements a, c, and d are not true.

VIII. ANSWER KEY: ESSAY QUESTIONS

1. First of all, the figures on the market value of output are in current dollars and thus are measures of the island's nominal GDP. The growth rate in nominal GDP between the first and second quarter is [($200,000)/$1,000,000] X 100 = 20%. The 20% figure, if annualized as is common for reporting of GDP growth rates, would be 20% X 4 = 80%. So, on an annualized basis, nominal GDP has increased by 80%. However, nominal GDP can increase because (1) output (production of volleyballs) has increased; (2) the price of volleyballs has increased; or (3) some combination of the two. Since inflation (increase in prices) does not constitute economic growth, the growth rate in nominal GDP should not be used to assess whether or not the economy has grown. The effects of higher prices on the nominal GDP growth rate must be taken out. Since you also know that inflation, on an annualized basis for your country was 80% between the first and second quarter of 2001, you can infer what has happened to the growth rate of output (real GDP). The growth rate of real GDP can be roughly measured as the difference between the growth rate of nominal GDP and the GDP deflator inflation rate. Thus, you would report that the growth rate in real GDP for the island was 0%. So, you would tell the president to sadly report that the economy did not grow. Moreover, the economy suffered double-digit inflation on the order of 80% on an annualized basis (or 20% = (80%/4) on a quarterly basis).

2. The four components of spending on GDP (I will consider U.S. GDP) are:

    (1) Consumption expenditures. This is spending by U.S. households on final goods and services, whether the goods and services are produced in the U.S. or abroad. That is, some consumption expenditures by U.S. households are for foreign-produced goods and services. For example, suppose that consumption expenditures in the U.S. totaled $5 trillion; further if $1 trillion of the spending was on foreign-produced goods and services, then we could say that households purchased $4 trillion worth of U.S. produced goods and services.

    (2) Investment expenditures. Investment expenditures has several components. The main component of investment spending is spending by businesses on plant and equipment. Businesses, of course, can purchase U.S.-produced equipment or foreign-made equipment. A second component of investment expenditures is residential housing. Purchases of new housing are considered investment expenditures even though households, not businesses, are typically the buyers. A third component of investment expenditures is "inventory investment." When businesses decide to add to their inventories from last year, they are investing in their inventory. Businesses may choose to build up their inventories in anticipation of a strong sales year.

(3) Government expenditures. This is spending by the government on goods and services for which there was productive effort. The government buys legal services from lawyers, paper from paper manufacturers, computers from computer manufacturers, guns from gun manufacturers, and so on. The government, too, can buy from U.S. manufacturers or from foreign manufacturers.

(4) Net Exports. This is spending by foreigners on U.S. made goods and services minus spending by U.S. entities on foreign-made goods and services. Since items (1), (2), and (3) above contain spending by households, businesses, and the government on foreign-made goods and services, these must be subtracted out to arrive at an estimate of how much spending was undertaken by U.S. households, businesses, and the government on only U.S. produced goods and services (i.e. U.S. GDP). However, since foreigners can purchase U.S. output just as U.S. residents purchase U.S. output, we must also include export spending in constructing a measure of GDP.

In sum, U.S. GDP is equal to consumption expenditures plus investment expenditures plus government expenditures plus exports minus imports.

The purchase of intermediate goods by businesses is not a component of GDP. To do so would lead to double-counting (which would lead to an overestimate of GDP). Here's why. Suppose you buy a computer system and pay $2,000 for it. The $2,000 price tag reflects the value of all of the production that went into producing the computer and making it available to a retail store where it can be sold to you. Thus, the $2,000 price tag is a measure of all of the production that has taken place. This number is used in computing GDP.

Suppose that of the $2,000 price tag on the computer system, $1,300 was due to the components used in the computer system. (We'll assume the components were produced in the U.S). If we included the $1,300 in addition to the $2,000 in computing U.S. GDP, we would be double-counting the value of production that has actually taken place. The $2,000 already reflects $1,300 worth of production.

Take It to the Net

We invite you to visit the O'Sullivan/Sheffrin page on the Prentice Hall Web site at:

http://www.prenhall.com/osullivan/

for this chapter's World Wide Web exercise.

CHAPTER 6
UNEMPLOYMENT AND INFLATION

I. OVERVIEW

In this chapter, you will learn about unemployment and inflation. You will learn about different types of unemployment and the problems they present for the economy. You will learn about the problems that inflation (and deflation) creates for a society. You will learn how the unemployment rate and the inflation rate are measured. You will see that these statistics may not always portray the most accurate picture of the state of the economy. You will learn that limitations to these statistics are caused by the difficulties in accurately measuring prices around the country and who exactly is unemployed. You will learn how the government compiles information on the unemployed. You will learn what the costs of unemployment are. You will also learn how the government compiles information on the consumer price index (CPI) and how this measure of the price level differs from the chain-type price index. You will learn why the percentage change in the CPI may overstate inflation.

II. CHECKLIST

By the end of this chapter, you should be able to:
- Define the unemployed.
- Define the labor force.
- Distinguish the unemployed from individuals who are not in the labor force.
- Define the labor force participation rate and distinguish it from the unemployment rate.
- Explain how the unemployment rate is calculated.
- Explain who would be considered unemployed.
- Define a discouraged worker and address whether or not a discouraged worker is considered unemployed.
- Define a marginally attached worker and address whether or he or she is considered unemployed.
- Describe the different types of unemployment (cyclical, frictional, and structural) and their causes.
- Define the natural rate of unemployment and "full employment."
- Discuss the Consumer Price Index (CPI).
- Discuss the types of goods included in the CPI.
- Use the CPI to estimate how much money would be needed to maintain a given standard of living across years.
- Compare the CPI to the chain-price index for GDP.
- Define inflation and explain how it hurts society.
- Explain why and by how much it is believed that the percentage change in the CPI overstates inflation.
- Explain some consequences of overstating the rate of inflation.
- Define deflation and the problems caused by it.

III. KEY TERMS

Labor force: The employed plus the unemployed.

Employed: People who have jobs.

Unemployed: People who are looking for work but do not have jobs.

Labor force participation rate: The fraction of the population over 16 years of age that is in the labor force.

Unemployment rate: The fraction of the labor force that is unemployed.

Individuals working part-time for economic reasons: Individuals who would like to work full time but are forced to take part-time jobs.

Marginally attached workers: Individuals who have worked in the past but stopped working for a variety of reasons.

Discouraged workers: Workers who left the labor force because they could not find jobs.

Frictional unemployment: The part of unemployment associated with the normal workings of the economy, such as searching for jobs.

Cyclical unemployment: The component of unemployment that accompanies fluctuations in real GDP.

Seasonal unemployment: The component of unemployment attributed to seasonal factors.

Structural unemployment: The component of unemployment reflecting a mismatch of skills and jobs.

Full employment: The level of employment that occurs when the unemployment rate is at the natural rate.

Natural rate of unemployment: The level of unemployment at which there is no cyclical unemployment.

Unemployment insurance: Payments received from the government upon becoming unemployed.

Consumer price index (CPI): A price index that measures the cost of a fixed basket of goods chosen to represent the consumption pattern of individuals.

Cost-of-living adjustments (COLAs): Automatic increases in wages or other payments that are tied to a price index.

Inflation rate: The percentage rate of change in the price level.

Shoe-leather costs: Costs of inflation that arise from trying to reduce holdings of cash.

Menu costs: Costs of inflation that arise from actually changing prices.

Unanticipated inflation: Inflation that is not expected.

Anticipated inflation: Inflation that is expected.

Hyperinflation: An inflation rate exceeding 50% per month.

IV. PERFORMANCE ENHANCING TIPS (PETS)

PET #1

To be considered unemployed, an individual must be 16 years or older, actively seeking paid employment, and must not be employed in a part-time job.

The government's definition about who is considered unemployed is very specific. Several preconditions must be satisfied before the government identifies an individual as unemployed. First, the individual must be 16 years or older. Second, the individual must be actively seeking paid employment. In fact, by the government's definition, the individual must have actively looked for work in the last four weeks. If an individual has not actively looked for work in the past four weeks, the individual would be classified as "not part of the labor force". Depending on their circumstances, they may be categorized as a 'discouraged worker' or as a 'marginally attached worker' but they would not be counted as unemployed. Finally, if an individual has a part-time job and is actively searching for another job, the government would not classify the individual as "unemployed" since the individual has a job.

PET #2

To be considered part of the labor force, an individual must either have a paying job (full-time or part-time) or be actively seeking employment.

This PET tells you that the labor force consists of those individuals with jobs (the employed) and those individuals who do not have a job and are looking for work (the "unemployed").

PET #3

Discouraged workers are not considered as unemployed because they are not actively seeking employment. Hence, they are also not considered part of the labor force. Since 'individuals working part time for economic reasons' do hold jobs and are thus employed, they are counted as part of the labor force but not as part of the unemployed. (Your professor may refer to 'individuals working part time for economic reasons' as 'underemployed.').

PET #4

*The consumer price index (CPI) in a base year is 100. The consumer price index in any year other than the base year may be greater or less than 100. The percentage change in the consumer price index between any two years gives the **cumulated** rate of inflation between those years. The*

Suppose the CPI in 2003 is 184. Further, suppose the base year for the CPI is 1985. You can conclude that between 1985-2003, there was increase in the CPI of 84% since the percentage change in the CPI over those years is 84%. Now, suppose the CPI in 2002 was 179.9. The percentage change in the CPI between 2002-03 would now be 2.3% = [(184 – 179.9)/179.9] X 100.

PET #5

The consumer price index (CPI) can be used to tell you how much money would be needed to maintain the same standard of living from one year to the next. It can also be used to tell you how much money would have been needed in previous years to maintain the standard of living currently maintained.

Suppose that in 2003, a typical family lived on $40,000 per year. Let's consider how much the family would need to maintain the same standard of living in 2004. We'll need some CPI numbers to do the calculation. Let the CPI in 2003 be 184 and the CPI for 2004 be 188. The family will need:

$40,000 X (188/184) = $40,870.

Suppose instead, we want to know how much money a family living on $40,000 a year in 2003 would have needed to live on in the base year. In this case, we simply divide the sum of money by the CPI in 2003 and multiply by 100 (or, alternatively divide by 1.84):

($40,000 / 184) X 100 = $21,739

($40,000 / 1.84) = $21,739

That is, a family living on $40,000 in 2003 would have needed $21,739 to have the same standard of living they have in 2003.

Now, we could ask how much money would a family living on $21,739 in the base year need to have in 2004 if the CPI in 2004 is 188. In this case, we would take the amount of money in the base year and multiply it by the CPI in 2004 divided by 100 (or, alternatively, multiply by 1.88):

($21,739 X 188) / 100 = $40,870

($21,739 X 1.88) = $40,870

That is, a family living on $21,739 in the base year would need $40,870 in 2004 to maintain the same standard of living they had in the base year.

The examples above illustrate how the CPIs in various years can be used to calculate the value of a given sum of money in those years.

V. PRACTICE EXAM: MULTIPLE CHOICE QUESTIONS

1. The labor force is defined as:
a) all persons age 16 and over who are currently employed in a paying job.
b) all persons age 16 and over who are either working for pay or have are actively seeking employment.
c) all persons willing and able to work for pay.
d) all persons of voting age who are working for pay.
e) the population minus those in the armed services.

2. Which one of the following statements is true?
a) the government counts anybody who does not have a job as "unemployed."
b) the unemployment rate is calculated as the number of unemployed individuals/labor force.
c) the labor force is equal to a country's population.
d) during the Great Depression, the unemployment rate reached a high of 10%.
e) all of the above are true.

3. The government considers a discouraged worker as:
a) someone who does not have a job but is actively seeking employment.
b) someone who is working at a job that is below their skill level.
c) not part of the labor force.
d) someone who has a part-time job but seeks full-time employment.
e) someone who has a job but is discouraged about getting a pay raise.

4. Frictional unemployment occurs when:
a) a worker can't find a job because he/she lacks the skills necessary to be employed.
b) a corporation transfers a worker to another city.
c) a worker quits one job in order to search for another.
d) a worker is laid off due to a downturn in the business cycle.
e) (c) and (d).

5. Which one of the following is an example of a structurally unemployed individual?
a) J. Martin, who lacks the skills necessary to be employed.
b) Lee, who lost his job as an art director because of a recession.
c) Jan, who has a Ph.D. in economics but is a bus driver.
d) Helena, who has just graduated from college and is searching for a job as an architect.
e) none of the above.

6. Which one of the following may be a reason why the unemployment rate doesn't reflect the true unemployment picture?
a) the unemployment rate does not count people who would like a job but cannot work due to transportation or child-care problems.
b) the unemployment rate is based on a telephone survey where individuals may not give truthful answers.
c) the unemployment rate does not count discouraged workers.
d) the unemployment rate counts part-time workers as employed.
e) all of the above.

7. Economists say that the economy is at "full employment" when:
a) the structural unemployment rate is zero.
b) the cyclical unemployment rate is zero.
c) the frictional unemployment rate is zero.
d) the natural unemployment rate is zero.
e) none of the above.

8. Which one of the following statements is true?
a) people with part-time jobs are counted as "unemployed."
b) a marginally attached worker is someone who is working but does not want to be.
c) the labor force participation rate is the percentage of the labor force that is employed.
d) all individuals over 16 years of age that do not have a job are considered unemployed.
e) married men and women tend to have the lowest unemployment rates.

9. Which one of the following statements is NOT correct?
a) the natural rate of unemployment is estimated to be 5 - 6.5% in the U.S.
b) the term "full employment" means that 100% of the labor force is employed.
c) cyclical unemployment increases during periods of falling GDP.
d) a teenager looking for work during the summer would be considered 'seasonally' unemployed.
e) the natural rate of unemployment is higher in Europe than it is in the United States.

10. An economy operating below the natural rate of unemployment will be likely to:
a) experience an increase in wages.
b) experience an increase in prices.
c) higher inflation.
d) a decline in claims for unemployment insurance.
e) all of the above.

11. The consumer price index is:
a) an index of the prices of a basket of goods and services purchased by a typical household.
b) the broadest price index.
c) an index of the prices of goods and services typically produced in an economy.
d) an index of retail prices.
e) a leading indicator of the producer price index.

12. Which one of the following statements is correct?
a) an inflation rate of 5% may arise even if some prices are falling.
b) inflation is the percentage change in the price level.
c) deflation occurs when the price level declines.
d) a CPI of 128 means that there has been 28% inflation since the base year.
e) all of the above.

13. Which price index is the most widely used by the government and the private sector?
a) producer price index.
b) consumer price index.
c) the GDP deflator.
d) the chain-type price index.
e) the core index.

14. Which one of the following statements is true of the Consumer Price Index?
a) it does not take account of the price of imported goods and services.
b) the goods and services used to construct the index do not change from month to month.
c) it does not take into account the price of used goods.
d) it understates the true rate of inflation.
e) all of the above are true.

15. Suppose that in 1994 the CPI was 150 and that in 1995 the CPI was 165. The inflation rate between 1994-95 would be:
a) 15%.
b) 10%.
c) 65%.
d) 5%
e) not enough information to answer question.

72   Chapter 6

16. Which one of the following is NOT true about the CPI rate of inflation?
a) it is currently believed to be overestimated by 0.5 – 1.5% points.
b) the CPI does not take into account the ability of consumers to substitute purchases of goods with higher prices for similar goods with lower prices.
c) it may not be an accurate measure of inflation for every household/person because consumption spending patterns may differ from that used to construct the CPI.
d) if the inflation rate is 3%, all prices must necessarily be rising by three percent a year.
e) it incorporates price changes of imported goods.

17. Use the information below to calculate the sum of money an individual would need in 2005 to maintain the same of standard of living they have in 2004.

Income in 2004 = $39,000

CPI in 2004 = 140

CPI estimated for 2005 = 170

a) $66,300
b) $54,600
c) $130,000
d) $47,357
e) cannot be determined without information on the base year CPI.

VI. PRACTICE EXAM: ESSAY QUESTIONS

1. Describe the different types of unemployment and discuss which type may be most problematic for a country.

2. Explain why the CPI overstates the true rate of inflation. What impact does this have for cost-of-living adjustments and social security payments?

VII. ANSWER KEY: MULTIPLE CHOICE

1. Correct answer: b.

Discussion: The labor force consists of the employed plus the unemployed. Thus, it is these individuals that are age 16 and over who currently have a job (the "employed") plus those individuals age 16 and over who do not have a job and have actively looked for or are looking for a job (the "unemployed").

Statement a is a definition of for individuals or are employed. Statement c is not a definition of the labor force since the labor force also counts individuals that are working. Statement d is not correct. Statement e is a definition of the civilian population.

2. Correct answer: b.

Discussion: Statement b is true. The unemployment rate is percentage (or fraction) of the labor force that is currently without a job and actively seeking employment.

Statement a is not true. The government only counts individuals who do not have a job but who are actively seeking a job as "unemployed." Individuals without a job and not seeking employment are counted as "not in the labor force." Statement c is not correct. A nation's labor force is not equal to its population. If it was, infants would be considered unemployed! Statement d is not correct. Unbelievable as it may seem, the unemployment rate was 25% meaning that one-fourth of the nation's labor force was unemployed during the Great Depression. That statistic is very high by historical standards and fortunately, the U.S. has not experienced unemployment like that since the Great Depression. It should be mentioned that by 1940 (11 years after the Great Depression commenced), the unemployment rate was 17% which is still rather high by post-World War II standards. Statement e is not correct since only statement b is correct.

3. Correct answer: c.

Discussion: Discouraged workers are individuals that have stopped searching for employment (because they are so discouraged about their prospects of actually finding work). Since these workers are not actively seeking employment, they are not considered unemployed and thus are not part of the labor force, either.

Statement a is not correct based on the discussion above. Statement b defines an individual who is "working part-time for economic reasons." Your professor may use the term "underemployed." Statement d does not define a discouraged worker. In fact, someone who has a part-time job is considered employed and part of the labor force. Statement e is included for a laugh:).

4. Correct answer: c.

Discussion: Individuals are considered to be "frictionally unemployed" under a few circumstances. One of those circumstances arises when an individual quits one job to search for another. Your textbook mentions several other instances that give rise to frictional unemployment.

Statement a is an example of structural unemployment. Statement b is not a statement about unemployment. Statement d is an example of cyclical unemployment. Statement e is not correct because statements c and d are not examples of frictional unemployment.

5. Correct answer: a.

Discussion: Statement a is an example of a structurally unemployed individual. Structural unemployment occurs because of a mismatch between the skills a worker possesses and the skills necessary to obtain a job. A structurally unemployed individual is someone who lacks the skills necessary to be employed.

Statement b is an example of a cyclically unemployed individual. Statement c is an example of an individual who has a job, albeit a job for which her skills are above the level used on the job. Thus, the individual is underemployed. Statement d is an example of a frictionally unemployed individual. A frictionally unemployed individual is someone who has either newly entered the labor market in search of a job, re-entered the labor market after an absence (perhaps to raise a child) in search of a job, or left their job in search of another job. Thus, Helena would be considered a new entrant into the labor market. She is frictionally unemployed because she has yet to find a job. Statement e is not correct because statement a is the answer.

6. Correct answer: e.

Discussion: There are many reasons why the unemployment rate may not necessarily reflect the true unemployment picture. Statements a-d are all reasons why the unemployment rate may be a potentially misleading indicator of the extent to which a nation's labor resources are being used.

7. Correct answer: b.

Discussion: An economy is said to be at "full-employment" when the cyclical rate of unemployment is zero. While the cyclical rate of unemployment is zero, it does not mean the frictional, structural, or natural rates of unemployment are zero. In fact, the term "full-employment" is associated with an unemployment rate greater than 0%. This is because there will naturally be in any healthy, functioning economy some individuals who are newly entering the labor market, re-entering the labor market, or searching for another job, either because of frictional or structural unemployment. That is, there will naturally always be some unemployment for frictional and structural reasons. For the U.S., the estimate of the natural unemployment rate which is the sum of the frictional and structural unemployment rates is 5.0-6.5%. Thus, full-employment is said to be achieved when the national unemployment rate is in the range of 5.0-6.5%.

8. Correct answer: e.

Discussion: Whereas married men and women tend to have the lowest unemployment rates, teenagers tend to have the highest unemployment rates. Thus, statement e is correct.

Statement a is not correct because even people with part-time jobs are counted as employed since they do have a job. Statement b is not true; a marginally attached worker is someone who has worked in the past, but has stopped working for a variety of reasons. Statement c is not correct; the labor force participation rate is calculated as the labor force (sum of employed plus unemployed individuals) divided by the population age sixteen and over. Statement d is not correct because only individuals over 16 years of age that have actively sought employment are considered unemployed. Thus, an individual who is 16 years or older, but is not looking for a job, is not counted as unemployed.

9. Correct answer: b.

Discussion: The term full-employment allows for there to be frictional and structural unemployment. Some unemployment is always to be expected in the natural functioning of an economy. Thus, 100% of the labor force will not typically be employed. This is a way of saying that there will always be some "natural unemployment" in an economy.

Statement a is correct since the current estimate of the natural unemployment rate for the U.S. is 5 - 6.5%.

Statement c is correct because a decline in GDP leads to job losses and higher cyclical unemployment. Statement d is correct because seasonal unemployment arises when people begin to look for work during the start of a particular season (summer, Christmas, etc) or lose their jobs because of the end of a particular season. Statement e is correct. Europe's natural rate of unemployment is estimated to be between 7-10%.

10. Correct answer: e.

Discussion: An economy operating below the natural rate of unemployment will have a negative cyclical unemployment rate. This means the unemployment rate is below what is considered 'natural' in a healthy, functioning economy. This means that firms are hiring aggressively and individuals will have an easier time getting hired. Consequently, wages will rise as firms begin to compete with each other for workers. As wages rise, the prices of goods and services those firms produce will rise. If this happens throughout the economy, inflation may result. Moreover, with the job market strong, claims for unemployment insurance will decline.

11. Correct answer: a.

Discussion: The consumer price index (CPI) is an index of the prices of a basket of goods and services purchased by a typical consumer. The goods and services in the basket do not change in calculating the CPI and for this reason, the basket of goods and services used in the calculation is said to be "fixed."

Statement b is not correct. The broadest price index is the chain price index for GDP. It is the broadest price index since it covers the prices of a broader range of goods and services than the CPI does. Statement c is a statement about the chain price index for GDP. Statement d is a made-up answer. Statement e is not correct. The producer price index (which your book does not mention) is viewed as a leading indicator (an "omen") of changes in the CPI.

12. Correct answer: e.

Discussion: Statement a is a correct statement because inflation measures what happens to the average level of prices. Since the price level is an average of prices of all different types of goods and services, it may turn out that some prices have actually fallen while other have risen in such a way that, on average, the price level may rise by 5%. Statement b is correct since inflation is measured as the percentage change in the price level. Statement c is correct since a decline in the price level is referred to as "deflation" (that is, negative inflation). Statement d is correct because in the base year, the CPI is 100. If the CPI is now 128, it implies that there has been 28% inflation between the base year and the current year.

13. Correct answer: b.

Discussion: The Consumer Price Index (CPI) is the price index that is most widely used by the government. The government uses the CPI to make cost-of-living adjustments to social security benefits it pays out to retirees. Such cost-of-living adjustments are given so as to keep the "real" or "purchasing power" value of the benefits the same from year to year. The private sector also uses the CPI to make cost-of-living adjustments to wages, particularly to union wages.

The producer price index (not discussed in your textbook) is a price index of goods and services used by producers. It is sometimes referred to as the "wholesale price index." The GDP deflator and the chain-type price index are price indices that are constructed from the prices of the goods and services in GDP. The core index is (not discussed in your textbook) is a price index that subtracts food and energy prices out of the CPI. Food and energy prices tend to be the most volatile (fluctuating) prices in the index.

14. Correct answer: b.

Discussion: The Consumer Price Index is based on a basket of goods and services that a typical household buys. The goods and services included in the basket do not change from month-to-month when the government collects the price data. Thus, the CPI is based on a fixed basket of goods and services.

Statement a is not correct because the CPI can include the price of imported goods and services. The chain-type price index and GDP deflator do not include the price of imported goods and services. Statement c is not correct because the CPI may include the price of used goods. Statement d is not correct; it is currently estimated that the percentage change in the CPI overstates the true rate of inflation by 0.5 - 1.5 percentage points. Thus, if the government reports a rate of inflation of 4%, the true rate of inflation is likely to be 2.5 - 3.5%.

15. Correct answer: b.

Discussion: The inflation rate is calculated as the percentage change in the CPI. The percentage change in the CPI is calculated as [(165-150)/150] X 100 = 10%. Thus, statement b is correct. None of the other statements are correct.

16. Correct answer: d.

Discussion: Statement d is not true of the CPI since an inflation rate of 3% does not necessarily imply that *all* prices are rising by 3%. Some prices could be rising by more than 3% and some by less than 3% with a reported inflation rate of 3%. All of the other statements are true.

17. Correct answer: d.

Discussion: To calculate the sum of money an individual would need to maintain the same standard of living in another year, the current sum of money, the current CPI, and what it will be in another year is needed. In this case, the calculation requires taking the sum of money and dividing it by the CPI in the current year. This "deflates" the sum of money back to the base year value. Then, that sum of money is "inflated" up to the year in question by using the CPI for that year. This involves performing the following calculation using the numbers given:

($39,000 / 140) X 170 = $39,000 X (170/140) = $47,357

VIII. ANSWER KEY: ESSAY QUESTIONS

1. The three types of unemployment are cyclical, frictional, and structural. The sum of the three is the unemployment rate. The sum of the frictional and structural unemployment rates is called the "natural rate of unemployment." Cyclical unemployment is caused by the ups and downs of the economy. Sometimes the economy booms and sometimes it goes into a recession. People who lose their jobs because the economy goes into a recession are categorized as cyclically unemployed. It is presumed that once the economy comes out of the recession, these people will be re-employed. Cyclical unemployment is of a fairly short-term nature, particularly in comparison to structural unemployment. Frictional unemployment occurs as people re-enter the labor force or enter the labor force for the first time (say upon graduation from high school or college). These people may be

unemployed for a time as they search for a job to which their skills are matched. Frictional unemployment also arises because people leave their jobs in search of another job -- perhaps a better paying one or one that is more satisfying. Frictional unemployment is also of a fairly short-term nature, particularly in comparison to structural unemployment. New entrants, re-entrants, and job switchers are part of a natural functioning economy. There will always be, at any point in time, these types of people looking for jobs. In other words, we should not expect that the frictional unemployment rate could be pushed to 0%. The third type of unemployment is structural unemployment. Structural unemployment occurs because of a mismatch between the skills a worker possesses and the skills necessary to obtain a job. Structural unemployment is of a longer-term nature. The structurally unemployed tend to have a more difficult time finding work and may even require re-training or new skills in order to find work. Structural unemployment is also a natural part of the economy in the sense that the structure of the economy changes over time and so, too, the demand for different types of workers. For example, the U.S. economy has become a more high-tech economy and the service industry has grown as an employer relative to the manufacturing industry. This structural change in the economy leads to unemployment in pockets of industry across the nation that are outmoded.

2. The CPI overstates the true rate of inflation because the basket of goods and services that are priced from month-to-month do not change. Implicitly, this means that consumers do not change their consumption spending patterns, either. However, consumers are able to alter and do alter their spending patterns in response to price changes. For example, suppose the price of a name-brand medicine goes up and that this brand is one of the goods in the basket used to construct the CPI. Consumers may switch to a generic brand of the medicine, thus avoiding the higher price for the name brand. However, the CPI will not register this switch to a lower price brand because it is constructed based on a fixed basket of goods and services. In fact, the CPI will increase because the price of the name-brand medicine that is included in the CPI has increased, even though consumers have been able to avoid the price increase. Thus, percentage changes in the CPI may overstate the actual rate of inflation to consumers.

The CPI may also overstate the rate of inflation because any increases in the prices of goods and services in the CPI are all considered to be inflationary. However, some prices increase because the good or service being purchased has improved. For example, suppose the new safety features of automobiles cause automobile prices to rise. An automobile today is now a different product from what it was in the past. It is a safer vehicle. The higher price tag should thus not be considered as inflationary because consumers are paying a higher price but getting more for their money.

For both of these reasons, it is estimated that percentage changes in the CPI overstate the true rate of inflation by 0.5% - 1.5%.

Cost-of-living adjustments and social security benefits are tied to the rate of change in the CPI. This means that they will be adjusted upward by the percentage increase in the CPI. For example, if the CPI inflation rate for 1996 was 2%, then social security benefits will automatically increase by 2%. This means that if a retiree was receiving a $1,000 per month social security payment, the payment would increase by 2% to $1,020. The same would be true for any worker or individual who has a payment tied to the CPI.

If the CPI currently overstates the true rate of inflation, then, in effect too much in social security benefits are being paid out. In the example above, if the true rate of inflation is actually 1%, then the retiree's benefit would only rise to $1,010 and the government would save $10 per month. While this may seem like a small saving for the government, multiply it by 12 months and the number of people receiving social security benefits. As you can imagine, the savings to the government (and ultimately the taxpayers) could end up being quite large.

However, retirees may argue that the CPI rate of inflation isn't relevant to compute their purchasing power. That is, the basket of goods and services used to construct the CPI is not the basket that they typically purchase. Since retirees are older, they may argue that they spend more of their income on medical services than that reflected in the CPI. Since medical fees are increasing at a much faster pace than, say entertainment or transportation prices, retirees may feel that the government should continue to make cost-of-living adjustments based on a number that overstates the true rate of inflation.

Take It to the Net

We invite you to visit the O'Sullivan/Sheffrin page on the Prentice Hall Web site at:
http://www.prenhall.com/osullivan/
for this chapter's World Wide Web exercise.

CHAPTER 7
THE ECONOMY AT FULL-EMPLOYMENT

I. OVERVIEW

In this chapter, you will learn about the factors that enable an economy that is already operating at full-employment to produce more output (GDP). You will learn that employment together with a given capital stock determine how much output an economy can produce. You will consider how the labor market and goods market operate when wages and prices are flexible. You will learn how changes to employment and/or the capital stock affect the full-employment level of output. The tools you will use to study the relationship between employment, the capital stock and output are the aggregate production function and a supply and demand model of the labor market. You will also discuss how real business cycle theory and how changes in technology can alter the full-employment level of output. You will also see that at the full-employment level of output is divided among competing sectors in the economy. You will learn that increases in government spending 'crowd out' or reduce spending by other sectors in the economy and that reductions in government spending 'crowd in' or permit greater spending by other sectors in the economy. That is, you will see how changes in government spending can lead to changes in consumption, investment and net exports. You will see that such government spending policies come at an opportunity cost when the economy is operating at its full-employment level.

II. CHECKLIST

By the end of this chapter you should be able to:

- Explain what factors determine the level of output an economy is capable of producing at full-employment.
- Describe what the 'classical model' for an economy assumes.
- Define what is meant by the term 'full-employment.'
- Define and graph a production function.
- Explain the shape of the production function and relate it to diminishing marginal returns.
- Discuss how changes in the capital stock affect the production function.
- Discuss labor demand and explain why it is negatively sloped when graphed against the real wage rate.
- Discuss labor supply and explain the substitution and income effects on the slope of the labor supply curve.
- Consider changes in the demand and supply of labor and their effect on the real wage, the price of output, and the full-employment level of output.
- Discuss the effects of a tax on labor on employment, the real wage, and output.
- Discuss the Laffer's idea on the effects of reducing tax rates.

- ❏ Discuss Real Business Cycle theory and explain how changes in technology can lead to changes in the full-employment level of output.
- ❏ Define crowding out and crowding in.
- ❏ Discuss the effects of crowding out and crowding in a closed and open economy.
- ❏ Explain what causes crowding out and crowding in and which sectors of the economy may be crowded out or crowded in as a result of an increase in government spending.

III. KEY TERMS

Classical model: Models that assume wages and prices adjust freely to changes in demand and supply.

Labor: Human effort, including both physical and mental effort, used to produce goods and services.

Stock of capital: The total of all the machines, equipment, and buildings in the entire economy.

Production function: The relationship between the level of output and the factors of production.

Income effect: As income rises, a worker may choose to work fewer hours and enjoy more leisure.

Substitution effect: An increase in the wage will raise the opportunity cost of leisure and lead to an increase in hours worked.

Real wage: The wage paid to workers adjusted for changes in prices.

Full-employment output: The level of output that results when the economy is producing at full employment.

Real business cycle theory: The economic theory that emphasizes how shocks to technology can cause fluctuations in economic activity.

Crowding out: The reduction in investment (or other component of GDP) in the long run caused by an increase in government spending.

Closed economy: An economy without international trade.

Crowding in: The increase of investment (or other component of GDP) in the long run caused by a decrease in government spending.

Open economy: An economy with international trade.

IV. PERFORMANCE ENHANCING TIPS (PETS)

PET #1

The production function is a graph relating output to the input labor. The capital stock is held fixed. Thus, changes in the capital stock will cause the production function to shift and changes in labor will cause movements along the production function.

You may wish to review PET #1 from Chapter 1 of the study guide.

An increase in the amount of labor that an economy uses will cause a movement out along the production function to higher levels of output. A decrease in the amount of labor will cause a movement down along the production function to lower levels of output.

An increase in the capital stock will shift the production function up (and to the left). The shift shows that for every amount of labor as before, more output is produced. A decrease in the capital stock works in reverse.

PET #2

The shorthand notation for a production function, Y = F(K,L) is also a shorthand notation for an equation that relates the amount of output to the amount of capital and labor an economy uses.

For example, Y = F(K,L) means that the amount of output an economy produces depends in some specific way on the amount of capital and labor used. A specific equation for Y = F(K,L) may be:

$$Y = 0.7 \times L + 0.3 \times K$$

Thus, if you are told that the amount of labor an economy has available is 1,000,000 units and the amount of capital an economy has available is 200,000, then you could determine how many units of output an economy could produce. You would plug in the numbers to get Y = 0.7 X (1,000,000) + 0.3 X (200,000) = 700,000 + 60,000 = 760,000 units of output.

PET #3

Crowding out occurs at the full-employment level of output because any increase in government purchases of output necessarily requires a reduction in purchases by some other sector(s) of the economy (consumers, businesses, foreign).

First of all, you may wish to replace the term "crowding out" with "reduction in" if it makes it easier for you to understand what crowding out is about. That is, when government spending increases, spending by other sectors of the economy will be reduced.

Let's look at some examples of crowding out. Suppose country A is operating at the full-employment level of output and at this level is producing $2 trillion worth of goods and services. Further, suppose that consumers purchase total $1.2 trillion; businesses purchases total $0.4 trillion; and government purchases total $0.6 trillion. Thus, total purchases equal $2.2 trillion which is more than the $2 trillion produced by country A. Thus, it must be that the foreign sector, i.e. exports minus imports, purchases total -$0.2. That is, $0.2 trillion of the $2.2 trillion purchased by consumers, businesses, and the government of Country A is satisfied through foreign supply.

Now, suppose the government increases its spending from $0.6 trillion to $1.0 trillion. With the economy operating at full-employment, only $2 trillion worth of output can be produced by Country A even though total spending by Country A's consumers, businesses, and government now totals $2.6 trillion.

82   Chapter 7

Something has to give -- consumer, business, and foreign sector spending will have to be re-arranged to accommodate the increase in government spending.

Let's look at one example of crowding out. Suppose country A's consumers and businesses do not change their spending behavior (so they continue to purchase 1.2 + 0.4 = $1.6 trillion) while government spending has increased to $1 trillion. Thus, country A's consumers, businesses, and government in total purchase $2.6 trillion worth of output. The $2.6 trillion worth of purchases by consumers, businesses, and the government must be satisfied through $2 trillion worth of production by country A supplemented with $0.6 trillion worth of (net) production from abroad. That is, country A must import $0.6 trillion more than it will export. Thus, country A's trade balance declines to -$0.6 trillion. That is, the trade deficit gets worse. In this sense, we would say that net exports are crowded out (reduced) by $0.4 billion because the trade balance worsens from -$0.2 trillion to -$0.6 trillion.

Let's look at another example of crowding out. Suppose that consumers and businesses both cut back their purchases by $0.2 trillion but that the trade deficit remains at -$0.2 trillion. Here, we would say that consumption and investment spending are crowded out (reduced) by a total of $0.4 billion (0.2 + 0.2). The crowding out of spending by the private sector accommodates the increased government spending. Thus, purchases by country A's consumers, businesses, and government would total $2.2 trillion (1.0 + 0.2 + 1.0). Since the country can only produce $2 trillion worth of output, the foreign sector brings in an additional $0.2 trillion (i.e. country A imports $0.2 trillion more than it exports) to satisfy the purchases of country A's residents.

IV. PRACTICE EXAM: MULTIPLE CHOICE QUESTIONS

1. Classical models in economics assume:
a) that wages and prices are completely flexible.
b) shocks to an economy are not long lasting.
c) an economy has a natural tendency to return to a state of full employment.
d) the potential or full-employment level of output is determined by the amount of capital and labor an economy has available.
e) all of the above.

2. An economy that operates at its full-employment or potential output level experiences:
a) cyclical unemployment only.
b) frictional unemployment only.
c) structural unemployment only.
d) frictional plus structural unemployment.
e) cyclical plus frictional unemployment.

3. The short run aggregate production function:
a) is negatively sloped.
b) shows that output increases but at a decreasing rate.
c) will shift down (to the right) as the stock of capital increases.
d) reflects increasing marginal returns.
e) shows how the level of output changes as more capital is employed, holding the stock of labor fixed.

4. Which one of the following would shift the demand for labor to the right (increase the demand for labor)?
a) an increased tax on workers that employers must pay.
b) a decrease in the real wage rate.
c) an increase in the capital stock.
d) an increase in the supply of workers.
e) a minimum wage.

5. Which one of the following statements is true of labor supply?
a) if the income effect dominates the substitution effect, the labor supply curve will be positively sloped.
b) if the income effect dominates the substitution effect, the labor supply curve will be negatively sloped.
c) a higher real wage rate may induce some workers to take on more leisure time and work less.
d) empirical estimates suggest that the labor supply curve is nearly horizontal.
e) (b) and (c).

6. Which one of the following statements is NOT true?
a) according to the substitution effect, an increase in the real wage rate causes workers to work more and take less leisure time.
b) according to the income effect, an increase in the real wage rate causes workers to work fewer hours and take more leisure time.
c) the substitution and income effects work in the same direction.
d) an increase in the capital stock makes workers more productive.
e) an increase in the capital stock will increase the demand for labor.

7. In an economy operating at the full-employment level of output, an increase in the demand for labor will _____ the real wage rate and _____ the full-employment level of output.
a) increase/increase.
b) increase/decrease.
c) decrease/decrease.
d) decrease/increase.
e) have an uncertain effect on/increase.

84 Chapter 7

8. In an economy operating at the full-employment level of output, immigration may:
a) increase labor supply.
b) reduce the equilibrium real wage rate.
c) raise the full-employment level of output.
d) cause a temporary rise in the unemployment rate.
e) all of the above.

9. Which one of the following could be responsible for decreasing the level of employment?
a) an increase in the capital stock.
b) a decrease in the capital stock.
c) a technological advancement.
d) a decrease in vacation time taken by workers.
e) an increase in the population.

10. Which one of the following statements is correct?
a) the Laffer curve illustrates that a cut in the tax rate could increase tax revenues collected by the government.
b) as more labor is hired along with more capital, diminishing marginal returns to output occurs.
c) one of the assumptions of classical models in economics is that wages are slow to adjust to changes in the demand and supply of labor.
d) a decrease in the stock of capital will cause the production function to shift up.
e) the income effect tells us that a higher wage rate will induce people to work more and take less time for leisure.

11. Which one of the following statements is true of real business cycle theory?
a) it emphasizes that shocks to human capital can cause fluctuations in real GDP.
b) it explains unemployment as arising from rigid wage adjustment.
c) a harmful "shock" to technology may cause an increase in the demand for labor.
d) a technological breakthrough will lead to an increase in the potential or full-employment level of output.
e) all of the above are true.

12. The equation that can be used to illustrate crowding out and crowding in an open economy is:
a) Y = C+I+G +NX
b) Y=C+I+G-NX
c) Y=C+I+G
d) Y=I+G+NX
e) Y=C+I+NX

13. Assuming a country is operating at the full-employment level of output, a government that increases its share of purchases of its country's GDP:
a) incurs an opportunity cost.
b) may find that its exports decline and its imports increase.
c) may find that investment spending declines.
d) may find that consumer spending declines.
e) all of the above.

14. Suppose you are given the following information on GDP and shares (percentages) of GDP purchased by consumers, businesses, the government, and the foreign sector:

GDP = $3 trillion.
Share of consumption expenditures = 50%
Share of investment expenditures = 15%
Share of government expenditures = 15%
Share of net exports = 20%.

Based on these numbers, which one of the following statements is true?
a) an example of crowding out would be if the share of consumption expenditures increased to 60% and the share of investment expenditures decreased to 5%.
b) an example of crowding out would be if the share of consumption expenditures increased to 75% and the share of net exports declined to -5%.
c) an example of crowding out would be if the share of government expenditures increased to 25% and consumption expenditures fell by 7% and investment expenditures fell by 3%.
d) an example of crowding out would be if all of the shares fell by, say, 5%.
e) if the share of government expenditures increased to 30% and investment expenditures increased to 20% but consumption expenditures decreased to 30%, we would conclude that the private sector, on net, had been crowded in.

VI. PRACTICE EXAM: ESSAY QUESTIONS

1. In the U.S. during the 1980s, the capital stock increased as did the supply of labor. Europe experienced similar events. What effects would these changes have on employment and GDP and what might explain why the U.S. experienced lower real wages whereas Europe experienced higher real wages?

2. What does it mean for a labor supply curve to be vertical? Compare and contrast the effects of a decrease in tax on labor on the real wage rate, employment, and output (GDP) for a labor supply curve that is vertical and one that is positively sloped.

86   Chapter 7

VII. ANSWER KEY: MULTIPLE CHOICE QUESTIONS

1. Correct answer: e

Discussion: Statement a is a Classical economists way of saying that markets (labor, capital, goods) will move to equilibrium quickly. Statement b means that shocks to an economy are not long lasting which is a way of saying that the economy adjusts quickly to negative circumstances and thus returns quickly to the full-employment level of output. That is, recessions should not be long lasting. Statement c means that the economy, without government intervention, will cure itself (quickly) of any economic downturns. Statement d means that the supply of factors of production (or resources) in an economy determines how much output can be produced at full-employment.

2. Correct answer: d.

Discussion: An economy that operates at its full-employment level of output does NOT have a zero rate of unemployment. There will, at any point in time, be some unemployment that is part of a natural-functioning, healthy economy. The unemployment rate that presides when the economy operates at the full-employment level of output is referred to as the "natural rate of unemployment." The natural rate of unemployment consists of frictional plus structural unemployment. Remember that frictional unemployment is due to new entrants, re-entrants, and job leavers searching for work. Structural unemployment is due to the mismatch of skills between workers and the needs of industry. These types of unemployment will occur even when the economy is operating at its potential level of output.

3. Correct answer: b.

Discussion: Statement b implies two things: (1) the aggregate production function is positively sloped; and (2) that the slope flattens out as the level of output produced increases. That is, the aggregate production function exhibits diminishing returns.

Statement a is not correct because the aggregate production function is positively sloped. Statement c is not correct; an increase in the stock of capital will be represented by an upward shift (to the left) in the aggregate production function. The shift shows that with more capital, more output can be produced for any level of labor employed than before. Statement d is not correct; the aggregate production function exhibits diminishing marginal returns. Statement e is not correct; the aggregate production function shows how output changes as the amount of labor employed changes, holding the capital stock fixed.

4. Correct answer: c.

Discussion: An increase in the capital stock will raise the productivity of workers and thus increase the benefit to firms of hiring workers. That is, firms would be willing to hire more workers at every wage rate than before. Alternatively, a rightward shift in demand also shows that firms would be willing to pay a higher real wage rate than before for every amount of labor. (You may wish to review PET #4 of Chapter 4 for insight).

Statement a is not correct; a tax on labor paid by employers will shift the demand for labor to the left. Statement b is not correct. A decrease in the real wage rate will cause a movement along the labor demand curve (not a shift of it). The decrease in the real wage rate will raise the quantity of labor demanded. Statement d is not correct. An increase in the supply of workers would be represented by a rightward shift in the labor supply curve, not a rightward shift in the labor demand curve. Statement e is not correct. A minimum wage will cause a movement along the labor demand curve, not a shift in it.

5. Correct answer: e.

Discussion: The income effect is that at higher real wage rates, workers earn more per hour earn more income, purchase more leisure, and therefore work less hours. In this case, higher real wage rates would be associated with lower employment, not higher employment. Thus, the labor supply curve would be negatively sloped. You also learned in this chapter that a higher real wage rate may induce some workers to work more (not less). That is, these workers substitute more work effort for less leisure time. If the substitution effect dominated, then the labor supply curve would be positively sloped.

Statement a is not correct based on the discussion above. Statement d is not correct; empirical estimates suggest that the labor supply curve is nearly vertical.

6. Correct answer: c.

Discussion: Statement c is not true because the income and substitution effects work in opposite directions. That is, a rise in the real wage causes workers to work more hours according to the substitution effect but causes workers to work fewer hours according to the income effect. Likewise, a *decline* in the real wage causes workers to work fewer hours according to the substitution effect but causes workers to work more hours according to the income effect. Thus, the income and substitution effect work in opposite directions.

Statements a, b, d, and e are all true.

7. Correct answer: a.

Discussion: An increase in the demand for labor will shift the demand for labor to the right (see multiple choice question 4 for review). An increase in the demand for labor, as for any good, will increase the price of labor, i.e. the real wage rate. Thus, the real wage rate will rise. The rightward shift in the demand for labor will also raise the amount of labor employed. With more labor employed and more capital available for production, the full-employment level of output must necessarily increase.

8. Correct answer: e.

Discussion: Immigration adds to an economy's available pool of workers, i.e. labor supply increases. As labor supply increases (rightward shift in labor supply), the real wage rate will decline and thus more workers will become employed. With more workers employed, the full-employment level of output will rise. However, it should be noted that immigration may cause a temporary increase in the unemployment rate as the immigrants search for jobs. In the classical model, the increase in the unemployment rate should be short-lived.

9. Correct answer: b.

Discussion: A decrease in the level of employment could be caused by the demand for labor decreasing (shifting left) or by the supply of labor decreasing (shifting left). Statement b is correct because a decrease in the capital stock makes workers less productive and thereby reduces the demand for labor. The reduced demand for labor results in fewer workers being hired.

Statements a and c are examples of factors that would increase the demand for labor and consequently increase the level of employment. Statements d and e are examples of factors that would increase the supply of labor. An increase in the supply of labor will raise the level of employment, too.

10. Correct answer: a.

Discussion: the Laffer curve illustrates a paradoxical concept that a *cut* in the tax rate could actually *increase* tax revenues collected by the government. The effect of the tax cut depends on the type of tax being cut as well as on the rate it is before the cut.

Statement b is not correct since diminishing marginal returns to output (production) occurs when one input, either labor or capital, is held fixed. In this chapter, the capital stock is held fixed. Thus, as more and more labor is hired, the amount of output produced by each additional worker declines. This is referred to as diminishing marginal returns. Statement c is not correct since one of the assumptions of classical models is that wages (and prices) are flexible and quick to adjust to changes in demand and supply. Statement d is not correct because a decrease in the capital stock will reduce the capacity of the economy to produce. This is represented by a downward shift in the production function. Statement e is not correct because the income effect tells us that a higher wage rate will induce people to take more leisure time, not less. Thus, they will also be inclined to work less.

11. Correct answer: d.

Discussion: According to real business cycle theory, a technological improvement or breakthrough (such as the computer revolution) will lead to an increase in the potential level of real GDP. This happens because the technological breakthrough shifts up the production function and at the same time increases the demand for labor. Both of these two events enable the output capacity of an economy to increase. Thus, the potential level of real GDP increases.

Statement a is not correct. The real business cycle theory claims that shocks to technology, not human capital, cause fluctuations in real GDP. Statement b is not correct. Real business cycle theory is not capable of explaining lasting periods of unemployment. Statement c is not correct. Adverse or harmful shocks to technology typically create decreases in the demand for labor. Statement e is not correct because not all of the statements are true.

12. Correct answer: a.

Discussion: In an open economy, the full-employment level of output is purchased by competing sectors – households, businesses, the government, and the foreign sector. The equation in statement a illustrates this concept. For example, if the full-employment level of output was $100 trillion with $25 trillion being purchased by households (C), $25 trillion by businesses (I), $25 trillion by the government (G), and $25 trillion by the foreign sector (NX), then an increase in government spending (G) would have to cause a reduction in spending by C, I, and/or NX.

Statement c is the equation that can be used to illustrate crowding out/in in a closed economy. A closed economy is one with no foreign sector and hence no net exports.

13. Correct answer: e.

Discussion: An increase in government spending incurs an opportunity cost because it crowds out spending by other sectors of the economy. Thus, an increase in government spending may incur an opportunity cost (giving up something) of decreased spending by consumers. That is, the economy, as a whole must give up some spending by consumers. The increased government spending also leads to crowding out of net exports (i.e. exports will decline but imports will rise) and investment spending. This is not to say that some groups of consumers or businesses will not be crowded in. For example, your book mentions that an increase in government spending on highways may crowd in (increase) some types of investment spending.

14. Correct answer: c.

Discussion: Crowding out is caused by an increase in government expenditures. Crowding out means that an increase in government spending causes a reduction in spending by consumers and/or businesses and/or through net exports. Thus, statements a and b cannot be correct because there is no basis for crowding out. Government spending has not changed. Statement d cannot be correct because government expenditures along with consumption and investment expenditures decline. Statement e is not correct because the share of government expenditures increased by 10% but investment expenditures increased by 5% while consumption expenditures declined by 20% so that in total, private sector spending was crowded out (reduced) by -15% = (+5% - 20%), not crowded in, on net. Statement d is the only statement that reflects crowding out. In this case, while government expenditures rise by 10%, consumption expenditures are reduced by 7% and investment expenditures by 3% for a total of a 10% reduction in private sector spending. That is, private sector spending is crowded out by the increase in government spending.

VIII. ANSWER KEY: ESSAY QUESTIONS

1. The increased capital stock makes labor more productive. As such, the marginal benefit to the firm of workers increase. An increase in the marginal benefit of workers is represented by a rightward shift in the demand for labor curve. As the demand for labor shifts to the right, the real wage rate increases and the level of employment increases as well.

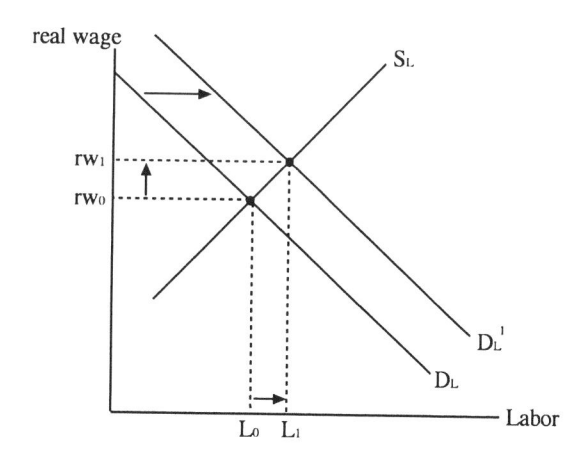

The increased supply of labor would be represented by a rightward shift in the labor supply curve. The increased supply of labor leads to a lower real wage rate (which induces firms to hire more workers) and a higher level of employment.

90   Chapter 7

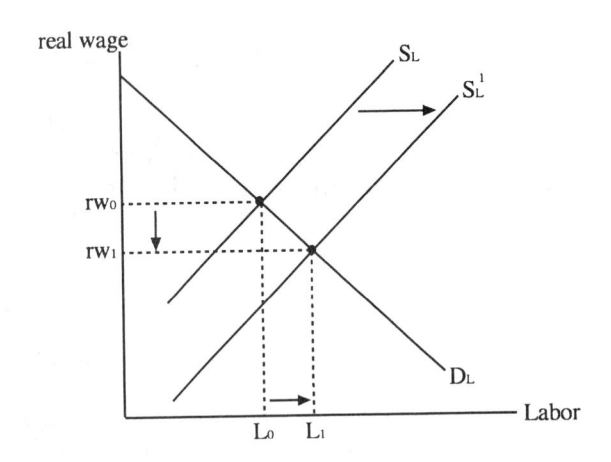

The two effects together suggest that unambiguously the level of employment will increase. However, the net effect on the real wage depends on the magnitude of the shift rightward in the demand for labor relative to the shift rightward in the supply of labor. A first case is that the increase in the demand for labor is larger than the labor supply increase. Here, the real wage rate will rise. A second case is that the increase in the demand for labor is smaller than the increase in the supply of labor. Here, the real wage will fall. Since the U.S. experienced an increase in employment alongside a decrease in the real wage, the second case must be applicable. In Europe, the level of employment increased as did the real wage. These combined effects would indicate that the first case is applicable.

2. If the labor supply curve is vertical, it means that a higher real wage rate does not induce more people to enter the labor force. That is, the real wage rate simply does not influence, in the aggregate, the labor force's choice between leisure and working. It has no effect, in the aggregate. Some people may choose to enter the labor force whereas others might work fewer hours (part-time) but the combined effect of everybody's decision leaves no net increase in employment as the real wage rate rises. What may be happening is that the income effect and the substitution effect are working to offset each other exactly. Remember that the income effect would, by itself, make the labor supply curve negatively sloped. However, the substitution effect would make it positively sloped. If the two effects "cancel" then a vertical labor supply curve may result. While a vertical labor supply curve indicates that changes in the real wage do not have an impact on the aggregate amount of labor supplied, it does not rule out the possibility of other factors influencing labor supply.

If labor supply is vertical and taxes on labor are reduced, this would translate into an increased demand for labor. However, the increased demand for labor would have no effect on the level of employment. To see this, look at the graph below.

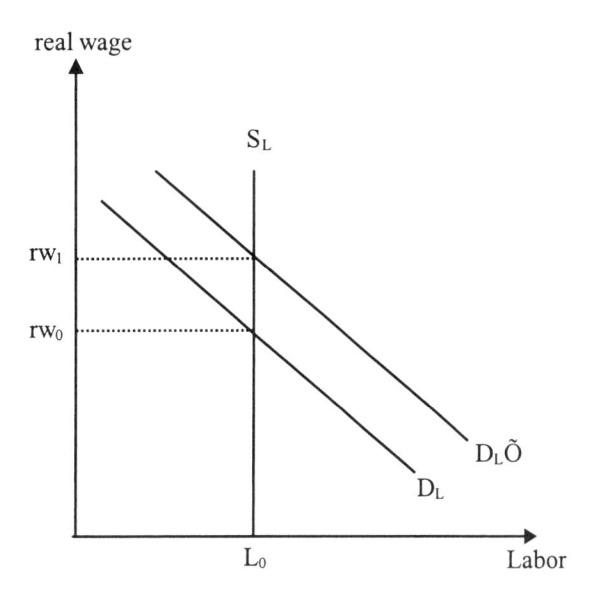

[Graph: real wage vs Labor, vertical S_L at L_0, two downward demand curves D_L and D_L', showing rw_0 and rw_1]

Notice that labor does not change but the real wage does.

By contrast, if the supply of labor is positively sloped, an increase in the demand for labor will raise the level of employment from L_0 to L_1 as illustrated in the graph below. The real wage will also rise as show in the graph below.

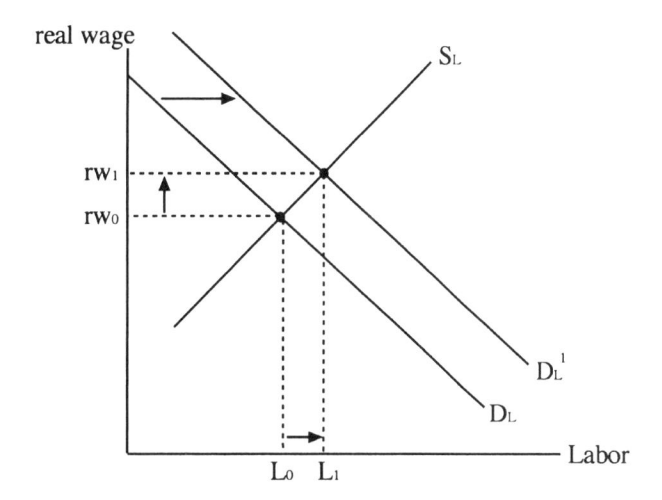

[Graph: real wage vs Labor, upward S_L, two downward demand curves D_L and D_L^1, equilibrium shifting from (L_0, rw_0) to (L_1, rw_1)]

As for the effects of a reduction in taxes on labor on the level of output, we can use the aggregate production function to compare the two cases. When labor supply is vertical, there is no increase in the amount of labor hired. Thus, there is no change in the amount of output able to be produced. Y_0 thus remains the level of output produced when labor supply is vertical and there is a decrease in taxes on labor. This is depicted by the graph below.

By contrast, when labor supply is positively sloped, a reduction in taxes on labor, by increasing the demand for labor and raising the employment level, leads to an increase in the level of output. The increased level of employment is represented by moving along the production function from L_0 to L_1 as shown below. As more labor is employed, more output can be produced. Thus, output rises from Y_0 to Y_1.

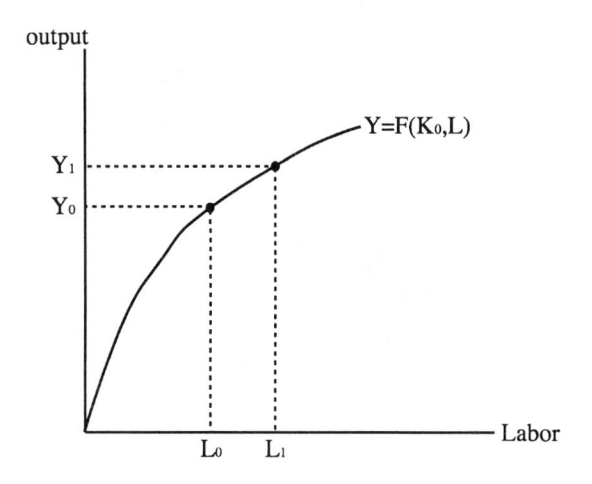

Take It to the Net

We invite you to visit the O'Sullivan/Sheffrin page on the Prentice Hall Web site at:
http://www.prenhall.com/osullivan/
for this chapter's World Wide Web exercise.

APPENDIX TO CHAPTER 7

I. OVERVIEW

In the appendix, you will use a simple model of an economy along with a graphic representation of it that develops the explicit relationship between saving, gross investment and depreciation, and capital deepening. In the simple model, the population will be held constant (zero growth rate) and there is assumed to be no government (and therefore no government spending, taxing, or policy) and no foreign sector (and therefore no exports or imports). You will learn that a country that saves more today increases its capital stock, capital per worker (i.e. capital deepening), real wages, and also its potential for future growth. You will learn that a higher rate of saving today comes at a sacrifice -- decreased consumption today. You will learn that the difference between the level of saving and the amount of depreciation determines the change in a country's capital stock. If the level of saving is just equal to the amount of depreciation, a country's net investment is zero. When this occurs, a country's economic growth through additions to the capital stock and capital per worker (capital deepening) will stop. You will learn that an increase in the saving rate of a country will lead to a higher capital stock and ultimately more output. You will learn that technological progress through raising output can increase the level of saving and thus lead to increases in the capital stock.

II. CHECKLIST

By the end of this appendix, you should be able to:

❑ Depict the process of economics with a Solow diagram.
❑ Explain how capital deepening is affected by saving relative to depreciation.
❑ Explain how a higher level of saving can lead to higher real wages and more output.
❑ Explain how technological progress enhances capital deepening.

III. KEY TERMS

Please see the key terms to this chapter.

IV. PERFORMANCE ENHANCING TIPS (PETS)

Please see the PETS to this chapter.

V. PRACTICE EXAM: MULTIPLE CHOICE QUESTIONS

1. Capital deepening will stop when a country's:
a) saving rate is equal to the rate of depreciation of the capital stock.
b) level of saving is equal to the amount depreciation of the capital stock.
c) gross investment is 1%.
d) consumption equals saving.
e) diminishing returns occurs.

2. If depreciation is greater than the level of saving:
a) technological progress will not occur.
b) real wages will rise.
c) output per worker (labor productivity) will decrease (assuming the size of the workforce does not change).
d) the capital stock will decline.
e) (c) and (d).

3. Technological progress leads to:
a) increases in output per worker.
b) increases in gross investment.
c) increases in the level of saving.
d) increases in real wages.
e) all of the above.

4. Which one of the following statements is NOT true of the Solow model?
a) as economy grows, the level of saving increases at an increasing rate.
b) capital per worker increases if the level of saving is greater than the amount of depreciation of a country's capital stock.
c) output increases but at a decreasing rate.
d) it may take decades for the process of capital deepening to come to an end.
e) all of the above are true.

VI. PRACTICE EXAM: ESSAY QUESTION

1. Explain how technological progress can enhance capital deepening.

VII. ANSWER KEY: MULTIPLE CHOICE QUESTIONS

1. Correct answer: b.

Discussion: Capital deepening arises when a country's capital stock is increased (relative to its workforce) so that the amount of capital per worker increases. Thus, one way in which capital deepening will stop is when a country stops adding to its capital stock. Statement b means that a country is saving just enough to fund replacement of worn out capital (depreciation) and no more. That is, a country's capital stock will not be increasing; it will remain at the same level (say $1 billion).

Statement a is not correct. It is the level of saving and amount of depreciation, not the saving rate (which is a percentage of income) or the depreciation rate (which is a percentage of the capital stock) which ultimately determine what will happen to a country's capital stock. Statement c is not true. Just because gross investment is equal to 1% does not mean that a country's capital stock will increase. Remember, it is net investment that matters in determining whether the capital stock will grow or not. Statement d is meaningless. The relationship between consumption and saving does not imply anything about what happens to a country's capital stock. Statement e is not correct. Diminishing returns has nothing to do with whether a country's capital stock will increase.

2. Correct answer: e.

Discussion: If depreciation is greater than the level of saving, a country's net investment will be negative which also means that a country's capital stock will decline. This has two implications. As a country's capital stock declines, and assuming the size of the workforce does not change, the amount of capital per worker will decline. With less capital per worker, workers will be less productive and so output per worker (labor productivity) will decline. Thus, statements c and d are true.

Statement b is not true because real wages would fall, not rise. This is because with less capital per worker, workers are less productive. If workers are paid based on how productive they are, their real wages will fall, not rise. Statement a is not true. Technological progress can occur independently of what is happening to the capital stock (and thus the relationship of depreciation to saving).

3. Correct answer: e.

Discussion: Technological progress increases the amount of output a country can produce with a given amount of labor and capital. Thus, output per worker will increase. With more output and therefore more income, the level of saving will rise. As the level of saving rises, a country is able to fund more gross investment. Since technological progress increases the amount of output per worker, workers' real wages will rise. (They are more productive and so will be paid accordingly).

4. Correct answer: a.

Discussion: Statement a is not true because as an economy grows, the level of saving increases but at a decreasing rate. This is because as an economy grows, output (and hence income) increases but at a decreasing rate. With a saving rate constant at, say, 10% of income, the level of saving will also increase as an economy grows, but at a decreasing rate.

Statement b is true. See the answer to question (2) for more detail. Statement c is true; it is another way of saying that there are diminishing returns to the aggregate production function. Statement d is true. Your book emphasizes that the process of capital deepening will eventually come to an end when the amount of depreciation is equal to the amount of saving of the country. However, it may take a long time for this equality to be fulfilled.

VI. ANSWER KEY: ESSAY QUESTION

1. Technological progress increases the amount of output a country can produce with a given amount of labor and capital. With more output and therefore more income, the level of saving will rise. As the level of saving rises, a country is able to fund more gross investment. As long as the increased level of saving exceeds that amount needed to replace worn out capital, the capital stock will increase. Thus, technological progress not only promotes economic growth on its own but also fosters the potential for more growth through capital accumulation.

Take It to the Net

We invite you to visit the O'Sullivan/Sheffrin page on the Prentice Hall Web site at:
http://www.prenhall.com/osullivan/
for this chapter's World Wide Web exercise.

CHAPTER 8
WHY DO ECONOMIES GROW?

I. OVERVIEW

In this chapter, you will learn how capital deepening and technological progress can affect a country's ability to grow. You will learn how saving and investment play a role in capital deepening as well as what determines technological progress. You will also learn how international trade and public policy ultimately affect economic growth through their effects on saving and investment. You will learn how research and development and investment in education may affect the growth rate a country is able to achieve. You will also see how population growth affects economic growth and real wages. You will use a production function to illustrate how capital deepening and technological progress alter the level of output a country is able to produce. You will be re-introduced to the difference between gross investment and net investment and will see why it is important in understanding the basis for economic growth. You will learn about growth accounting which is an attempt to estimate the contributions of capital deepening, labor growth, and technological progress to economic growth. You will learn about productivity and how capital deepening and technological progress affect productivity and real wages. You will learn about the sources of technological progress and how policy can be directed at enhancing technological progress. You will also learn that institutions can contribute to economic growth by promoting the willingness to work, save, and invest in a society. You will also learn about real GDP per capita as a basis for comparing living standards across countries.

II. CHECKLIST

By the end of this chapter, you should be able to:

❑ Define economic growth.
❑ Use the Rule of 70 to analyze how long it will take a country to double its standard of living if it grows at X% per year.
❑ Use the Rule of 70 to analyze what growth rate it would have to achieve in order for its standard of living to double in X years.
❑ Discuss how a country's standard of living can be measured and some problems with making direct comparisons to another country's standard of living.
❑ Define capital deepening and illustrate its effects on real wages, the production function, and the level of output.
❑ Explain how saving and investment are related.
❑ Explain the distinction between gross and net investment. Explain which type of investment is important to economic growth.
❑ Explain the effect of population growth on output per worker and discuss ways in which policy can be used to mitigate the effect.
❑ Explain how government spending and a trade deficit can be used to enhance capital deepening.

98   Chapter 8

- Define technological progress.
- Discuss growth accounting.
- Define labor productivity.
- Discuss what has happened to U.S. labor productivity since the 1970s and offer possible explanations.
- Discuss the five causes of technological progress.
- Define creative destruction.
- Give some examples of government policy that would raise the rate of technological progress.
- Discuss how the government can influence incentives in an economy and how they can contribute to or deter economic growth.
- Define human capital.
- Discuss the importance to education and health and fitness on productivity and growth.
- Discuss the merits of a public policy aimed at educating a society versus improving the sanitation system of a country.
- Explain 'new growth theory.'

III. KEY TERMS

Human capital: The knowledge and skills acquired by a worker through education and experience and used to produce goods and services.

Technological progress: An increase in output without increasing inputs.

Capital deepening: Increases in the stock of capital per worker.

Real GDP per capita: Gross domestic product per person adjusted for changes in prices. It is the usual measure of living standards across time and between countries.

Growth rate: The percentage rate of change of a variable.

Rule of 70: A rule of thumb that says that output will double in 70/x years where x is the percentage rate of growth.

Convergence: The process by which poorer countries "catch up" with richer countries in terms of real GDP per capita.

Saving: Total income minus consumption.

Growth accounting: A method to determine the contribution to economic growth from increased capital, labor, and technological progress.

Labor productivity: Output produced per hour of work.

Creative destruction: The process by which competition for monopoly profits leads to technological progress.

New growth theory: Modern theories of growth that try to explain the origins of technological progress.

IV. PERFORMANCE ENHANCING TIPS (PETS)

PET #1

Real GDP per capita is a country's real GDP level divided by its population. It is not an appropriate measure of what a typical individual's before or after-tax real income is.

Real GDP per capita is not a useful measure of average income for a working individual or household. The reason is that the calculation for real GDP per capita assumes that the dollar figure for real GDP is a measure of the income that accrues to every individual in the population, whatever their age, and whether they are working or not. Also, real GDP, while an approximate measure of national income, is not a good measure of personal income (i.e. before-tax household income) or of disposable income (i.e. after-tax household income) -- income that accrues to working individuals. In fact, real GDP exceeds aggregate real personal and aggregate real disposable income by a substantial amount. Thus, when this chapter reports that real GDP per capita in the U.S. was $29,010 in 1997, it does not imply that on average, every working individual earns $29,010. It also does not imply that on average, a family of four's before or after-tax real income is $116,040 ($29,010 X 4).

PET #2

GDP per capita (per person) is not necessarily the best measure of the standard of living of a country's residents.

GDP per capita is often used as a measure of comparing the standards of living across countries; high GDP per capita countries are presumed to have higher standards of living than low GDP per capita countries. However, the use of GDP per capita to compare living standards does not take into account quality of life issues like crime, pollution, traffic congestion, access to health care, status of the educational system, etc. Thus, the country with the highest GDP per capita may not necessarily offer the highest "quality of life."

PET #3

The Rule of 70 can be used to determine either the time periods it will take for a variable to double or the growth rate necessary for a variable to double in X time periods.

For example, suppose you are told that the U.S. growth rate is 3% per year and that the Japanese growth rate is 5% per year. Which country's real GDP will double more quickly? Using the rule of 70, it will take the U.S. approximately 23 years (70/3) to double its real GDP whereas Japan's real GDP will double in 14 years (70/5). For another example, suppose you are told that Canada has undertaken an ambitious economic plan. One goal is for real GDP to double in 10 years. What growth rate must Canada sustain each year for 10 years in order to achieve the goal? Using the rule of 70, the answer would be 7% per year (70/10 years).

One word of caution: if the growth rate is stated on a monthly or quarterly basis, the time period to double should be stated in monthly or quarterly terms (instead of yearly) as well. For example, suppose the government reported that they expected real GDP to grow at 2% each quarter. Using the rule of 70, at that growth rate, it would take 70/2 = 35 quarters for real GDP to double. Thirty-five quarters is 8.75 years.

PET #4

The pool of savings available to fund investment in Country A can come from the savings of country A's residents or from the savings of foreign countries' residents who lend their savings to country A.

Suppose that U.S. residents in total save $500 billion a year, $450 billion of which is placed in the U.S. and the remaining $50 billion which is lent to other countries. Further, suppose that foreigners save $1 trillion a year, $100 billion of which is lent to the U.S. On net, the U.S. pool of private saving will be $450 billion + $100 billion = $550 billion. This pool of saving will be available to fund private and/or government investment projects.

PET #5

Net investment is the change in a country's capital stock after taking account of depreciation. Thus:
  net investment = gross investment - depreciation.

You can also re-arrange the equation above as:
  gross investment = net investment + depreciation.
  depreciation = gross investment - net investment.

PET #6

Net investment that is positive is the addition to a nation's stock of capital above and beyond its current level. Net investment that is zero means that a nation's stock of capital is neither increasing nor decreasing beyond its current level. Net investment that is negative means that a nation is not investing enough to replace capital that is being worn out.

To illustrate the difference between gross investment and net investment, consider the stock of shoes that you currently have. Suppose you have 10 pairs of shoes. Over the course of the year, 3 of the pairs wear out (depreciate) and are no longer any good. If you buy 7 more pairs of shoes that year, your gross investment in shoes is 7 pairs. However, because you are replacing 3 pairs that have worn out, your net investment in shoes is 4 pairs. That is, at the end of the year, you will now have 14 pairs of shoes. You have, on net, added 4 (7-3) pairs to the stock of 10 pairs of shoes that you started out with.

Suppose instead that you bought 3 pairs of shoes that year. While three pairs would be your gross investment, your net investment would be zero. You have only replaced what you have worn out. Thus, you are no better off at the end of the year since your stock of shoes remains at 10 pairs.

Now, suppose that you bought 1 pair of shoes that year. While three pairs would be your gross investment, your net investment would be -2 (1-3). You have not invested enough to replace the 3 pairs of shoes worn out. Thus, your stock of shoes will decline from 10 pairs to 8 pairs.

The same is true for a country. A country whose net investment is zero will not be adding to its capital stock and so will not experience the benefits of capital deepening; a country that is not replacing its worn out capital will see its capital stock shrink and will not experience the benefits of capital deepening.

PET #7

In order for a country to grow through capital deepening, its saving must be greater than the depreciation of the capital stock.

This PET is just an application of PETS #5 and #6. That is, a country must save enough to ensure that its level of net investment is positive (greater than zero).

V. PRACTICE EXAM: MULTIPLE CHOICE QUESTIONS

1. Which one of the following statements is NOT true of real GDP per capita?
a) if a country's real GDP per capita grows at 2% per year, it will take 35 years for real GDP per capita to double.
b) it is difficult to compare real GDP per capita across countries because of differences in consumption patterns.
c) it is difficult to compare real GDP per capita across countries because of differences in currencies.
d) if a country's real GDP per capita doubled in 7 years, it must have grown at 7% per year.
e) If a country's real GDP per capita is $10,000 and it is growing at 5% per year, it will be $20,000 in 14 years.

2. Which one of the following statements is NOT true?
a) there has been a convergence of real GDP per capita among the developed (industrialized) countries.
b) there is strong evidence that less developed countries grow at faster rates than developed countries.
c) real GDP per capita may decline if the growth rate in real GDP is less than the population growth rate.
d) the average growth rate in real GDP per capita between 1960-2001 for the U.S. was about 2%.
e) the level of real GDP per capita amongst countries will eventually converge if the low real GDP per capita countries grow at rates faster than the high real GDP per capita countries.

3. Suppose the economy was expected to grow at 4% a year for the next five years. If GDP this year is $100 billion, what will it be at the end of five years?
a) $120 billion.
b) $121.67 billion.
c) $104 billion.
d) $537.82 billion.
e) $305.18 billion.

4. Suppose that you would like to see your salary double in ten years. What must the growth rate of your salary be each year in order for you to achieve your goal?
a) 7%.
b) 1.7%.
c) 1.4%.
d) 10%.
e) 14%.

5. Suppose that a country's real GDP was growing at a rate of 5% per year. How many years would it take for the country's real GDP to double?
a) 10 years.
b) 20 years.
c) 14 years.
d) 40 years.
e) cannot be determined without more information.

6. Labor productivity depends on the amount of _____ an economy has.
a) machines.
b) buildings (or factories).
c) equipment.
d) technology.
e) all of the above.

7. In an economy with no government or foreign sector:
a) saving must equal gross investment.
b) saving must equal net investment.
c) saving must equal depreciation.
d) saving will be less than investment.
e) saving will be greater than investment.

8. A change in a country's capital stock is equal to:
a) the level of gross investment.
b) the level of net investment.
c) the rate of depreciation of a country's capital stock.
d) the level of saving.
e) (a) and (d).

9. Which one of the following statements is true of capital deepening?
a) for a fixed amount of capital, increases in a country's work force will lead to increases in the amount of output per worker.
b) a government that uses its tax revenues to fund the construction of new highways and bridges is not engaging in capital deepening because the government creates a budget deficit.
c) trade deficits always hurt the ability of a country to deepen its capital stock.
d) capital deepening will stop when depreciation is zero.
e) capital deepening is a source of economic growth.

10. Which one of the following would NOT be an example of technological progress?
a) discovery of a new tax loophole which enables companies to reduce the amount of taxes they pay to the government.
b) the invention of the computer.
c) the invention of a conveyor belt.
d) the discovery of converting steam to energy.
e) the invention of the washing machine.

11. Which Nobel-prize winning economist developed a method for measuring technological progress?
a) Franco Modigliani.
b) Milton Friedman.
c) Robert Solow.
d) Sir Charles Godfrey.
e) Gerard Debreu.

12. Which one of the following statements is true of growth accounting?
a) technological progress has accounted for roughly 1% of the growth rate in U.S. output.
b) growth accounting determines how much of a country's growth in output is due to growth in worker productivity and to growth in prices (inflation).
c) a country whose main source of growth in output is through technological progress will typically be able to enjoy a higher level of consumption than a country whose main source of growth is through increases in the capital stock.
d) the slowdown in U.S. labor productivity has been explained by a reduced rate of capital deepening.
e) the effect of advances in information technology on labor productivity is easily measured.

13. Which one of the following has been considered a potential source of technological progress?
a) research and development in fundamental sciences.
b) monopolies that spur innovation.
c) inventions designed to reduce costs.
d) the scale of the market.
e) all of the above have been considered potential sources of technological progress.

14. Which one of the following statements is NOT true?
a) technological progress enables a country to produce more output with the same amount of labor and capital.
b) education can promote technological progress.
c) creative destruction is the process of replacing plant and equipment before it has fully depreciated.
d) patents may promote technological progress.
e) the protection of intellectual property rights may promote technological progress.

15. Suppose country A's real GDP per capita is $10,000 and country B's real GDP per capita is $20,000. If country A's real GDP per capita is growing at 7% per year while country B's real GDP per capita is growing at 3.5% per year, after how many years will country A's real GDP per capita exceed country B's real GDP per capita?
a) 10 years.
b) 60 years.
c) 80 years.
d) 7 years.
e) 20 years.

16. To foster economic growth, governments should:
a) enforce property rights.
b) make sure that contracts are abided.
c) prevent corruption.
d) ensure that education leads to higher income and better jobs.
e) all of the above.

17. Which one of the following would be an example of an investment in human capital?
a) purchase of an automated assembly line.
b) sending a crew of factory workers to a year-long training program.
c) buying stock in a biotechnology firm.
d) installing a new sewer system in the rural part of a country.
e) (b) and (d).

18. Which of the following is NOT a true statement about real GDP per capita?
a) Real GDP per capital is not a useful measure of average income for a working individual.
b) Real GDP per capital is not an appropriate measure of the typical individual's before tax income
c) Real GDP per capital is not an appropriate measure of the typical individual's after tax income
d) Real GDP per capita is calculated only using persons in the population that work.
e) Real GDP per capita is calculated by dividing a country's real GDP by its population.

VI. PRACTICE EXAM: ESSAY QUESTIONS

1. Explain why the citizens of a country that experiences economic growth through only technological progress may enjoy a better standard of living than a country that experiences economic growth only through an increase in the capital stock.

2. Discuss the different sources of technological progress.

VII. ANSWER KEY: MULTIPLE CHOICE QUESTIONS

1. Correct answer: d.

Discussion: Statement d is not true. Using the rule of 70, if a country's real GDP per capita doubled in 7 years, it must have been growing at 10% per year, not 7% per year.

All of the other statements are true. Differences in consumption patterns and the prices of goods across countries must be evaluated in arriving at a correct comparison of real GDP per capita. Thus, statements b and c are true. Statements a and e are applications of the rule of 70. Statement a is true because with a growth rate of 2% per year, it will take 35 years (70/2) for a country's real GDP per capita to double. Statement e is true because using the rule of 70 tells us that the country's real GDP per capita will double in 14 years (70/5). Thus, if its GDP per capita is now $10,000, it will be $20,000 in 14 years.

2. Correct answer: b.

Discussion: Statement b is not true. Economists have found only weak evidence that less developed countries have grown at a rate faster than developed countries.

Statement a is true for developed countries. Statement c is necessarily true. Since real GDP per capita is equal to a country's real GDP divided by its population, then an increase in the population growth rate that exceeds the growth rate in real GDP will necessarily lead to a decline in real GDP per capita. Statement d is true. Statement e is true. (For a numerical example of the principle, see the answer to question 15).

3. Correct answer: b.

Discussion. The formula to use is GDP in year n = current GDP X $(1 + \text{growth rate})^n$. Thus, GDP after five years will be $100 billion X $(1.04)^5$ = $100 billion X 1.2167 = $121.67 billion. Based on this, none of the other statements are correct.

106   Chapter 8

If you used $100 billion X (1.40), you would incorrectly get $537.82 billion.

4. Correct answer: a.

Discussion: You must use the Rule of 70 to arrive at the answer. The Rule of 70 is: Number of years to Double = 70/growth rate. Since you know the number of years to double is ten years, you have 10 = 70/growth rate. Thus, the growth rate must be 7% in order for your goal to be achieved.

5. Correct answer: c.

Discussion: The Rule of 70 can be used to answer this question, as it was used to answer question 4. Using the Rule of 70 (see PET #4), the years it would take real GDP to double is calculated by dividing 70 by 5. Since 70/5 is equal to 14, it will take real GDP fourteen years to double.

6. Correct answer: e.

Discussion: The productivity of labor (how much output each worker is able to produce over a given time period) is affected by the amount (including quality and age) of machines that the workers use; by the building or factory (including quality and age) that workers work in; by the equipment they have to work with (tools, computers, fax machines, etc); and by the state of technology.

7. Correct answer: a.

Discussion: A country's saving (in the absence of a government or foreign sector) is used by (lent to) businesses who in turn purchase plant and equipment, i.e. invest or add to the capital stock. The investment by businesses may be undertaken to replace worn out capital (depreciation) or to purchase new capital. Gross investment is the sum of these two activities and saving provides the funds necessary for both.

Statements d and e cannot be true of an economy that does not have a government or a foreign sector. It is necessarily true that saving must equal (gross) investment.

8. Correct answer: b.

Discussion: A country's capital stock will change when its net investment changes. If net investment is positive, a country's capital stock will increase. This is because the country will not only be replacing worn out capital, it will be adding more new plant and equipment to its capital stock. If net investment is negative, a country's capital stock will decrease. This is because the country will not even be totally replacing its worn out capital. Remember that net investment is gross investment minus depreciation. You may wish to review PET #7 of this chapter for more detail.

9. Correct answer: e.

Discussion: Capital deepening is an increase in the amount of capital available per worker. Since capital deepening enables workers to produce more output per day, capital deepening leads to economic growth (increases in output).

Statement a is not true. For a fixed amount of capital, increases in a country's work force will lead to a decline in capital per worker (i.e. total capital/number of workers), not an increase. Statement b is not true. When a government spends your tax dollars on such things as highway and bridge construction (or research and development, or education for that matter), it is adding to the stock of capital (physical or human) and thereby engaging in capital deepening. Statement c is not true. A country that runs a trade deficit may incur the trade deficit because it is importing a lot of plant and equipment (capital). Thus, a trade deficit is not necessarily a bad thing for a country since it can promote capital deepening. This, of course, assumes that the country is deficit spending on capital goods not on consumption goods. Statement d is not true. Capital deepening will stop when net investment is zero (i.e. when gross investment equals depreciation).

10. Correct answer: a.

Discussion: Technological progress is defined as progress that enables a country to produce more output with the same amount of capital and labor. The discovery of a new tax loophole does not add to the amount of output a country can produce with the same amount of capital and labor. It simply keeps dollars in the hands of businesses and out of the hands of the government.

11. Correct answer: c.

Discussion: None necessary.

12. Correct answer: c.

Discussion: Your book discusses a comparison of the growth rates achieved by Hong Kong and Singapore. The discussion points out that technological progress enables the citizens of a country to consume more than a country that grows through increases in the capital stock. This is because increases in the capital stock are funded from saving. That is, in order to increase the capital stock, a country must save more. This means that a country must consume less. Thus, a country that experiences growth because of increases in the capital stock is probably a country where the level of consumption is not very high. In contrast, if growth occurs through technological progress (which presumably is not being funded from saving), then a country does not have to reduce its consumption level in order for growth to occur.

Statement a is not true. Technological progress has accounted for roughly 35% of the growth rate in U.S. output. That is, with a U.S. growth rate in output of 3% a year, 1% of that 3% is attributed to technological progress, i.e. 1/3 = 33% of the growth rate is attributed to technological progress. Statement b is not true. Growth accounting determines how much of a country's growth in output is due to growth in the capital stock, the labor force, and technological progress. Statement d is not true. The slowdown in U.S. labor productivity has not been explained by a reduction in the capital stock. A number of explanations (discussed in your text) have been offered but none seem to do a good job of explaining why U.S. labor productivity has declined since the 1970s. Statement e is not true. The effect of advances in information technology on labor productivity have been very difficult to quantify. This, in part, is due to the fact that the information technology advances primarily affected the service sector where output per worker is much harder to quantify than, say, for the manufacturing sector.

13. Correct answer: e.

Discussion: Research and development, either private or government-funded leads to technological advances not only within the industry conducting the research and development but for other related industries. Monopolies, particularly those granted through patents, can spur innovation. Monopoly status confers the possibility of long-term profits to a firm which in turn spurs a firm to innovate. Secondly, as other firms try to break the monopoly status by producing a similar product (a process called "creative destruction"), other innovations are generated. Inventions that are designed to reduce costs are another source of technological progress. Here again, the profit-maximizing motive of the firm can promote innovation. A firm that reduces its costs through innovation will see bigger profits. The scale of the market also spurs innovation. The possibility that a product, once developed, will be mass marketed (e.g. disposable diapers) also creates an incentive to innovate. That is, if firms see a huge profit potential in an innovative product, they will produce it.

14. Correct answer: c.

Discussion: Creative destruction is a process whereby firms compete with an innovating monopolist by introducing a new, better, version of the product, which generates more innovation.

Statement a is true and means that technological progress can increase the productivity of labor, as well as capital. Statement b is true. Your book discusses a case in which education (investment in human capital) is thought to be the key to technological progress. A more educated society is a more intelligent society and a more intelligent society is more likely to innovate than one that is not as well educated. Statement d is true. Successful patents guarantee an innovator profits for a long period of time. The incentive to reap profits thus leads to innovation and technological progress. Statement e is true. If property rights are not protected, neither are profits from innovations. Thus, without property rights, there is a reduced incentive to innovate and technological progress is likely to be shunted.

15. Correct answer: e.

Discussion: Country A's real GDP per capita will double to $20,000 in 10 years (70/7). In another 10 years, it will double from $20,000 to $40,000. Country B's real GDP per capita will double in 20 years (70/3.5). Thus, country B's real GDP per capita will be $40,000 in 20 years. After the 20th year, assuming country A will continue to grow at 7% a year while country B grows at 3.5% a year, it must be true that country A's real GDP per capita will surpass country B's real GDP per capita after the 20th year.

16. Correct answer: e.

Discussion: To foster economic growth, a country must foster an environment where there are incentives to work, save, invest, innovate, and get educated. Moreover, the efforts to work, save, invest, innovate, and get educated must prove to be worthwhile. Otherwise, they will not be undertaken. Governments must enforce property rights so that there is an incentive to innovate. Without assurance that property rights will be protected, individuals may fear that any product that may develop will be stolen from them. Governments must also make sure that contracts are abided. Otherwise, transactions that may be worthwhile may not happen. For example, suppose a business needs to take out a loan to build a new factory. If contracts are not abided, a bank may be less willing to offer the business a loan fearing that the business may not abide by the contract. If the bank fears it will not be paid back according to the terms of the loan contract, it may not be willing to make the loan. Governments must also prevent corruption since corruption rewards those who steal and takes away from those who work, save, invest, innovate, and get educated. Corruption makes it less worthwhile to undertake economic transactions that are productive. Thus, fewer productive transactions will be undertaken. Governments should also ensure that an activity like getting an education leads to opportunity. Otherwise, there will be no incentive to get educated. Imagine if you graduated from college but couldn't find a job, perhaps because all of the 'good' jobs were going to friends and relatives of government officials. This would harm your incentive to get educated in the first place. Your decision would not only negatively impact your economic future but, if nationwide, citizens act as you do, the economy will be negatively impacted, too.

17. Correct answer: e.

Discussion: Statements (b) and (d) are both examples of investments in human capital. Investments in human capital come in two forms: investments in the education of a workforce and investments in the health and fitness of a workforce. Mandatory attendance to a four-year college would be one example of an investment in the education of a country's workforce. For some countries, mandatory attendance through grade eight is an investment in a country's workforce. Investment in food supplies to a country's population (it's hard to be productive when you're chronically hungry) as well as in its sewer and water infrastructure is another.

Statement a is an example of investment in a country's capital stock. Statement c is an example of "financial investment".

18. Correct answer: d.

Discussion: Statement d is not true. GDP per capita is calculated by dividing a country's real GDP by its population. The population includes all persons, regardless if the individual is working.

All of the other statements are true. a through c state the cautions about interpreting GDP per capita and e states how the measure is calculated by dividing real GDP by the population

VIII. ANSWER KEY: ESSAY QUESTIONS

1. Technological progress enables a country to produce more output with the same amount of capital and labor as before. Because more output can be produced without any increase in the capital stock, a country's citizens do not have to reduce their consumption spending (i.e. increase the level of their saving today) in order to fund additions to the capital stock. Thus, citizens can consume a higher share (percentage) of output than citizens of a country that grows through additions to its capital stock. In this way, we might say that the citizens are able to enjoy a better standard of living. When a country experiences economic growth through additions to its capital stock, its citizens are in effect sacrificing current consumption (i.e. they are saving more today) so that businesses can purchase new plant and equipment with the saving. The purchases of new plant and equipment benefit society as a whole in the future by enabling the country to grow at a faster rate than it would have if its citizens had not been willing to reduce consumption spending today. However, there is a cost to the citizens in that their standard of living may not be as enjoyable because of reduced consumption. So, technological progress permits economic growth without the sacrifice of reduced consumption in the present whereas economic growth through additions to the capital stock comes at a cost.

This, of course, assumes that technological progress is not funded through saving. Some types of technological progress (innovations) may arise without any necessary increase in saving required. If they did, then what is true of economic growth through additions to the capital stock would be true of economic growth through technological progress.

A good example of the sacrifices that a country's citizens must make in terms of reduced consumption spending is present-day Russia. The country is trying to rebuild itself and requires a lot of new, updated plant and equipment. The funds to pay for the new plant and equipment must come from somewhere. They must come from the saving of Russian citizens who lend their saving to businesses (i.e. business borrow from the citizens). Another way to look at the problem is to apply the principle of crowding out. If a country can only produce $X of output, it must be divided up between consumers and businesses (assuming no government). Thus, if a country wants to add to its capital stock, businesses must be able to increase their spending on plant and equipment which means consumers must reduce their spending on consumption goods since the country as a whole can only produce a limited amount of output.

2. Technological progress has many sources. Technological progress can occur through the research and development efforts of the government or the privately sector. Sometimes research and development has spillover benefits for other industries which can, in turn, promote further technological progress. Technological progress also arises through the creative, educated, and talented minds of a nation's workforce. Thus, education (particularly in engineering and the sciences) can promote technological progress. The granting of patents to firms that innovate (which gives the firm a monopoly status) also promotes technological progress. A firm's desire to innovate is affected by the potential profit reward. A firm that is awarded a patent has more assurance that the profits it will earn on its innovation will not, at least for a time, be reduced by other firms competing with it. A legal framework for the protection of intellectual property rights also promotes technological progress through assuring innovative firms that profits they make from new ideas will be justly protected. This also helps to ensure that innovative firms will have a continued desire to innovate. Without such protection, firms may decide that the payoff from innovating is not enough and so technological progress is held back. Technological progress can also be influenced by the market potential. A bigger market presents a bigger potential profit opportunity. This is why free trade, which is a way of broadening a firm's market potential, may also encourage technological progress. Just think of the profit opportunities if U.S. firms were able to freely export to China, the world's biggest market and almost 30 times the size of the U.S. market! Now, there's an incentive to come up with new and improved products! Technological progress also occurs through a firm's desire to reduce its costs (and thereby increase its profits).

A careful look at the list above suggests that innovation and therefore technological progress is fundamentally prompted by two things: an educated society and a profit motive.

Take It to the Net

We invite you to visit the O'Sullivan/Sheffrin page on the Prentice Hall Web site at:

http://www.prenhall.com/osullivan/

for this chapter's World Wide Web exercise.

CHAPTER 9
AGGREGATE DEMAND AND AGGREGATE SUPPLY

I. OVERVIEW

In this chapter, you will learn why the economy doesn't always operate at full employment. That is, you will learn about explanations for fluctuations in output – periods of recessions as well as periods of economic expansion. Along the way, you will learn a little about the Great Depression and how economic thinking regarding wages, prices, and policy has evolved since that time. The model you will use to understand the behavior of real GDP (and other economic variables) over time is the model of aggregate demand and aggregate supply. You will use this model to study the short and long run effects of changes in aggregate demand and aggregate supply on output and the price level. You will learn what causes aggregate demand and aggregate supply to shift and what determines the slope of each curve. You will be introduced to multiplier analysis. You will learn that multiplier analysis can be used to understand by how much and why an initial change in spending changes the level of GDP (output). You will learn about "shocks" that can move an economy in one direction or another and the short and long run effects of such shocks. You will also learn how changes in government spending and the money supply can affect the behavior of real GDP in one direction or another, at least in the short run. You will learn about these policies' effects in the long run. You will learn why, in a market-based economy, the price system may not act to coordinate economic activities.

II. CHECKLIST

By the end of this chapter, you should be able to:

❑ Explain the key problem of the Great Depression.
❑ Explain the difference between auction prices and custom prices and the implications for bringing about market equilibrium.
❑ Explain why wages and prices may be 'sticky.'
❑ Describe the aggregate demand curve and graph it.
❑ Explain the components of aggregate demand.
❑ Explain why the aggregate demand curve is negatively sloped when graphed against the price level.
❑ Describe the 'wealth effect.'
❑ Explain what factors shift the aggregate demand curve and in which direction.
❑ Explain the multiplier effect.
❑ Describe the consumption function and the marginal propensity to consume.
❑ Explain how the marginal propensity to consume relates to the multiplier effect.
❑ Give an equation for the multiplier.

- ❑ Compare and contrast the long run and short run aggregate supply curves.
- ❑ Illustrate the effects of changes in aggregate demand on the price level and the level of output using the long run aggregate supply curve.
- ❑ Explain what determines the level of output in the long run.
- ❑ Illustrate the effects of changes in aggregate demand on the price level and the level of output using the short run aggregate supply curve.
- ❑ Explain how recessions occur.
- ❑ Compare and contrast the effects of shifts in aggregate demand on output and the price level in the short run and the long run.
- ❑ Give some examples of supply shocks, i.e. explain what factors cause the short run aggregate supply curve to shift and in which direction.
- ❑ Describe the effects of shifts in short run aggregate supply on output and the price level.

III. KEY TERMS

Economic fluctuation: Movements of GDP above or below normal trends.

Short run in macroeconomics: The period of time that prices do not change very much.

Aggregate demand curve: The relationship between the level of prices and the quantity of real GDP demanded.

Wealth effect: The increase in spending that occurs because the real value of money increases when the price level falls.

Multiplier: The ratio of the total shift in aggregate demand to the initial shift in aggregate demand.

Consumption function: The relationship between the level of income and consumption spending.

Autonomous consumption spending: The part of consumption that does not depend on income.

Marginal propensity to consume (MPC): The fraction of additional income that is spent.

Aggregate supply curve: The relationship between the level of prices and the quantity of output supplied.

Long-run aggregate supply curve: A vertical aggregate supply curve. It reflects the idea that in the long run, output is determined solely by the factors of production.

Short-run aggregate supply curve: A relatively flat horizontal supply curve. It reflects the idea that prices do not change very much in the short run and that firms adjust production to meet demand

Supply shocks: External events that shift the aggregate supply curve.

Stagflation: A decrease in real output with increasing prices.

IV. PERFORMANCE ENHANCING TIPS (PETS)

PET #1

Changes in output in the short run economic model are associated with changes in employment.

For example, if an economy produces more output (i.e. real GDP increases), employment is expected to have increased. If an economy produces less output (i.e. real GDP decreases), employment is expected to have decreased.

PET #2

Economic fluctuations are defined as changes in the level of output (real GDP) over time.

Economic fluctuations are also referred to as "the business cycle" which was discussed in an earlier chapter.

PET #3

Shifts in aggregate demand are caused by factors that lead to changes in spending other than changes in the price level.

This is just an application of PETS #1 and #6 from Chapter 4 of the study guide, which you may want to review. Since aggregate demand is composed of spending by households (consumers), businesses (firms), the government, and the foreign sector, any change in these spending components not caused by a change in the price level will be represented by a shift in aggregate demand. These spending components may change for a variety of reasons (change in taxes, interest rates, money supply, exchange rate, etc).

For example, suppose the interest rate increases. A rise in the interest rate makes it more costly for households and businesses to borrow money to fund their purchases. Thus, a rise in the interest rate may reduce consumption and business spending. This would be represented by a leftward shift in the aggregate demand curve.

PET #4

Shifts in the short run aggregate supply curve are caused by factors that lead to changes in the cost of inputs used to produce output.

Labor and oil are key inputs used in the production of just about everything. Changes in the cost of labor (wages) as well as changes in the price of oil are represented by shifting the short run aggregate supply curve. Increases in input costs (wages or price of oil) are represented by a leftward shift in the short run aggregate supply curve. Decreases in input costs are represented by rightward shifts in the short run aggregate supply curve.

114   Chapter 9

PET #5

Shifts in the long run aggregate supply curve are caused by factors that lead to changes in an economy's capacity to produce output.

An economy's capacity to produce depends on a number of factors: the size and productivity of its labor force, the age and amount of the capital stock, and the state of technology. Changes in these factors will be represented by a shift in the aggregate supply curve. While your book does not consider these effects on the long run aggregate supply curve in this chapter, your professor may introduce them at this point and you in later chapters the long run aggregate supply curve will be shifted.

For example, suppose the government increases spending on highways and telephone lines. An improvement in the capital stock means that an economy will be able to produce more output with its given set of resources than before. The improvement to the nation's capital stock would then be represented by a rightward shift in the aggregate supply curve.

V. PRACTICE EXAM: MULTIPLE CHOICE QUESTIONS

1. According to Keynes, the main cause of the Great Depression in the U.S. was:
a) insufficient demand for goods and services.
b) excess capacity in production.
c) the stock market crash.
d) unemployment.
e) low real wages.

2. Which one of the following statements is NOT true?
a) Keynesian economic thought deals with the behavior of the economy in the long run.
b) 'sticky' prices means that prices adjust downward slowly.
c) in the short run, the economy may be operating above or below the full employment (potential) level of output.
d) the economic coordination problem is that in the short run, prices may not accurately reflect demand and supply conditions.
e) the wages of most workers are 'sticky.'

3. In which market would the price be least likely to be "sticky"?
a) wages of union teachers.
b) steel rods.
c) fresh fruit.
d) trucks.
e) wages of government workers.

4. A consequence of sticky airplane prices in the aircraft industry would be:
a) a shortage or surplus of airplanes.
b) a shortage or surplus of labor in the aircraft industry.
c) a shortage or surplus of aircraft parts.
d) a vertical production function.
e) (a), (b), and (c).

5. Which one of the following is a reason for why the aggregate demand curve is negatively sloped?
a) a decrease in the price level raises the purchasing power of money and wealth.
b) a decrease in the price level raises interest rates which reduces spending.
c) an increase in the price level raises exports.
d) an increase in the price level reduces the amount of output produced.
e) a decrease in income causes people to save more.

6. Which one of the following would shift the aggregate demand curve to the left (decrease aggregate demand)?
a) an increase in the money supply.
b) an increase in government spending.
c) an increase in exports.
d) an increase in taxes.
e) a decline in the capital stock.

7. A decrease in government spending is represented by shifting aggregate demand to the _____ and an increase in spending by foreigners on goods and services produced in our country is represented by shifting aggregate demand for our country to the _____.
a) right; right.
b) left; left.
c) left; right.
d) right; left.
e) need more information to answer the question.

8. The multiplier effect:
a) is that an initial increase in spending will cause the aggregate demand curve to shift by more than the initial increase in spending.
b) happens because consumption (household spending) depends positively on income.
c) arises because an initial increase in spending generates production and income.
d) arises because the marginal propensity to consume is positive.
e) all of the above.

116 Chapter 9

9. The marginal propensity to consume is:
a) consumption/income.
b) change in consumption/change in income.
c) income/consumption.
d) change in income/change in consumption.
e) change in consumption/change in interest rate.

10. If the marginal propensity to consume is 0.75, an initial increase in spending of $100 billion will cause consumer spending to rise by ____ at the first round and total spending to rise by ____ when the multiplier process is complete.
a) $75 billion; $133 billion.
b) $25 billion; $400 billion.
c) $75 billion; $400 billion.
d) $25 billion; $133 billion.
e) $133 billion; $400 billion.

11. If the marginal propensity to consume is 0.8, the multiplier must be:
a) 5
b) 4
c) 1.25
d) 8
e) 0.5

12. The short run aggregate supply curve is ____ and the long run aggregate supply curve is _____.
a) negatively sloped; vertical.
b) positively sloped; vertical.
c) vertical; positively sloped.
d) vertical; negatively sloped.
e) positively sloped; negatively sloped.

13. In the short run, an increase in aggregate demand will increase _____ and in the long run will increase _____.
a) the price level and output/the price level.
b) the price level and output/output.
c) output/the price level.
d) the price level/the price level.
e) output/the price level and output.

14. Which one of the following statements is true?
a) in the short run model, the level of output is determined by demand.
b) in the long run model, the level of output is determined by demand.
c) in the long run model, the aggregate supply curve is horizontal.
d) where aggregate demand and aggregate supply intersect is the full-employment level of output.
e) (b) and (c).

15. In the short run, a drop in oil prices will lead to:
a) a lower price level with no change in output.
b) a lower price level and a higher output level.
c) a lower price level and a lower output level.
d) a higher price level and a higher output level.
e) a higher price level and a lower output level.

16. A negative supply shock may cause:
a) the short run aggregate supply curve to shift left.
b) the price level to rise.
c) the level of output to decline.
d) stagflation.
e) all of the above.

VI. PRACTICE EXAM: ESSAY QUESTIONS

1. Explain the short and long run effects of an increase in the money supply on the price level and output. Assume the economy is initially operating at the potential level of real GDP. Be sure to address why the results are different.

2. Explain the short run effects of an increase in the price of oil on the price level and output. Assume the economy is initially operating at the potential level of real GDP.

VII. ANSWER KEY: MULTIPLE CHOICE QUESTIONS

1. Correct answer: a.

Discussion: Keynes thought that the Great Depression was caused by too little spending taking place in the U.S. economy. This insufficient demand for goods and services lead to a reduced demand for workers which consequently led to a very high unemployment rate.

Statements b, c, and e may be consequences (not causes) of the Great Depression. While the stock market crash may have been partly responsible for the Great Depression, it is not the reason that Keynes stressed.

2. Correct answer: a.

Discussion: Statement a is not true since Keynesian economic thought deals with the behavior of the economy in the *short* run.

Statement b is correct since the use of the word 'sticky' implies that prices (and wages) adjust slowly to changes in demand or supply. Statement c is correct; in the short run an economy may operate above the full-employment level of output (with inflation likely to result) and an economy may operate below the full-employment level of output (recession). In the *long* run, it is assumed that the economy is operating at the full employment level of output. Statement d is correct since transactions are more difficult to coordinate when prices do not signal problems of increased or decreased demand and supply. Statement e is true since most wages are negotiated for a contract period.

3. Correct answer: c.

Discussion: When prices are "sticky," it means that prices don't move up or down immediately in response to changes in demand or supply. Such price stickiness may be due to contracts that have been set that fix the price at which a good or service sells for a period of time. Thus, wages of union and government workers (and most workers in general) are considered sticky. The price for durable goods like steel rods, trucks, etc. are also typically set by a contract. Even prices on pre-printed brochures and menus may be sticky since businesses may not be able to quickly change the price for their output when there is a shift in demand or supply. Fresh fruit, however, is a good that is much less likely to be sticky.

4. Correct answer: e.

Discussion: The consequence of sticky prices is that when demand and/or supply shift, the price does not immediately change. Consequently, an excess demand or supply can be created. An example of completely sticky prices are price ceilings and price floors discussed in Chapter 4. You may wish to review PETS #8 and #9 of Chapter 4 of the study guide. If a shortage or surplus of airplanes emerges, then the amount of labor and aircraft parts used in producing airplanes will also be affected. If wages in the aircraft industry and prices in the aircraft parts industry are not sticky, then a shortage or surplus may not arise. A production function shows the relationship between output and labor for a given capital stock and state of technology. It has nothing to do with sticky prices.

5. Correct answer: a.

Discussion: When the price level drops, the average level of prices of goods and services declines. This means goods and services are less costly to consumers. This, in turn, means that the purchasing power of consumers' money and wealth (how many goods and services they can buy) will have increased. Since the real value of consumers' money and wealth has increased, they will be inclined to buy more when the price level drops. This is a way of saying that aggregate demand is negatively sloped. As the price level drops, the amount of total output desired to be purchased will increase.

Statement b is incorrect because a decline in the price level lowers interest rates, not raises them. Statement c is incorrect because an increase in the price level implies that exports are becoming more expensive to foreign residents. Thus, an increase in the price level would reduce exports, not raise them. Statement d is incorrect; the relationship between the price level and the amount of output produced is an aggregate supply concept, not an aggregate demand concept. Statement e is incorrect; aggregate demand shows the relationship between the price level and the amount of output in total demanded by an economy. It does not show the relationship between income and saving.

6. Correct answer: d.

Discussion: A leftward shift in the aggregate demand curve means that aggregate demand for goods and services has declined. An increase in taxes would reduce the amount of spending in the economy and thus translate to a decrease in aggregate demand for goods and services.

Statements (a), (b), and (c) are all events that would raise the amount of spending in an economy and thus would be represented with a rightward shift in the aggregate demand curve. Statement e is an aggregate supply concept. A decline in the capital stock (a factor of production) would be represented by an upward shift in the short run aggregate supply curve and a leftward shift in the long run aggregate supply curve.

7. Correct answer: c.

Discussion: In the short run, a decrease in government spending is a decline in aggregate demand. This is represented by a leftward shift in aggregate demand. By contrast, an increase in spending by foreigners (a rise in net exports) is an increase in aggregate demand. This is represented by a rightward shift in aggregate demand.

8. Correct answer: e.

Discussion: The multiplier effect (which you will learn more about in later chapters) hinges on the fact that spending generates production and income, and that changes in income lead to further changes in spending. The fact that changes in income lead to further changes in spending is expressed through the consumption function. The consumption function is an equation that shows that changes in income will cause consumer spending to change. Rises in income lead to increases in consumption and declines in income lead to declines in consumption. This positive relationship between income and consumption is reflected in a marginal propensity to consume that is positive. Thus, an initial increase in spending (say, by the government) will cause production and income to rise. As income rises, consumer spending increases. This further adds to the increase in spending (aggregate demand) initiated by the government. Thus, the aggregate demand curve ends up shifting by more than by the increase in government spending alone.

9. Correct answer: b.

Discussion: The marginal propensity to consume shows that changes in income lead to changes in consumption (spending by households). The marginal propensity to consume is positive which means that additional increases in income lead to additional increases in consumer spending and vice-versa for decreases in income.

Statements a and c are not correct because the marginal propensity to consume is about the relationship between *changes* in income and consumer spending, not just the amounts. Statement d is not correct because the numerator and denominators need to be reversed. Statement e is not correct because the interest rate is not a factor in the marginal propensity to consume.

120 Chapter 9

10. Correct answer: c.

Discussion: If the marginal propensity to consume is 0.75, an initial increase in spending of $100 billion will generate $100 billion more worth of income. Thus, consumer spending will rise by $75 billion (= 0.75 X $100 billion). When the multiplier process is complete, total spending will have increased by the multiplier X $100 billion. Since the marginal propensity to consume is 0.75, the multiplier is [1/(1-0.75)] = 1/(0.25) = 4. Thus, total spending will have increased by 4 X $100 billion = $400 billion. Thus, none of the other answers can be correct.

11. Correct answer: a.

Discussion: The formula for the multiplier is [1/(1-MPC)] where the MPC is the marginal propensity to consume. With an MPC equal to 0.8, the multiplier must be [1/(1-0.8)] = 1/0.2 = 5.

12. Correct answer: b.

Discussion: The short run aggregate supply curve is positively sloped, but relatively flat. The positive slope shows that increases in production (output) correspond to higher price levels, and vice-versa. The long run aggregate supply curve is vertical (and positioned at the full-employment level of output). The vertical aggregate supply curve illustrates that in the long run, changes in aggregate demand do not lead to increases in production (output).

13. Correct answer: a.

Discussion: To see this, look at the graphs below. Your text represents the short run with a relatively flat aggregate supply curve and the long run with a vertical aggregate supply curve. Compare what happens to the price level and output (real GDP) in the short and long run when aggregate demand increases.

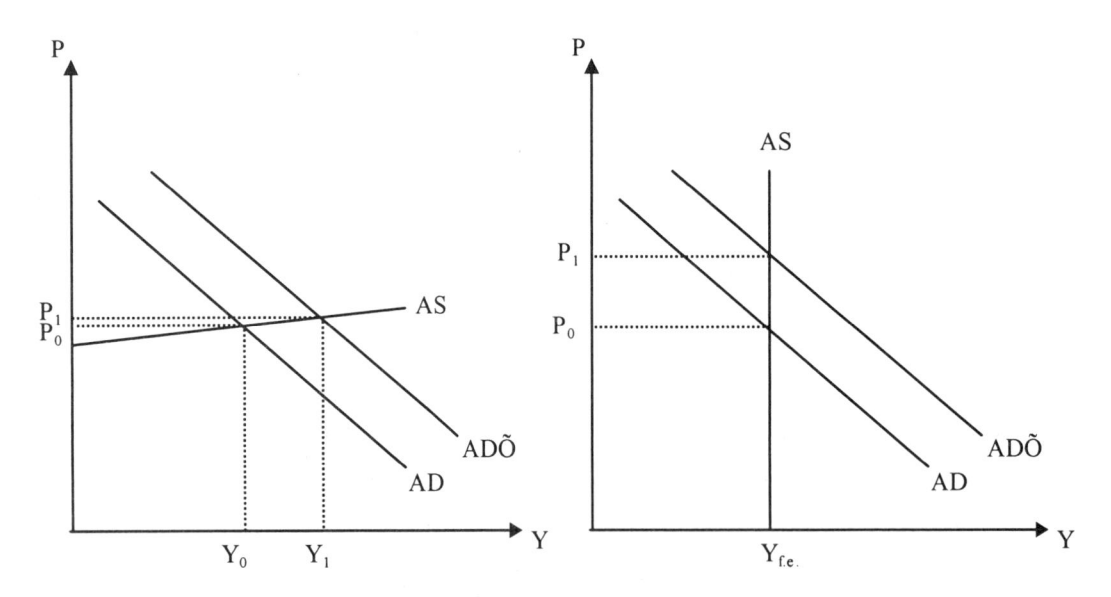

As you can see, in the short run, output increases with a modest increase in the price level. In the long run, the economy is assumed to be producing at full-capacity (full-employment, or potential). This means that physically, the economy does not have the resources to produce any more. Thus, when aggregate demand increases, businesses cannot respond by, in the aggregate, producing any more output. However, with buyers wanting to purchase more output, they will compete with each other for the limited output by offering to pay a higher price for it (much like at an auction). Ultimately, the price level rises. It rises by enough to keep aggregate demand equal to the amount the economy is able to produce. Thus, the price level rises in the long run with no change in the level of output produced.

Given the discussion above, statements b, c, d, and e cannot be correct.

14. Correct answer: a.

Discussion: The short run model is a "demand-driven" model meaning that the level of output an economy produces is determined by the demand for the goods and services it produces. Low demand will mean a low output level.

Statement b is not true; in the long run model, the level of output is determined by the factors of production an economy has. Statement c is not true; in the long run model, aggregate supply is represented as a vertical line. Statement d is not true; the intersection of aggregate demand and supply produce an "equilibrium" output level but the equilibrium output level may not be the full-employment output level. For example, the full-employment output level may be $1.5 trillion worth of goods and services whereas the intersection of aggregate demand and supply produce an output level of $1 trillion.

15. Correct answer: b.

Discussion: A drop in oil prices is an example of a supply shock. Oil is a key input into production and when its price changes, it affects the aggregate supply curve. In effect, the lower price of oil makes production less costly. This would be represented by a downward shift in the short run aggregate supply curve (i.e. the same amount of output can be produced as before, but now at a lower price level). As the short run aggregate supply curve shifts down along the aggregate demand curve, you will see that the equilibrium price level will drop and the equilibrium output level will rise. Output rises because the lower price level creates a real wealth, interest rate, and trade effect which all lead to increased spending. Since the cause of the increased spending is a drop in the price level (which is graphed on the axis), the increased spending is represented by a movement along the aggregate demand curve (not a rightward shift in it). With increased spending, businesses respond by producing more which is why output rises.

Given the discussion above, none of the other statements are correct.

16. Correct answer: e.

Discussion: A negative supply shock is something that causes the short run aggregate supply curve to shift to the left. Thus, statement a is correct. Typically, negative supply shocks are associated with rises in input prices – like an increase in wages, the price of oil, or the price of capital. Reductions in technology could also be considered a negative supply shock. In any case, a leftward shift in the short run aggregate supply curve will lead to a higher price level and a lower level of output. Thus, statements b and c are correct. The joint occurrence of a higher price level (inflation) and a lower level of output (recession, stagnating economy) is referred to as 'stagflation.' Thus, statement d is also correct.

VIII. ANSWER KEY: ESSAY QUESTIONS

1. In the short run, prices are sticky and output is demand determined. Thus, the increase in the money supply which raises spending by households and businesses leads to an increase in aggregate demand.

122 Chapter 9

As aggregate demand shifts out to the right, with prices sticky, there is hardly any change in the price level. This is represented by the aggregate demand curve shifting rightward along a relatively flat aggregate supply curve as below which moves the economy from point A to point B:

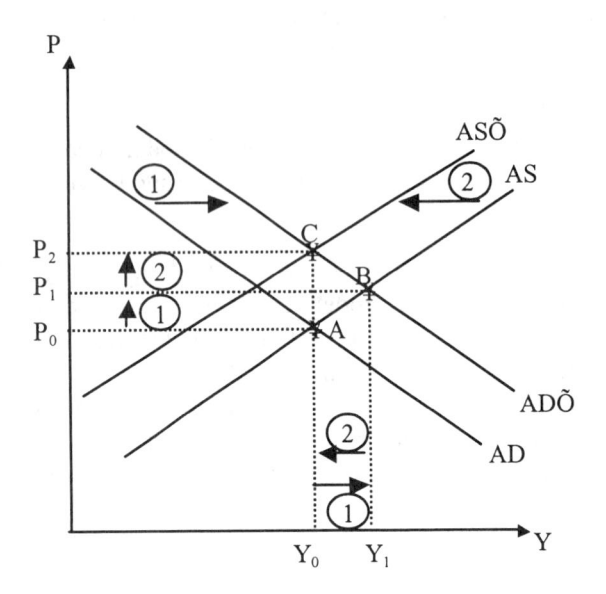

However, in the short run, businesses respond to the increased demand by producing more output and so the level of output produced rises. It rises from Y_0 to Y_1. The price level rises modestly from P_0 to P_1.

However, the economy cannot continue to operate for a sustained period of time above its full-employment or potential level of output. The increase in aggregate demand cannot be satisfied for a long period of time given the production capability of the economy which is at Y_0. This is because the full-employment level of output is determined by supply conditions -- labor, capital, and technology and these have not changed. So, in the long run, given the increases in demand for goods and services as well as for labor, prices and wages will begin to rise. The rise in wages and other input prices is represented by a leftward shift in the aggregate supply curve as marked in the graph above. Thus, eventually, the economy returns to the potential level of output, Y_0, but with a higher price level, P_2. (movement from B to C).

2. An increase in the price of oil is represented by a leftward shift in the short run aggregate supply curve. Oil is a key input into production and an increase in its price raises the price of nearly all goods and services. The oil price increase is represented by a leftward shift in the short run aggregate supply curve illustrating that at all output levels, the price level would now be higher than before the oil price increase. See the graph below.

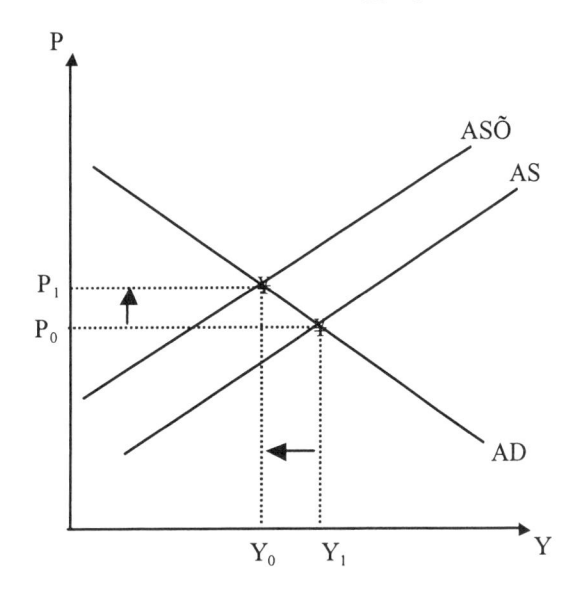

As the aggregate supply curve shifts leftward along the aggregate demand curve, the effect is to raise the price level, as you might have expected. At the same time, there is a corresponding decline in the level of output the economy is capable of producing. Thus, the oil price increase creates two problems in the economy: a higher price level (inflation) and a reduction in real GDP (more unemployment). This was the experience of the U.S. economy in 1973 and again in 1979.

Take It to the Net

We invite you to visit the O'Sullivan/Sheffrin page on the Prentice Hall Web site at:

http://www.prenhall.com/osullivan/

for this chapter's World Wide Web exercise.

CHAPTER 10
FISCAL POLICY

I. OVERVIEW

In this chapter, you will be introduced to one type of economic policy – fiscal policy. You will learn that fiscal policy is enacted through changes in government spending and taxation and that the purpose of fiscal policy is to help stabilize the economy, i.e. to keep the economy operating at the full-employment level of output (GDP). You will see that fiscal policy actions are represented through their effects on the aggregate demand curve. You will use multiplier analysis, introduced in the previous chapter, to consider the effects of changes in government spending and taxation on GDP (output). You will learn that stabilizing the economy through fiscal policy actions is not an exact science. You will learn that there are problems with using fiscal policy to achieve desired economic objectives. Along the way, you will learn about the federal budget – federal government spending and taxation, and the related issue of the federal government deficit. You will learn about the broad categories of government spending and the broad categories of government revenues collected through taxation. You will be introduced to concerns commonly voiced about government budget deficits. You will also learn about the history of fiscal policy in the United States from the 1930s through the present day.

II. CHECKLIST

By the end of this chapter, you should be able to:

- Explain the effect of an increase in government spending or a cut in taxes on aggregate demand.
- Explain the effect of a decrease in government spending or an increase in taxes on aggregate demand.
- Explain how a change in government spending directly affects aggregate demand whereas a change in taxes indirectly affects aggregate demand.
- Define 'expansionary' and 'contractionary' fiscal policy.
- Illustrate the effects of expansionary and contractionary fiscal policy using an aggregate demand and aggregate supply diagram.
- Discuss the multiplier effects of a change in government spending or taxation.
- Discuss the limits to stabilization policy.
- Define 'inside' and 'outside' lags and provide some examples of each.
- Explain how the need to forecast makes policymaking more difficult.
- Discuss federal spending in the United States and the broad components of spending by the government.
- Discuss the difference between discretionary spending by the government and entitlement and mandatory spending.
- List the main components of entitlements and mandatory spending by the U.S. government.
- Describe what is means for a government spending program to be 'means-tested.'

- ❑ Discuss the sources of revenue the government earns through collecting taxes.
- ❑ Define the terms 'budget deficit' and 'budget surplus.'
- ❑ Explain why the federal government budget is more likely to go into a deficit during downturns in the economy and a surplus during upturns.
- ❑ Define 'automatic stabilizers.'
- ❑ Explain how the government spending and taxations system can be 'automatically stabilizing' during economic downturns and upturns.
- ❑ Discuss why it might be appropriate to cut taxes and increase government spending, worsening the budget balance, during a recession.
- ❑ Discuss the main concerns with a prolonged (or persistent) government budget deficit.
- ❑ Describe the use of fiscal policy in U.S. history from the 1960s - present.
- ❑ Explain the difference in effect between permanent and temporary tax cuts.
- ❑ Explain how proponents of tax cuts during the Reagan Administration viewed tax cuts differently than what was traditional thinking about them.

III. KEY TERMS

Fiscal policy: Changes in taxes and spending that affect the level of GDP.

Expansionary policies: Government policy actions that lead to increases in output.

Contractionary policy: Government policy actions that lead to decreases in output.

Stabilization policies: Policy actions taken to bring the economy closer to full employment or potential output.

inside lags: Lags in implementing policy.

Outside lags: The time it takes for policies to work.

Econometric models: Mathematical computer-based models that economists build to capture the actual dynamics of the economy.

fiscal year: The calendar on which the federal government conducts its business, which runs from October 1 to September 30.

Entitlement and mandatory spending: Spending that Congress has authorized by prior law.

Social Security: A federal government program to provide retirement support and a host of other benefits.

Medicare: A federal government health program for the elderly.

Medicaid: A federal government health program for the poor.

Discretionary spending: The spending programs that Congress authorizes on an annual basis.

Means-tested: Based on the income of individuals or families.

Social insurance taxes: Taxes levied on earnings to pay for Social Security and Medicare.

Individual income taxes: Taxes levied on the income earned by individuals.

Withholding: Taxes collected directly from the paychecks of workers.

Estate and gift taxes: Taxes levied on the estates and gifts of individuals.

Corporate tax: A tax levied on the earnings of a corporation.

126 Chapter 10

Federal excise taxes: Taxes levied directly on the sale of selected products by the federal government.

Custom duties: Taxes levied on goods imported to the United States

Supply-side economics: A school of thought that emphasizes the role that taxes play in the supply of output in the economy.

Laffer curve: A relationship between tax rates and tax revenues that illustrates that high tax rates do not always lead to high tax revenues if they discourage economic activity.

Budget deficit: The difference between spending and revenues for a government.

Budget surplus: The difference between revenues and spending for a government—the opposite of a budget deficit.

Automatic stabilizers: Taxes and transfer payments that stabilize GDP without requiring policymakers to take explicit action.

Crowded out: The reduction in a component of GDP that results when government spending is increased or taxes are decreased.

Permanent income: An estimate of a household's long-run average level of income.

IV. PERFORMANCE ENHANCING TIPS (PETS)

PET #1

Fiscal policy actions are represented by shifts in the aggregate demand curve. Increases in government spending increase aggregate demand and are represented by a rightward shift in the aggregate demand curve. The same is true of a tax cut (which leads to an increase in consumer spending). Decreases in government spending decrease aggregate demand are a represented by a leftward shift in the aggregate demand curve. The same is true of an increase in taxes (tax hike).

PET #2

A change in government spending of $X will have a bigger impact on income and output than a change in taxes of $X because government spending works directly on total spending whereas taxes work indirectly on total spending through consumption spending.

V. PRACTICE EXAM: MULTIPLE CHOICE QUESTIONS

1. Fiscal policy is defined as:
a) the use of interest rates to influence spending (aggregate demand) and GDP.
b) the use of exchange rates to influence spending (aggregate demand) and GDP.
c) the use of government spending and taxation to influence spending (aggregate demand) and GDP.
d) the use of automatic stabilizers to help stabilize the economy.
e) the use of financial regulations to influence spending (aggregate demand) and GDP.

2. An increase in government spending will:

a) shift the aggregate demand curve to the left.
b) shift the aggregate demand curve to the right.
c) shift the aggregate supply curve to the left.
d) shift the aggregate supply curve to the right.
e) shift aggregate demand to the right and aggregate supply to the left.

3. An increase in taxes will:
a) shift the aggregate demand curve to the left.
b) shift the aggregate demand curve to the right.
c) shift the aggregate supply curve to the left.
d) shift the aggregate supply curve to the right.
e) shift aggregate demand to the left and aggregate supply to the right.

4. In an economy operating below the full-employment level of output, appropriate policy action might be to:
a) increase taxes.
b) decrease government spending.
c) decrease taxes.
d) increase government spending.
e) (c) and (d).

5. In an economy operating above the full-employment level of output, appropriate policy action might be to:
a) increase taxes.
b) decrease government spending.
c) decrease taxes.
d) increase government spending.
e) (a) and (b).

6. In an economy operating below the full-employment level of output, a tax cut would likely lead to:
a) a rightward shift in aggregate supply.
b) a leftward shift in aggregate demand.
c) an increase in the price level.
d) a decline in output.
e) a leftward shift in aggregate supply.

7. Which one of the following statements is true of contractionary fiscal policy?
a) it is likely to be used when the economy is overheating and inflation is a concern.
b) it occurs when government spending and taxes are increased together.
c) it occurs when government spending and taxes are decreased together.
d) it will cause the level of output to increase.
e) it will create a budget deficit.

8. Which one of the following statements is NOT true?
a) stabilization policies are aimed at maintaining an output (GDP) level at potential (or full-employment).
b) expansionary fiscal policy is used when recession is a threat.
c) good policymaking depends on good forecasts.
d) difficulty with recognizing what state the economy is in is an example of an inside lag in policymaking.
e) lags in implementing policy are referred to as outside lags.

9. Which one of the following statements is true?
a) outside lags may cause policy to take effect after the economy has recovered from its problems.
b) good policymaking will dampen fluctuations in GDP.
c) inside lags may occur because data is poor quality or may not be readily available to policymakers.
d) inside lags may occur because it takes time for policymakers to implement a policy.
e) all of the above are true.

10. Current statistics on the U.S. budget show that:
a) federal government spending is approximately 33% of GDP.
b) federal government taxes collected were approximately 30% of GDP.
c) federal spending amounts to approximately $7,400 per person in the United States.
d) federal spending on national defense accounts for approximately 10% of GDP.
e) federal spending on social security accounts for approximately 10% of GDP.

11. Which one of the following statements is NOT true?
a) entitlement and mandatory spending account for approximately one-fourth of all federal spending.
b) fiscal policy relies on changes in discretionary spending.
c) entitlement and mandatory spending is spending that was authorized by Congress under prior laws and remains in effect until the laws are changed.
d) a means-tested program means that government outlays to participants of the program depend, in part, on the income of the participant.
e) the challenges of an aging society may mean that social security and government-funded health care programs may need to be changed.

12. Federal excise taxes are:
a) levied on the sale of particular products.
b) levied on goods imported in to the United States.
c) the single largest component of federal tax revenues collected by the government.
d) also known as death taxes.
e) taxes withheld from workers' paychecks.

13. A supply-side economist believes all but which one of the following?
a) a cut in the tax rate could increase tax revenues collected by the government.
b) a very high tax rate might discourage people from working.
c) very high tax rates may reduce the level of economic activity.
d) a tax on labor may lead to higher employment.
e) all of the above.

14. A budget deficit:
a) is never appropriate for a government to run.
b) may be necessary during times of recession.
c) may lead to reduced investment spending, if run persistently.
d) reduces the amount of government borrowing.
e) (b) and (c).

15. Automatic stabilizers:
a) are part of the tax and transfer payment system.
b) work without enacting any laws.
c) help stabilize the business cycle.
d) tend to reduce spending during economic expansions and raise spending during economic contractions.
e) all of the above.

16. Which one of the following statements is true?
a) fiscal policy was actively used during the Great Depression.
b) President Kennedy applied fiscal policy to the U.S. economy through a tax cut.
c) Clinton passed a major tax cut during his term but these led to budget surpluses.
d) the tax cuts introduced by President Reagan in the early 1980s were proposed as part of a fiscal policy prescription.
e) all of the above are true.

17. A temporary tax cut is:
a) expected to be very expansionary.
b) not expected to have much affect on spending and output.
c) will raise permanent income.
d) an example of an automatic stabilizer.
e) none of the above.

VI. PRACTICE EXAM: ESSAY QUESTIONS

1. Explain the circumstances under which expansionary fiscal policy would be used and the circumstances under which contractionary fiscal policy would be used.

2. Suppose that you are chair of the Council of Economic Advisors and must make a recommendation to the President about what policy actions may need to be taken given that the economy is suffering a severe recession. What might you recommend and why?

VII. ANSWER KEY: MULTIPLE CHOICE QUESTIONS

1. Correct answer: c.

Discussion: Fiscal policy is defined as the use of government spending and taxation to influence spending (aggregate demand) and GDP.

Statement a is true of monetary policy, which you will learn about later. Statement b is not correct because fiscal policy is not about changing exchange rates. Statement d is not correct because fiscal policy is not about automatic stabilizers, it is about the use of making discretionary changes in government spending and taxation. Statement e is not correct.

2. Correct answer: b.

Discussion: An increase in government spending will shift the aggregate demand curve to the right. The aggregate demand curve represents spending by households (consumption), businesses (investment), the government sector, and the foreign sector (exports minus imports). An increase in government spending adds to aggregate demand. An increase in aggregate demand is represented by a rightward shift in the aggregate demand curve.

Based on the discussion above, none of the other statements can be correct.

3. Correct answer: a.

Discussion: An increase in taxes will reduce spending by households. That is, consumer spending will decline since higher taxes will reduce the amount of income they have to spend. Since consumer spending is part of aggregate demand, the increase in taxes and consequent reduction in consumer spending will cause a decline in aggregate demand. This is represented by a leftward shift in the aggregate demand curve.

Based on the discussion above, none of the other statements can be correct.

4. Correct answer: e.

Discussion: In an economy operating below the full-employment level of output, appropriate policy action might be to decrease taxes and increase government spending. Thus, statements c and d are both correct. When an economy is operating below the full-employment level of output, there will be unemployment in excess of the natural rate of unemployment. Thus, policy moves to increase spending (either directly by increasing government spending or indirectly by cutting taxes and thereby increasing consumer spending) will lead to more production and hence the need for more workers. This will help return the economy to the full-employment level of output.

5. Correct answer: e.

Discussion: In an economy operating above the full-employment level of output, appropriate policy action might be to increase taxes and reduce government spending. Thus, statements a and b are both correct. When an economy is operating above the full-employment level of output, it is straining its resources and this will lead to increases in the prices of them, and thus increases in the prices of goods and services they help produce. Thus, there is worry that inflation will be created. In an effort to avoid inflation, policymakers might desire to take pressure off prices by reducing aggregate demand. An increase in taxes, by reducing consumer spending, and a reduction in government spending will both reduce aggregate demand and help prevent inflation.

6. Correct answer: c.

Discussion: In an economy operating below the full-employment level of output, a tax cut would likely lead to an increase in consumer spending and thus an increase in aggregate demand. Thus, statements a, b, and e are not correct. The tax cut, by increasing aggregate demand will also *increase* the level of output, not decrease it. Thus, statement d is not correct. Statement c is correct because an increase in aggregate demand, which is represented by a rightward shift in aggregate demand, will cause a slight increase in the price level as aggregate demand shifts out along the positively sloped aggregate supply curve.

7. Correct answer: a.

Discussion: Contractionary fiscal policy is likely to be used when the economy is overheating and inflation is a concern, as discussed in the answer to question 5. Thus, statement a is correct.

Since the purpose of contractionary fiscal policy is to reduce spending, contractionary fiscal policy occurs when either government spending is decreased and/or taxes are increased. Thus, statements b and c are not correct. Statement d is not correct since contractionary fiscal policy reduces spending, and thus reduces the level of output. Statement e is not correct. Contractionary fiscal policy, by reducing government spending and raising taxes is likely to create a budget surplus rather than a deficit.

8. Correct answer: e.

Discussion: Statement e is not true since lags in implementing policy are referred to as inside lags. An outside lag is the lag associated with the time it takes for the policy to begin to take effect in the economy. Statements a – d are all true.

9. Correct answer: e.

Discussion: Statements a – d are all true. Outside lags may cause policy to take effect after the economy has recovered from its problems and can potentially make the economy more unstable. Good policymaking will dampen fluctuations in GDP by moderating the upturns and downturns. Inside lags may occur for a few reasons. Inside lags can occur because data is poor quality or may not be readily available to policymakers and also because it takes time for policymakers to implement a policy. For example, fiscal policy requires approval by Congress. It may take time for Congress to actually agree on a policy and put it into practice.

10. Correct answer: c.

Discussion: Current statistics on the U.S. budget show that federal spending amounts to approximately $7,400 per person. Thus, statement c is true.

Statement a is not true. Federal government spending is approximately 20% of our GDP. Statement b is not true since federal government taxes collected are approximately 16% of GDP. Statement d is not true since federal spending on national defense is approximately 4% of GDP. Statement e is not true since social security accounts for approximately 4% of GDP.

11. Correct answer: a.

Discussion: Statement a is correct since it is NOT true. Entitlement and mandatory spending account for approximately *one-half*, not one-fourth, of all federal spending. Federal spending is approximately 20% of GDP with a bit more than 10% coming from entitlements and mandatory spending.

Statements b – e are all true.

12. Correct answer: a.

Discussion: Federal excise taxes are levied on the sale of particular products. Thus, statement a is correct.

Statement b is an example of custom duties, which are levied on goods imported into the United States. Regarding statement c, federal excise taxes represent a small proportion of overall taxes collected by the government. In fact, the single largest component of federal tax revenues is individual (household) income taxes. Statement d is not true of excise taxes. "Death" taxes are also known as estate and gift taxes since they are often paid upon the death of an individual. Statement e is not true since taxes withheld from workers' paychecks are called 'social insurance taxes.' These taxes fund social security and medicare.

13. Correct answer: d.

Discussion: A supply-side economist does NOT believe that a tax on labor may lead to higher employment. A supply-side economist would be concerned that a tax on labor would lead to lower employment by making workers more costly to firms.

Supply-side economists do believe that it is possible for a cut in the tax rate to generate more tax revenues for the government, not less, because economic activity by workers and firms will increase, generating more income. Thus, the income base on which tax revenues are collected will rise and could potentially lead to more tax revenues for the government despite the tax rate cut. Supply-siders also believe that cuts in tax rates may encourage people to work more (not less). That is, supply-siders believe the substitution effect on labor supply dominates the income effect.

14. Correct answer: e.

Discussion: Statement e is true since statements b and c are both true. A budget deficit may be necessary during times of recession. That is, a cut in taxes and an increase in government spending, both of which may lead to a budget deficit, are fiscal policy actions that help increase spending and aggregate demand and can help an economy recover from a recession. Thus, statement b is true. On the other hand, as statement c mentions, a budget deficit if persistently run, can reduce or 'crowd out' spending by businesses on plant an equipment. That is, a budget deficit may reduce investment spending. This can happen because if a government persistently needs to borrow from the private sector, it competes more and more with businesses who typically need to borrow to fund their investment spending. With a limited pool of saving available from which to borrow, the increased borrowing by the government may mean reduced borrowing by businesses.

Given the reasons offered above, statement a is not correct. As the discussion above indicates, it may be appropriate for a government to run a budget deficit. Indeed, some feel that war times also justify running a budget deficit. Statement d is not true since a budget deficit *increases,* not reduces, the amount of government borrowing.

15. Correct answer: e.

Discussion: None necessary.

16. Correct answer: b.

Discussion: President Kennedy applied a tax cut to the U.S. economy on the advice of Walter Heller, then chair of the Council of Economic Advisors. The belief was that the U.S. economy could be doing better than it currently was and that a tax cut would help get the economy to grow and thus bring the unemployment rate down.

Statement a is not correct. While the writings of John Maynard Keynes, who advocated the use of government spending during economic downturns, were known during the Great Depression, his views were not put into practice in the U.S. until the 1960s. Statement c is not correct. President Clinton initiated a tax *increase*, not a decrease, which later led to budget surpluses. Statement d is not correct. The tax cuts introduced by President Reagan were billed as part of the "supply-side" prescription for the U.S. economy, not as fiscal policy. Undeniably, they would carry demand side effects. But, the view was that the tax cuts would promote work effort and additions to the capital stock which would thereby enhance the growth of the U.S. economy.

17. Correct answer: b.

Discussion: A temporary tax cut is recognized by people to be temporary and thus is not expected to have a lasting impact on their income. Thus, people do not alter their spending behavior much in response to the tax cut. In fact, some studies suggest that people tend to save most of a temporary tax cut. Thus, the temporary tax cut has little effect on spending and consequently little effect (through the multiplier) on output.

Statement a is not correct because the policy is not likely to be very expansionary as discussed above. Statement c is not correct; a temporary tax cut raises temporary income. Statement d is not correct; an automatic stabilizer does not require legislative action as a temporary tax cut would.

VIII. ANSWER KEY: ESSAY QUESTIONS

1. Expansionary fiscal policy may be used when the economy is in a recession (producing below the full-employment level of output) or threatens to go into a recession. In this situation, a burst of spending may be needed to help get out of a recession or avoid it altogether. Expansionary fiscal policy can be enacted two ways, or some combination thereof. The government can increase government spending and/or cut taxes. Both of these policies influence total spending (aggregate demand). Obviously, an increase in government spending raises total spending and increases aggregate demand. A tax cut leads to an increase in spending by the group whose taxes have been cut (individuals or businesses). In either case, more spending is generated. With more spending and more demand for goods and services, businesses respond by producing more output (GDP). This helps restore the economy to the full-employment level of output. The graph below illustrates the effects of expansionary fiscal policy move in a case where the economy is operating below the full-employment level of output.

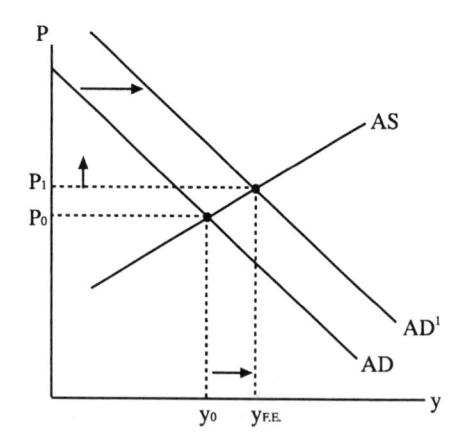

Contractionary fiscal policy may be used when the economy is operating above the full-employment level of output. In such a situation, the likely outcome is an increase in the price level (inflation). In order to avoid the possibility of inflation, the government may use contractionary fiscal policy as a way of taking pressure off prices. In this case, contractionary policy would involve increasing taxes and/or cutting government spending. As a consequence, the contractionary policy leads to a reduction in total spending (aggregate demand). The reduction in aggregate demand helps take pressure off prices and thereby helps to avoid inflation. The graph below illustrates the effects of contractionary fiscal policy in the case where the economy is operating above the full-employment level of output.

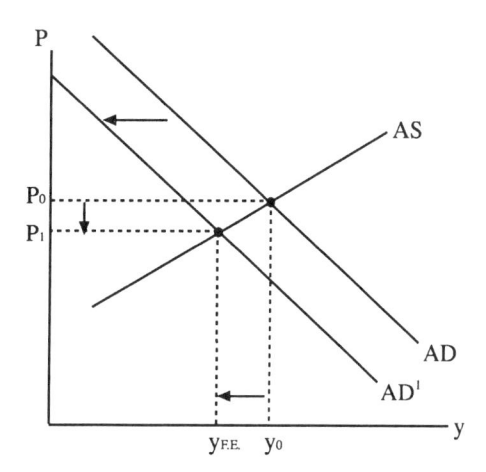

2. As chair of the Council of Economic Advisors and having knowledge of economics confined to material that I've learned up through this chapter, I would be inclined to advise expansionary fiscal policy. Expansionary fiscal policy can be carried out in two ways – through increases in government spending and/or permanent cuts in taxes. An increase in government spending works directly on spending and in comparison to an equal dollar tax cut is more stimulative to output. For example, a $50 billion increase in government spending will raise output by more than a $50 billion cut in taxes. This is because the $50 billion tax cut does not generate $50 billion worth of spending; it generates less than $50 billion worth of spending. If the marginal propensity to consume is 0.8, a $50 billion tax cut will increase spending by $40 billion which is $10 billion less than if government spending is used instead. Thus, the initial spending stimulus to the economy is smaller and for a given multiplier, its effects on output will also be smaller.

However, this is not to say that a tax cut is inferior to government spending as a tool of policymakers. If my Council deems it necessary to unleash $50 billion worth of spending into the economy, we could cut taxes by more than $50 billion. In fact, if we cut taxes by $62.5 billion, we will generate the desired $50 billion increase in spending (0.8 X $62.5). One difference with the tax cut policy compared to an increase in government spending is that it is the private sector that is doing the spending and not the government. Some people may find this preferable. On the other hand, a tax cut (holding government spending constant) will increase the budget deficit by $62.5 billion whereas an increase in government spending (without cutting taxes) will increase the budget deficit by $50 billion. In any case, I'd let the President make the choice – that's what he's been elected to do anyway.

I would warn the President that the effects of the expansionary fiscal policy may not turn out to be what my staff and I have estimated. The reason is that the budget deficit that is created in an effort to get the economy out of the recession may have some bad side effects on the economy that are not considered in the simple model that I am using to formulate policy. For example, if the budget deficit makes people more worried about the economy and therefore more cautious about spending, then the spending effects may not be as big as assumed. Also, if the expansionary fiscal policy creates a budget deficit which leads to crowding out of investment spending, it may not be as effective. Also, the fiscal policy may take time to work. If it takes too long for Congress to act on the policy, the economy may have already recovered from the recession. Consequently, the expansionary fiscal policy could actually generate inflation. That is, if the economy is already on the rebound by the time the fiscal policy is enacted, the increased spending caused by the policy could actually create more pressure on prices.

Take It to the Net

We invite you to visit the O'Sullivan/Sheffrin page on the Prentice Hall Web site at:

http://www.prenhall.com/osullivan/

for this chapter's World Wide Web exercise.

CHAPTER 11
THE INCOME-EXPENDITURE MODEL

I. OVERVIEW

In this chapter, you will learn about the income-expenditure model of the economy, often referred to as a Keynesian economic model. This model is based on important insights by Keynes. The model demonstrates how demand, production, and income are interrelated. Demand for goods and services generates production and income, and income generates demand for goods and services. The model makes a number of simplifying assumptions – one of which is that prices do not change at all in response to changes in aggregate demand. This simplification is done in order to highlight the effect of spending on output and relatedly, income. As you will see, the model emphasizes that changes in spending or aggregate demand can influence the level of output in the short run. You will see that changes in spending by households, businesses, the government and the foreign sector determine how much is in total produced in an economy. Since production generates income, you will see that changes in spending thereby lead to changes in income (hence the 'income-expenditure' model). You will learn that these changes in income lead to further changes in spending, and so on. You will revisit multiplier analysis and learn how an initial dollar change in spending can lead to a multiple dollar change in the level of income and output. The income-expenditure model will also be developed using graphs.

II. CHECKLIST

By the end of this chapter, you should be able to:

- Discuss the fundamental economic problem that Keynes addressed and the 'cure' he suggested.
- Discuss the basic point of the income-expenditure model.
- Explain what a 45° line does in a graph.
- Discuss situations of macroeconomic equilibrium and disequilibrium using the income-expenditure diagram.
- Discuss the role of inventories in situations of macroeconomic disequilibrium.
- Explain the consumption function and the equation for the consumption function.
- Explain autonomous consumer spending.
- Define the marginal propensity to consume and the marginal propensity to save.
- Explain how the marginal propensity to consume and marginal propensity to save are related.
- Explain what factors might cause the consumption function to shift (increase or decrease).
- Explain how a change in the marginal propensity to consume would affect the slope of the consumption function.
- Write out equations for the macroequilibrium conditions, based on assumptions regarding government, taxes, and a foreign sector.

138 Chapter 11

- Define the multiplier.
- Describe how the multiplier works in an economy.
- Consider how the magnitude of the marginal propensity to consume affects the magnitude of the multiplier. Relatedly, consider how the magnitude of the marginal propensity to save affects the magnitude of the multiplier.
- Compare the effects on output and income of an increase (or decrease) in government spending of $X to a cut in taxes of $X.
- Define the government spending multiplier, the tax multiplier, and the balanced budget multiplier.
- Define automatic stabilizers and explain what they do.
- Explain how the marginal propensity to consume, the multiplier, and the slope of the expenditure line are affected when consumption is made to depend on after-tax income.
- Write the equation for the multiplier when consumer spending depends on after-tax income.
- Explain how changes in the tax rate affect the magnitude of the multiplier.
- Discuss factors besides automatic stabilizers that contribute to stability in the economy.
- Explain how exports affect planned expenditure (total spending) in an economy.
- Explain how imports affect planned expenditure (total spending) in an economy.
- Define the marginal propensity to import.
- Write the equation for the multiplier assuming a country is able to import.
- Explain how the magnitude of the multiplier is affected by the magnitude of the marginal propensity to import.
- Show how an aggregate demand curve can be derived by evaluating macroequilibrium points in the income-expenditure diagrams at various price levels.

III. KEY TERMS

Planned expenditures: Another term for total demand for goods and services.

Equilibrium output: The level of GDP at which the demand for output equals the amount that is produced.

Consumption function: The relationship between the level of income and consumption spending.

Autonomous consumption: The part of consumption that does not depend on income.

marginal propensity to consume: The fraction of additional income that is spent.

Savings function: The relationship between the level of income and the level of savings.

Inventory cycle: The process by which an increase in demand would lead firms to produce more for their inventories, thereby increasing demand further.

marginal propensity to import: The fraction of additional income that is spent on imports.

IV. PERFORMANCE ENHANCING TIPS (PETS)

PET #1

In the income-expenditure model with prices and the price level fixed, output is also a measure of income. Thus, the two terms "output" and "income" may be used interchangeably.

PET #2

In the income-expenditure diagram, the purpose of the 45 degree line is to permit you to read output (income) off of the vertical axis to more easily compare it to the level of total spending that occurs at that income level.

To understand this, look at the graph below.

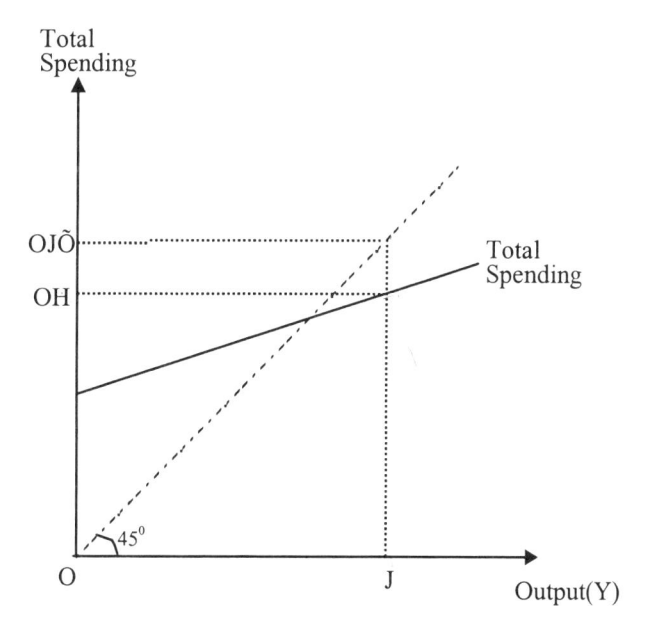

A comparison of total spending to income (output) at income (output) level OJ may at first appear difficult to do since spending is measured on the vertical axis but income is measured on the horizontal axis. However, you can measure income on the vertical axis by drawing a line from income level OJ up to the 45 degree line and over to the vertical axis. Mark this as OJ'. This is a measure of income read off of the vertical axis. Since total spending at income level OJ is read by taking that income level up to the spending graph and over to the vertical axis (marked OH), you can see that income and output (OJ') exceed total spending (OH). Thus, you could conclude that businesses' inventories will be building up since too much has been produced relative to how much is in total being purchased by the economy.

PET #3

The difference between consumption spending (C) and imports (M) is defined to be spending by households on domestic goods and services.

In a model with exports and imports, consumption spending is defined as spending by households on domestic and foreign-produced goods and services. If consumption figures reported for the U.S. are $45 billion, part of that $45 billion is spending on U.S. made goods and services and part on foreign-made goods and services. If imports are reported to be $5 billion, then the difference between consumption and imports will define the amount of spending by U.S. households on U.S. made goods and services only. In this case, the amount would be $40 billion.

PET #4

The relationship between changes in spending, output, and the multiplier is given by the formula:

Δy = multiplier X initial Δ in spending

Given any two of these three pieces of the formula, you should be able to figure out the third.

For example, suppose you are told that the multiplier is 2.5 and that income and output have decreased by $100 billion. What might be the cause? A change in spending of $100/2.5 = $40 billion might be the cause. It may be that government spending declined by $40 billion or that investment spending declined by $40 billion, etc.

Suppose you are told that the marginal propensity to consume is 0.9 and the marginal propensity to import is 0.3. Further, you are told that investment spending has increased by $20 billion. What will be the effect on income and output? Since you know the marginal propensity to consume and the marginal propensity to import, you can compute the multiplier as 1/1-(0.9-0.3) = 1/0.4 = 2.5. With the increase in investment spending of $20 billion, you can compute the change in income and output as 2.5 X $20 billion = $50 billion.

Suppose you are told that government spending has increased by $10 billion and that income and output increased by $20 billion. What must the multiplier's value be? Using the formula in bold above, the multiplier would be $20 billion/$10 billion = 2.

PET #5

Autonomous consumption, investment spending, government spending, exports are components of planned expenditure (or total spending) that are assumed to NOT depend on the level of income. This means that changes in income (output) will not cause changes in these spending components. However, changes in these spending components can cause changes in income (output).

For example, suppose you are given the following information:

$C = 100 + 0.9 \times (y - T)$
$I = 150$
$G = 200$
$X = 20$
$M = 0.1 \times y$

Based on this information, the multiplier for the economy is 1/1-(0.9-0.1) = 1/0.2 = 5. Suppose you are told that government spending increases by $20 billion. Based on multiplier analysis, income and output will rise by 5 X $20 billion = $100 billion. While the increase in government spending leads to an increase in income and output, the increase in income will not affect the Ca, I, G, X since these expenditures do not depend on the level of income. However, overall consumption (C) and overall imports (M) will be affected because they depend on the level of income as the equations above show. The extent to which they depend on the level of income is given by the marginal propensity to consume (0.9) and the marginal propensity to import (0.1). If income increases by $100 billion, since the marginal propensity to consume is 0.9, consumption spending will increase by 0.9 X 100 = $90 billion. Also, since the marginal propensity to import is 0.1, imports will increase by 0.1 X 100=$10 billion. The $90 billion increase in consumption spending is spending by households on domestic and foreign goods. Since imports (spending on foreign goods) have increased by $10 billion, the increase in spending on domestic goods is $80 billion ($90 - $10).

PET #6

There are several formulas for the multiplier. Each formula depends on the variables are assumed to be functions of income.

The simplest formula that your book introduces is a multiplier formula of 1/(1-b) where b is the marginal propensity to consume. This formula applies to a model in which there are either no taxes and no imports or taxes and imports are autonomous (i.e. do not depend on the level of income). For example, if b = 0.8, then the multiplier is 1/0.2 = 5.

The next multiplier formula your book introduces is one in which taxes depend on the level of income so T = t X y. In this case, the multiplier's formula is 1/[1- bX(1-t)]. For example, if b = 0.8 and the tax rate is 0.1, the multiplier is 1/[1 - 0.8X(1 - 0.1)] = 1/[1 – 0.8 X 0.9] = 1/1-0.72 = 1/0.38 = 2.63

Then, your book introduces a multiplier formula where taxes are autonomous (i.e. do not depend on the level of income) but there are imports which do depend on the level of income so M = m X y. In this case, the multiplier's formula is 1/[1-(b-m)]. For example, if b = 0.85 and m = 0.10, the multiplier is 1/[1 - (0.85 – 0.10)] = 1/1 - 0.75 = 1/0.25 = 4.

PET #7

The magnitude of the multiplier depends on the marginal propensity to consume (b), the marginal propensity to import (m), and the tax rate (t).

A bigger marginal propensity to consume will increase the magnitude of the multiplier and vice-versa. A bigger marginal propensity to import will decrease the magnitude of the multiplier and vice-versa. A bigger tax rate will decrease the magnitude of the multiplier and vice-versa.

For example, suppose b = 0.9 and m = 0.1, and that the tax rate is zero. The multiplier will be 1/1-(0.9 - 0.1) = 1/0.2 = 5. Now, suppose marginal propensity to consume decreases to 0.85. What will the multiplier's value be? The multiplier will be 1/1 - (0.85-0.1)= 1/0.25 = 4.

Now, suppose that the marginal propensity to import decreases to 0.05 while the marginal propensity to consume remains at 0.9. The multiplier will be 1/1 - (0.9-0.05) = 1/0.15 = 6.67.

Now, suppose that the tax rate is no longer zero but 10% (i.e. t = 0.10). Also, for simplicity, assume that the marginal propensity to import is zero. When taxes do not depend on income, the multiplier would be 1/1-0.8 = 1/0.2 = 5. When taxes depend on income, the multiplier will be 1/1-0.8 X (1-0.1) = 1/1-0.72 = 1/0.38 = 2.63.

PET #8

A change in government spending of $X will have a bigger impact on income and output than a change in taxes of $X because government spending works directly on total spending whereas taxes work indirectly on total spending through consumption spending.

Remember that in the income-expenditure model, the level of output an economy produces depends on planned expenditures, i.e. total spending. An increase in government spending will thus increase the level of output. The amount that output will increase depends on the size of the multiplier.

For example, suppose the marginal propensity to consume is 0.75 and the marginal propensity to import is 0. The multiplier is 1/1 - (b-m) = 1/1 - (0.75-0) = 1/0.25 = 4. Now, suppose government spending increases by $25 billion. The increase in income and output will be 4 X 25 = $100.

Compare this increase in income and output to a cut in taxes of $25 billion (the same amount by which government spending has increased). You know that the cut in taxes will increase consumption spending. The amount by which consumption spending will increase is NOT $25 billion. The reason is that the marginal propensity to consume is 0.75. In this case, consumption spending will increase by 0.75 X $25 billion = $18.75 billion. The remainder of the tax cut will be saved (25 - 18.75 = 6.25). Income and output will increase by the multiplier times the change in consumer spending. Thus, income and output will increase by 4 X $18.75 = $75 billion. As you can see, the cut in taxes is not as expansionary on spending and thus on output as is an equivalent increase in government spending.

V. PRACTICE EXAM: MULTIPLE CHOICE QUESTIONS

1. Which one of the following statements is true of the graph below?

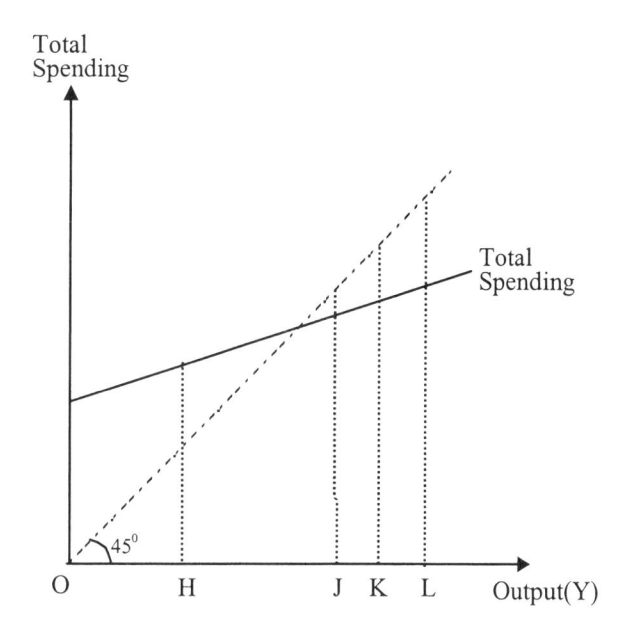

   a) at output level OH, inventories are accumulating.
   b) at output level OK, total spending exceeds output.
   c) output level OJ is the equilibrium level of output.
   d) at output level OL, inventories are accumulating.
   e) at output level OH, consumption equals saving.

2. Which one of the following statements is true about the consumption function below?

   C = 20 + 0.75 X (y - T)

   a) the marginal propensity to save must be 1.75.
   b) if income is 250 and taxes are 50, then consumption is 150.
   c) if income is 400 and taxes are 120, then saving must be 50.
   d) the slope of the consumption function is 0.25.
   e) the autonomous level of consumption cannot be determined without information on income and taxes.

3. Which one of the following would cause the consumption function to shift down?
   a) an increase in stock prices.
   b) a decrease in income.
   c) a decrease in wealth.
   d) a fall in interest rates.
   e) (b) and (c).

4. Which one of the following is true of equilibrium in an economy in which there is no government and no foreign sector?
a) I = S.
b) C = S.
c) C = I.
d) Y = C.
e) Y = I.

5. Which one of the following statements is true of the multiplier?
a) it is greater than 1.0.
b) it will increase with an increase in the marginal propensity to consume.
c) it will increase with a decrease in the marginal propensity to import.
d) it gives the multiple by which output will change in response to a change in, e.g. investment spending.
e) all of the above are true.

6. Assume the marginal propensity to consume is 0.90 and that there are no imports. Based on this, the marginal propensity to save is ___ and the multiplier is ___.
a) 0.10; 1.11.
b) 0.10; 10.
c) 1.9; 1.11.
d) 1.9; 10.
e) cannot be determined; 10.

7. Given a multiplier of 2, a decrease in investment spending of $40 billion will:
a) increase equilibrium output by $80 billion.
b) decrease equilibrium output by $80 billion.
c) increase equilibrium output by $20 billion.
d) decrease equilibrium output by $20 billion.
e) decrease equilibrium output by $40 billion.

8. An increase in investment spending of $16 billion will cause output to rise by ___ assuming the multiplier is 2.5:
a) $16 billion.
b) $6.4 billion.
c) $64 billion.
d) $40 billion.
e) $12 billion.

9. If an increase in government spending of $50 billion creates an increase in output of $200 billion, then the multiplier must be:
a) 4.
b) 2.5.
c) 1.4
d) 4.44.
e) 0.25.

10. Suppose the President would like to increase the level of output an economy produces by $100 billion, no more and no less. Further, suppose the multiplier is 3. Which one of the following policy options would work?
a) increase government spending by $33.33 billion.
b) increase taxes by $33.33 billion.
c) increase government spending by $300 billion.
d) increase government spending by $100 billion.
e) increase government spending by $33.33 billion and reduces taxes by $33.33 billion.

11. Suppose Congress decides to cut taxes by $25 billion. Further assume the marginal propensity to consume is 0.80. Also assume that this is a closed economy with no imports. Based on this information, consumption spending will initially change by ____ and output will change by ____.
a) +$20 billion; +$100 billion.
b) -$20 billion; -$100 billion.
c) +$25 billion; +$125 billion.
d) +$125 billion; +$625 billion.
e) +31.25 billion; +$39.06 billion.

12. A fiscal policy of increasing government spending by $50 billion and increasing taxes by $50 billion will (assuming the marginal propensity to consume is 0.5 and the marginal propensity to import is 0):
a) decrease autonomous consumption by $25 billion.
b) raise output by $100 billion.
c) create a budget deficit.
d) raise output by $50 billion.
e) (a) and (d).

13. Automatic stabilizers:
a) are part of the tax and transfer payment system.
b) work without enacting any laws.
c) help stabilize the business cycle.
d) tend to reduce spending during economic expansions and raise spending during economic contractions.
e) all of the above.

14. Which one of the following is a factor that contributes to the stability of the economy?
a) consumers base their spending decisions on short-run income.
b) firms' and consumers' belief that the government will keep the budget balanced in economic upturns and downturns.
c) improved inventory management practices.
d) a reduction in government transfer payments during downturns.
e) all of the above.

15. Which one of the following statements is true?
a) an increase in income will reduce imports.
b) if the multiplier is 2 and exports increase by $10 billion, output will increase by $20 billion.
c) an increase in the marginal propensity to import will increase the multiplier.
d) a cut in tax rates will reduce the slope of the consumption function.
e) (b) and (c).

16. If the marginal propensity to save is 0.4 and the marginal propensity to import is 0.25, the value of the multiplier is:
a) 1.54
b) 2.86
c) 1.18
d) 6.67
e) cannot be determined without information on the marginal propensity to consume.

17. Keynes argued that the fundamental problem causing world depression was:
   a. Insufficient taxes.
   b. Insufficient income.
   c. Insufficient savings.
   d. Insufficient demand.
   e. All of the above.

VI. PRACTICE EXAM: ESSAY QUESTIONS

1. Explain why an initial increase in spending leads to a multiple expansion in output. What role does the magnitude of the marginal propensity play? Use a simple model with a government but no foreign sector.

2. Using the income-expenditure model with a government sector, illustrate and explain how an increase in taxes (T) by $100 billion would affect the level of income and output. Assume the initial level of income and output is $800 billion. Further, assume the marginal propensity to save is 0.25.

VII. ANSWER KEY: MULTIPLE CHOICE QUESTIONS

1. Correct answer: d.

Discussion: At output (income) level OL, the amount the economy produces, OL, is greater than the amount of output in total purchased at that income level. Total spending at income level OL is read off the vertical axis and is OM, as shown below.

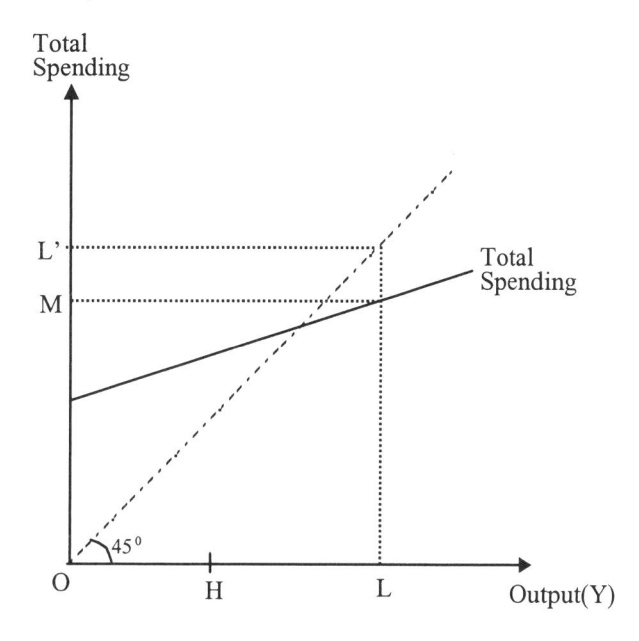

To compare this spending level to the output level, use the 45 degree line to measure the OL output level on the horizontal axis off of the vertical axis. The output level read off of the vertical axis is OL'. Since OL' is greater than OM, output exceeds total spending which means that businesses inventories will be piling up (accumulating).

Statement a is not correct because at output level OH, spending exceeds current output and so inventories are being depleted. Statement b is not correct because output is greater than total spending. Statement c is not correct. The equilibrium level of output occurs where the 45 degree line and the total spending line intersect. Statement e is not correct. There is not enough information in the graph provided to say anything about the relationship between consumption and saving.

2. Correct answer: c.

Discussion: If income is $400 and taxes are $120, then disposable income is $280. The consumption function shows that the marginal propensity to consume is 0.75. Thus, 0.75 X $280 of disposable income will be used by households to buy goods and services (consume). This amount is $210. Since autonomous consumption is $20, then total consumption based on a before-tax income level of $400 is $230. Since income is $400 and $230 is spent on goods and services and $120 is spent on taxes, the remainder is saved. Thus saving is ($400 - $230 - $120) = $50.

Statement a is not correct. The marginal propensity to save (MPS) is 1 minus the marginal propensity to consume. Thus, the MPS is 0.25. Statement b is not correct based on the discussion above. Statement d

148 Chapter 11

is not correct. The slope of the consumption function is 0.75 as is given in the equation for consumption. Statement e is not correct because the autonomous level of consumption is given in the equation. It is equal to the value of consumption that would occur even if income were zero and in this case is $20.

3. Correct answer: c.

Discussion: A shift down in the consumption function means that for every level of income, consumer spending is now lower. That is, autonomous consumption spending has declined. A decrease in wealth could cause consumers to be more frugal and thus spend less at every level of income than they had been willing to spend before.

Statement a is not correct. An increase in stock prices would increase wealth and thus lead to an increase in autonomous consumption which would shift the consumption function up. Statement b is not correct because a decrease in income would be represented by a movement down along the consumption function, not by a shift in it. Remember that since income is graphed on the axis, changes will cause movements along the consumption function but not shifts in it. You may wish to review PET #1 of Chapter 1 of the practicum. Statement d is not correct. A fall in interest rates makes it less costly for households to borrow in order to buy a new car or a new home. Thus, lower interest rates will lead to an increase in autonomous consumption which would be represented by an upward shift in the consumption function. Statement e is not correct because statement b is not correct.

4. Correct answer: a.

Discussion: macroequilibrium occurs where total output (y) is equal to total spending. Total spending in an economy where there is no government and no foreign sector is just the sum of spending by households (C) and businesses (I). Thus, y = C + I. Furthermore, since output equals income and since there is no government, there are also no taxes. Thus, income can be either spent (C) or saved (S). Thus, y = C + S. By substitution in the equilibrium condition, C + S = C + I which means S = I.

5. Correct answer: e.

Discussion: The multiplier is greater than 1.0. This means that some initial change in spending will have a bigger impact on output than the initial change in spending. For example, if spending increases by $20 billion, output and income will increase in the first round by $20 billion but will then continue to increase as more spending and hence more production and income are generated. Thus, output will increase by more than the initial $20 billion increase in spending. The multiplier's value depends on the marginal propensity to consume and import (and on the tax rate). A bigger marginal propensity to consume means that after the first-round increase in income of $20 billion, more consumption will occur than with a lower marginal propensity to consume. With more consumption occurring, more output and income will be generated in the second, third, fourth....spending rounds. This can be described by saying that the multiplier will be bigger for a bigger marginal propensity to consume. A bigger marginal propensity to import means that after the first round increase in income of $20 billion, more imports will be purchased than with a lower marginal propensity to import. With more income being used to buy foreign-made goods and services, less income is left available to buy domestic-made goods and services. Thus, with less spending on domestic goods and services, less domestic production and income will be generated. That is, the multiplier will decrease as the marginal propensity to import increases.

6. Correct answer: b.

Discussion: Since you know the marginal propensity to consume is 0.9, the marginal propensity to save must be 0.1. That is because the marginal propensity to consume and the marginal propensity to save sum to 1.0 (MPC + MPS = 1). Next, the multiplier is 10 based on the formula for the multiplier which is [1/(1-MPC)] = 1/(1-0.90) = 1/0.10 = 10. Notice that the multiplier can also be determined from the formula 1/MPS. In this question, the formula would be 1/0.10 = 10. Both methods of calculating the multiplier give you the same information. But, make sure you remember that the denominator is either (1-MPC) or just the MPS. Don't confuse the denominator as 1/MPC and (1-MPS) or you could end up with the wrong answers!

Statement a gets the MPS correct but gives the wrong multiplier. You would have gotten a multiplier of 1.11 if you had incorrectly calculated it as 1/MPC, i.e. 1/0.9. Statement c gets the multiplier and the MPS wrong. Statement d gets the MPS wrong but the multiplier correct. And statement e is not true because you can figure out the MPS by knowing what the MPC is.

7. Correct answer: b.

Discussion: First, you should be able to rule out answers a and c since a decrease in investment spending will lead to a decrease in output, not an increase. Next, you should be able to rule out answer e since the multiplier is a number that is not equal to 1. Given that the multiplier is 2, the $40 billion reduction in investment spending will circulate through the economy with multiplier effects leading to a reduction in output and income of $80 billion. You may wish to review PET #4 of this chapter to see how to use the formula.

8. Correct answer: d.

Discussion. Since you know the multiplier is 2.5 and you are told that investment spending increases by $16 billion, you can use formula (see PET #4) to figure out the change in output. The change in output will be 2.5 X $16 billion = $40 billion. In this type of question, you should always look for an answer about the change in output to be greater than the change in initial spending (in this case, investment spending). Thus, you could narrow the answers down to statements that give a change in output greater than $16 billion. That is, statements a, b, and e will not be correct.

Warning: In questions where there is an increase in government spending and an increase in taxes by the same amount, the change in output will be the same amount as the fiscal policy move. That is, if government spending and taxes both increase by $10 billion, then output will rise by $10 billion. The same holds true if the question gives equal decreases in government spending and taxes. That is, if government spending and taxes both decrease by $26 billion, then output will decrease by $26 billion. However, if government spending increases and taxes decrease (or vice-versa), you cannot answer that output will change by the same amount as the policy move.

9. Correct answer: a.

Discussion: The multiplier is figured out by using the formula from PET #4. In this question, you know that the change in output is $200 billion and that the change in spending is $50 billion. That is, by plugging these numbers into the formula you would have:

$200 billion = multiplier X $50 billion.

From this, you can calculate that the multiplier must be $200 billion/$50 billion = 4.

150 Chapter 11

10. Correct answer: a.

Discussion: Since you are given the multiplier and the desired change in output, all you need to do is to apply the formula reviewed in PET #4. With a multiplier of 3, any spending increase of $33.33 billion will lead to an increase in output of $100 billion.

Statement b cannot be correct because an increase in taxes would reduce spending and thus would decrease output, not increase it. Statement c is not correct because an increase in government spending of $300 billion will lead to an increase in output of $900 billion. Statement d is not correct because an increase in government spending of $100 billion will lead to an increase in output of $300 billion. Statement e is not correct. The increase in government spending of $33.33 billion will increase output by $100 billion and the cut in taxes of $33.33 billion will raise consumption spending by the MPC times $33.33 billion. In total, output would rise by more than $100 billion since more than $33.33 billion worth of initial spending will take place.

11. Correct answer: a.

Discussion: A tax cut works initially to affect consumption spending. However, consumption spending doesn't change by the full amount of the tax cut since part of the tax cut (refund, if you prefer to think of it that way) will be saved. Since you know the marginal propensity to consume is 0.80, then 0.8 of the $25 billion tax cut will be spent. Thus, there will initially be an increase in consumption spending of 0.80 X $25 billion = $20 billion. The remaining $5 billion will be saved (0.20 X $25 billion). Now, since you know that the change in consumption spending initially is $20 billion, you can figure out the effect on output. But, you need the multiplier. Fortunately, you are told the MPC is 0.80. Thus, the multiplier will be $1/(1-0.8) = 1/0.2 = 5$. The change in output, using the formula from PET #4 will be 5 X $20 billion = $100 billion.

12. Correct answer: e.

Discussion: The increase in taxes of $50 billion will cause consumers to cut back on their spending. Thus, autonomous consumption will decline. By how much? Since the marginal propensity to consume is 0.5, autonomous consumption spending will decline by 0.5 X $50 billion = $25 billion. This reduction in consumption will have a multiplier effect on output. Since the MPC is 0.5 (and the marginal propensity to import and the tax rate is zero), the multiplier is $1/(1-0.5) = 2$. Thus, the fall in consumption spending of $25 billion will lead to a $50 billion fall in output. However, government spending has increased at the same time that taxes have been increased. The increase in government spending will work to raise output. By how much? Since the multiplier is 2, the increase in government spending of $50 billion will lead to an increase in output of $100 billion. On net, with output rising by $100 billion but declining by $50 billion (via the tax increase), output will increase by $50 billion. This is an example of the balanced budget multiplier. The balanced budget multiplier is 1 which means that any increase in spending of $X will lead to an $X increase in output.

Since taxes and government spending increase by the same amount, the budget will not go to a deficit (or surplus, either) but will remain in balance.

13. Correct answer: e.

Discussion: None necessary.

14. Correct answer: c.

Discussion: Improved inventory management practices have helped stabilize the economy (moderating both upturns and downturns). By forecasting where demand for products will be in the future and keeping inventories matched to those demands, firms are able to more finely tune their inventory levels to demand conditions. This means firms will be less likely to be faced with unwanted inventory and the need to lay off workers. This helps stabilize employment and output.

Statement a is not correct. When consumers base their spending on *long run*, not short run income, the economy will be more stable. Statement b is not correct. When consumers and firms believe that the government will use its taxing and spending authority to counteract downturns in demand which can lead to recession and upturns in demand which can lead to inflation, spending by consumers and firms becomes more stable. This contributes to stability in the economy, too. If consumers and businesses believed, instead, that the government desired to keep its budget in balance, consumers and firms would recognize that this government policy would not help stabilize the economy and this would make spending by consumers and firms less stable. Statement d is not correct. Increases, not cuts, in transfer payments (and other types of government spending) are what help stabilize overall spending and thus help stabilize the economy (GDP) during downturns in the economy. Statement e is not correct since all of the statements are not correct.

15. Correct answer: b.

Discussion: Exports are an autonomous component of spending and constitute spending by foreigners on goods produced by another country. Thus, if our exports increase by $10 billion, that means there is more spending on our goods. With a multiplier of 2, output will increase by $20 billion.

Statement a is not correct. Imports depend on income. Since the marginal propensity to import is positive, it means that increases in income will lead to increases in imports and decreases in income will lead to decreases in imports. Statement c is not correct; an increase in the marginal propensity to import will reduce the multiplier, not raise it. (See the answer to question 5 for more detail). Statement d is not correct. A cut in tax rates raises the slope of the consumption function. A lower tax rate means that, effectively, there is more income available for consumers to spend.

16. Correct answer: a.

Discussion: The formula for the multiplier when there is a marginal propensity to consume (b) and import import (m) is given by $1/[1 - (b-m)]$. The question, however, does not provide the marginal propensity to consume but rather the marginal propensity to save. However, the marginal propensity to consume is equal to 1 minus the marginal propensity to save. So, the marginal propensity to consume is 1 − 0.4 = 0.6. Knowing this, we can now compute the multiplier as $1/[1 - (0.6 - 0.25)] = 1/[1 - (0.35)] = 1/0.65 = 1.54$.

17. Correct answer: d.

Discussion: John Maynard Keynes thought that the fundamental problem causing the world depression was an insufficient demand for goods and services. Firms would not increase their production and put the unemployed back to work unless there was sufficient demand for the foods and services they produced but consumers and firms would not demand enough goods and services unless the economy improved and their incomes were higher. He argued that fiscal policy (increasing government spending or cutting taxes could increase total demand for goods and services and bring the economy back to full employment. All the other explanations are incorrect.

VIII. ANSWER KEY: ESSAY QUESTIONS

1. An initial increase in spending of say, $30 billion dollars, will initially lead to an increase in output and income of $30 billion. (With more output being produced, more income is generated). This is not the end of the effects on the economy of the initial increase in spending. Since income has now increased by $30 billion, consumers (households) will go out and spend more. Just how much more they spend depends on the magnitude of the marginal propensity to consume (MPC). If the MPC is 0.9, households will spend an additional 0.9 X 30 = $27 billion. Their spending, of course, generates production and income in an amount equal to $27 billion. At this point, output has now increased by $57 billion which is more than the initial $30 billion increase in spending. The multiplier effect continues because the additional $27 billion worth of income propels more spending in an amount equal to 0.9 X 27 = $24.3 billion which further activates production and income by $24.3 billion. At this point, output has now increased by $81.3 billion in total. This is the multiplier effect in action and is dependent on how much consumers like to spend of additional income they receive. In the end, the multiplier formula dictates that the initial $30 billion increase in spending, given an MPC of 0.9, will lead to a $300 billion increase in output. This is because the multiplier is 1/1-0.9 = 1/0.1 = 10. If the MPC had been 0.6, then less spending would occur for each increase in income. For example, after the initial increase in output and income of $30 billion, only 0.6 X 30 = $18 billion in spending and hence output and income would be generated. This is $9 billion less (27 - 18) than is generated when the MPC is 0.9. Thus, a smaller MPC creates a smaller multiplier effect which shows up in a smaller multiplier. In this case, with an MPC of 0.6, the multiplier would be 1/1-0.6 = 1/0.4 = 2.5. For an extreme, if the MPC was 0 (which means that when consumers receive additional income they do not spend any of it), the multiplier would be 1 and the total increase in output coming from the initial $30 billion increase in spending would be $30 billion. There would be no multiplier effect.

2. A lump-sum increase in taxes (T) of $100 billion will lead to a reduction in planned expenditures (total spending) by reducing consumer spending. The increase in taxes reduces the amount of after-tax income that consumers have to spend. The amount by which consumer spending declines in response to the decline in after-tax income depends on the marginal propensity to consume. In this question, you are provided with the marginal propensity to save. However, you can determine the marginal propensity to consume by subtracting the marginal propensity to save from 1.0. So, the marginal propensity to consume is 0.75. An MPC of 0.75 means that a $1 change in income will lead to a $0.75 change in consumer spending. That is, if consumers receive $1 more in income, they will spend $0.75. Likewise, if consumers receive $1 less in income, they will spend $0.75 less. Applying the MPC to the national economy where the tax *increase* amounts to $100 billion implies that nationally, consumer spending will *decline* by $75 billion (0.75 X $100 billion). Thus, planned expenditures (total spending) will also decline, initially, by $75 billion. However, this is not the end of the story. The initial $75 billion decline in spending causes an initial decline in output and hence income of $75 billion, too. This decline in income leads to further declines in spending by consumers. That is, the multiplier effect starts to take hold. By calculating the multiplier and knowing the amount of the initial change in spending, you can calculate by how much output and income will, in total, decline by. The multiplier's value is given by the formula 1/[1 − b] which, in this case, is equal to 1/ [1 − 0.75] = 1/ 0.25 = 4. Now, using PET #4, you can calculate the total effect on output resulting from the $100 billion increase in taxes. Remember that the $100 billion increase in taxes has caused consumer spending to initially decline by $75 billion. Thus, the total effect on output and income is 4 X -$75 billion which is -$300 billion. That is, output and income decline by $300 billion as a result of an increase in taxes of $100 billion.

The income-expenditure diagram below illustrates the discussion above.

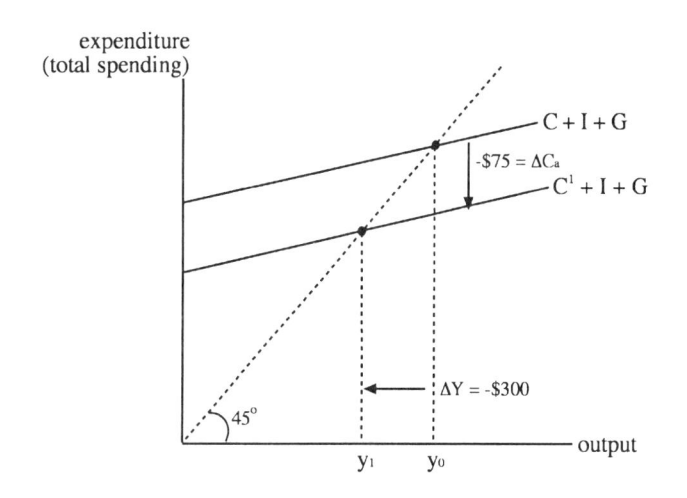

[Diagram: Income-expenditure diagram with expenditure (total spending) on the vertical axis and output on the horizontal axis. A 45° line is shown. Two parallel upward-sloping lines labeled $C + I + G$ (upper) and $C^1 + I + G$ (lower) intersect the 45° line. The vertical drop between them is labeled $-\$75 = \Delta C_a$. The horizontal shift is labeled $\Delta Y = -\$300$, from y_0 to y_1.]

Take It to the Net

We invite you to visit the O'Sullivan/Sheffrin page on the Prentice Hall Web site at:
http://www.prenhall.com/osullivan/
for this chapter's World Wide Web exercise.

CHAPTER 12
INVESTMENT AND FINANCIAL INTERMEDIATION

I. OVERVIEW

In this chapter, you will learn about the factors that affect investment in an economy. You will be given a broader definition of investment than that used in GDP accounts. You will see that the interest rate, the inflation rate, a firm's stock price, and the current state of the economy can affect how much investment and individual or business may be willing to undertake. You will re-encounter the real-nominal principle and see how it affects the costs of borrowing and lending. You will learn why higher interest rates tend to reduce the level of investment spending in an economy, how tax incentives can be used to influence investment spending, and how stock prices influence the level of investment spending. You will learn what financial intermediation is and how it can facilitate investment in an economy by overcoming a coordination problem. You will learn that financial intermediaries pool the saving funds from individuals and households and lend them to borrowers. You will also learn that financial intermediaries help reduce the risk of lending and borrowing because of diversification.

II. CHECKLIST

By the end of this chapter, you should be able to:

- ❑ Explain why investment is volatile.
- ❑ Discuss what percentage of GDP is investment spending.
- ❑ Explain the multiplier-accelerator model of investment spending.
- ❑ Define the present value of a payment and apply the principle of opportunity cost to it.
- ❑ Write the formula for calculating a present value.
- ❑ Calculate a present value.
- ❑ Explain the relationship between interest rates and the present value of money.
- ❑ Explain the difference between nominal and real interest rates/returns.
- ❑ Calculate nominal and real interest rates.
- ❑ Explain why savers may be hurt by inflation and why borrowers may benefit by inflation.
- ❑ Define the expected real interest rate/return.
- ❑ Explain why investment spending and the interest rate are negatively related.
- ❑ Describe the neo-classical theory of investment and the Q-theory of investment.
- ❑ Explain three ways a firm could finance a new project.
- ❑ Explain why the stock market and investment rise and fall together.
- ❑ Define a financial intermediary and describe its function.

- ❑ Define liquidity and why it is important.
- ❑ Define diversification and explain its affects on risk.
- ❑ Give some situations in which financial intermediaries failed to function and what role the government can play in preventing such malfunctions.

III. KEY TERMS

Accelerator theory: The theory of investment that says current investment spending depends positively on the expected future growth of real GDP.

Procyclical: Moving in same direction as real GDP.

Multiplier-accelerator model: A model in which a downturn in real GDP leads to a sharp fall in investment, which triggers further reductions in GDP through the multiplier.

Present value: The maximum amount a person is willing to pay today to receive a payment in the future.

Nominal interest rates: Interest rates quoted in the market.

Real interest rate: The nominal interest rate minus the inflation rate.

Expected real interest rate: The nominal interest rate minus the expected inflation rate.

Neoclassical theory of investment: A theory of investment that says both real interest rates and taxes are important determinants of investment.

Retained earnings: Corporate earnings that are not paid out as dividends.

Corporate bond: A bond sold by a corporation to the public in order to borrow money.

Q-theory of investment: The theory of investment that links investment spending to stock prices.

Liquid: Easily convertible to money on short notice.

Financial intermediaries: Organizations that receive funds from savers and channel them to investors.

Deposit insurance: Federal government insurance on deposits in banks and savings and loans.

Bank run: Panicky investors trying to withdraw their funds from a bank they believe may fail.

IV. PERFORMANCE ENHANCING TIPS (PETS)

PET #1

Remember that in economics, investment spending is largely spending on plant and equipment. It is NOT the purchase of stocks and bonds and other financial assets (which economists would refer to as saving).

PET #2

One way to think about the present value of a given sum of money ($X) is to ask yourself how much you would have to put into an interest-bearing asset (such as a bank account) today if you wanted to have $X in t years. The amount you will need to put into a bank account will depend on the interest rate that you can earn.

156 Chapter 12

For example, suppose you would like to have $10,000 five years from now. Further, suppose the current interest rate is 6%. How much would you have to deposit in an account today so that in five years the interest earnings plus the amount you deposit add up to $10,000? The answer to the question is a calculation of the present value of $10,000 (in five years at an interest rate of 6%).

$$\text{Present value} = \$10,000/(1+0.06)^5 = \$10,000/(1.338) = \$7,474$$

Thus, if you put $7,474 into an interest-bearing account earning 6% per year and you left that money in the account for five years, you would have $10,000 in five years.

The present value equation tells you that $7,474 today is equal to $10,000 in five years assuming the interest rate is 6% per year.

PET #3

The present value of a given sum of money ($X) in t years decreases for higher interest rates and increases for lower interest rates.

Returning to the example from PET #2, suppose you would like to have $10,000 in five years but that the interest rate is now 7%. What is the present value of $10,000, now?

Using the formula gives:

$$\text{Present value} = \$10,000/(1.07)^5 = \$10,000/(1.403) = \$7,128$$

In the previous example in PET #2, the present value was $7,474 when the interest rate was 6%. Thus, this example illustrates that a higher interest rate results in a lower present value. The present value is lower with a higher interest rate, because with a higher interest rate, more interest earnings are accumulated over the years. That is, a given deposit (the present value amount) grows more quickly to the desired sum of money with a higher interest rate. This means that a smaller sum of money can be put away today when the interest rate is higher. The reverse holds true for a lower interest rate.

PET #4

Investors are borrowers.

An investor is an individual or business who borrows funds from savers (either directly or indirectly). The investor uses the borrowed funds to undertake an investment project for which the borrower expects the payoff from the project to be large enough to not only pay back the saver but to also have made a profit.

PET #5

The real interest rate is equal to the nominal interest rate minus the rate of inflation. You can equivalently say that the nominal interest rate is equal to the real interest rate plus the rate of inflation.

For example, suppose you are told that the nominal interest rate is 7% and that the inflation rate is 3%. The real interest rate is 4%. Likewise, if you are told that the real interest rate is 4% and the inflation rate is 3%, the nominal interest rate must be 7%.

PET #6

The real interest rate determines the level of investment spending, not the nominal interest rate.

For example, compare two cases: (1) a nominal interest rate of 15% when the inflation rate is 10%; and (2) a nominal interest rate of 8% when inflation is 2%. In case (1), the real interest rate is 5% and in case (2), the real interest rate is 6%. Thus, even though in case (1), the nominal interest rate is higher, the real cost of borrowing is lower. Thus, the real interest rate is a better indicator of the true cost of borrowing funds for investment spending.

PET #7

The accelerator model of investment spending assumes that investment spending depends on expected output (income), much like the consumption spending is assumed to depend on income.

An accelerator model of investment spending could be represented by writing out an investment function:

$$I = g + h \times Ey$$

where $h > 0$, g is autonomous Investment, and Ey is expected output. Since h is greater than zero, it means that expected increases in output and income (y) lead to increases in investment spending. The amount by which a $1 increase in expected output changes investment spending is given by h. You should recognize that "h" plays the same role that "b" plays in the consumption function of Chapter 25. You could say that "h" is the marginal propensity to invest. For example, if h = 0.25, every $1 increase in expected output (income) will generate $0.25 worth of investment spending.

V. PRACTICE EXAM: MULTIPLE CHOICE QUESTIONS

1. Which one of the following statements is NOT true of investment?
a) the payoff is typically uncertain or unknown.
b) an increase in the real interest rate raises investment spending.
c) according to the accelerator model, expected growth and investment spending are positively related.
d) investment spending is procyclical.
e) investment spending is a volatile component of GDP.

2. The multiplier-accelerator model:
a) emphasizes how increases in investment spending can plunge the economy into a recession.
b) is that acceleration in the growth of the economy can trigger increases in interest rates which lead to reductions in investment spending.
c) is that investment spending is a function of "animal spirits."
d) explains how a downturn in real GDP can lead to a sharp fall in investment which will in turn trigger further reductions in GDP.
e) none of the above.

3. What is the present value associated with receiving $5,000 in ten years assuming the interest rate is currently 4% per year?
a) $7,401
b) $12,500
c) $481
d) $3,000
e) $3,378

4. Which one of the following statements is true?
a) a higher interest rate is associated with a higher present value.
b) the amount "$25,000 in 3 years" is less than the amount "$22,000 today" assuming the interest rate is 8% per year.
c) an increase in the number of years until a given sum of money is accumulated raises the present value.
d) if you wanted to have $100,000 in thirty years and the interest rate was currently 5%, you would have to put $35,000 into an interest-bearing account.
e) if the interest rate is 10% per year, the present value of $3,000 in two years is equal to $2,400.

5. Interest rates quoted by banks and that appear in the newspaper are:
a) nominal interest rates.
b) real interest rates.
c) inflation-adjusted interest rates.
d) official interest rates.
e) federal funds rates.

6. Which interest rate would be likely to be the highest?
a) a six-month interest rate on a U.S. government treasury security.
b) a one-year certificate of deposit rate offered by a bank.
c) a ten-year interest rate on the bond of a very stable, healthy corporation.
d) a ten-year interest rate on a loan to a start-up business.
e) a ten-year interest rate on a U.S. government treasury security.

7. If you put $1,000 of your savings into a one-year certificate of deposit that offers a nominal interest rate of 5.31%, then:
a) your real return will be 7.31% if the inflation rate was -2% that year.
b) your real return will be 3.31% if the inflation rate was -2% that year.
c) your real return will be -10.62% if the inflation rate was -2% that year.
d) your real return will be 10.62% if the inflation rate was -2% that year.
e) your real return will be 2.655% if the inflation rate was -2% that year.

8. Which one of the following statements is correct?
a) nominal interest rate = real interest rate + inflation rate.
b) nominal interest rate = real interest rate - inflation rate.
c) real interest rate = nominal interest rate + inflation rate.
d) real interest rate = nominal interest rate/inflation rate.
e) inflation rate = real interest rate - nominal interest rate.

9. Based on the investment schedule below, how many of the projects would be undertaken assuming an interest rate of 6%?

Investment	Cost	Return
A	$1,000	$1,030
B	$2,000	$2,100
C	$500	$550
D	$5,000	$5,250
E	$300	$306

a) one project would be undertaken.
b) two projects would be undertaken.
c) three projects would be undertaken.
d) four projects would be undertaken.
e) five projects would be undertaken.

10. The Q-theory of investment is that:
a) real interest rates and taxes play a key role in determining investment spending.
b) investment spending increases when stock prices are high.
c) the quantity of output a firm sells will determine its investment spending.
d) the GDP of a nation will determine the overall level of investment spending.
e) changes in investment spending are both quick and typically made quarterly.

11. Which one of the following is a method a firm could use to finance an investment in a project?
a) use its retained earnings.
b) borrow from a bank.
c) sell corporate bonds to the public.
d) sell new shares (stock) in the firm to the public.
e) all of the above.

12. Which one of the following statements is NOT true?
a) higher stock prices typically lead to higher investment.
b) if people expect future dividends paid on shares of stock to be high, the price of the stock will be high.
c) optimistic expectations about stock prices can cause stock prices to be high.
d) a rise in real interest rates raises investment spending.
e) if the cost to invest in a project is less today than the present value of the future earnings from the project, the investment should be undertaken.

13. Which asset would be most liquid?
a) real estate.
b) an antique car.
c) money in a bank account.
d) money in an individual retirement account.
e) money in a pension fund.

14. Which one of the following is NOT a function of a financial intermediary?
a) channels funds from savers to borrowers (investors).
b) pooling of funds from savers.
c) reduce the risk of placing saving in financial assets.
d) providing liquidity to households at reduced cost.
e) all of the above.

15. Which one of the following statements is true?
a) the savings and loan crisis of the 1990s was due to the big U.S. budget deficit.
b) deposit insurance guarantees saving up to $1,000,000.
c) savings and loan institutions were very profitable during the 1970s when there was high inflation.
d) deposit insurance was created to prevent bank runs from recurring.
e) banks keep 100% of the funds provided by savers on hand.

16. Investment spending:
f) Is a constant percentage of GDP.
g) Can fluctuate dramatically as a percentage of GDP:
h) Changes very slowly over time.
i) Changes rapidly over short periods of time
j) b and d

VI. PRACTICE EXAM: ESSAY QUESTIONS

1. Explain why real interest rates are more closely related to investment spending than nominal interest rates are. Also, explain how high real interest rates affect investment spending and output.

2. Explain how banks, by funding diverse investment projects, can reduce the risk of losing money on the total amount funded.

162 Chapter 12

VII. ANSWER KEY: MULTIPLE CHOICE QUESTIONS

1. Correct answer: b.

Discussion: Statement b is incorrect because an increase in real interest rates reduces, not raises, investment spending.

Statements a is correct and means that investment spending is risky. It also means that when savers lend their funds to investors (borrowers), their savings are subject to risk, as well. Statement c is correct. The accelerator model suggests that when businesses expect the economy to boom, investment spending will increase now and when they expect the economy to go into a recession, they will reduce investment spending now. Statement d means that when output (real GDP) increases, investment spending increases and vice-versa. Statement e means that investment spending fluctuates a lot more than some of the other spending components of GDP.

2. Correct answer: d.

Discussion: The multiplier-accelerator model links investment spending to changes in output through the multiplier (as discussed in the previous chapter) and further adds that when output changes, investment spending, in turn, changes again setting off further changes in output.

Statement a is not correct; increases in investment spending would help to push the economy up, i.e. to do better. Statement b is not correct because the multiplier-accelerator model does not address the role of interest rates. Statement c is not correct. Keynes coined the term "animal spirits" which meant that sharp swings in the moods of investors could trigger sharp swings in investment spending. Statement e is not correct because statement d is correct.

3. Correct answer: e.

Discussion: The present value of $5,000 in ten years assuming the interest rate is 4% per year is calculated as $5,000/(1.04)^{10}$ = $5,000/1.48 = $3,378.

4. Correct answer: b.

Discussion: Statement b is correct since the present value of $25,000 in three years assuming the interest rate is 8% per year is $25,000/(1.08)^3$ = $25,000/1.26 = $19,841. Since this amount is less than $22,000 today, answer b is a correct statement.

Statement a is not correct – a higher interest rate is associated with a *lower* present value. Statement c is not correct. An increase in the number of years until a given sum of money is accumulated reduces the present value. This is because an increase in the number of years allows for more time for interest earnings to accumulate. Thus, a lower sum of money needs to be put away today to achieve a given amount in the future. That is, the present value is lower the longer is the time over which the money is held in an account (or tied up). This can be seen from looking at the formula for calculating a present value. Statement d is not correct. If you wanted to have $100,000 in thirty years when the interest rate is currently 5%, you would have to put $23,148 into a bank account today. This is equal to $100,000/(1.05)^{30}$ = $100,000/4.32. Statement e is not correct. The present value of $3,000 in two years when the interest rate is 10% per year is $3,000/(1.10)^2$ = $3,000/1.21 = $2,479.

5. Correct answer: a.

Discussion: Nominal interest rates are often referred to as quoted or stated rates. Real interest rates are inflation-adjusted interest rates.

6. Correct answer: d.

Discussion: The interest rate that would be likely to be the highest would be the one corresponding to the financial instrument that is most risky. In order to induce savers to provide funds to borrower for risky projects, borrowers must be willing to pay a higher interest rate in order to compensate the savers for their willingness to share the risk. A loan to a start-up business is obviously more risky than any of the other financial instruments listed in statements a, b, c, or e.

7. Correct answer: a.

Discussion: The real interest rate or real return is the nominal interest rate (what is actually paid) minus the inflation rate. In this case, the inflation rate is negative meaning that the economy is experiencing deflation -- the price level is declining. Thus, the real interest rate (the purchasing power of the interest proceeds) will be greater than 5.31% because at the end of the year, prices will be, on average, 2% lower and so the saver will find that the interest proceeds stretch farther in terms of what they can be used to purchase. Thus, the real return is 7.31% = (5.31% - (-2%)).

8. Correct answer: a.

Discussion: The nominal interest rate is the sum of the real interest rate plus the inflation rate. Statement a can also be re-written to say that the real interest rate is equal to the nominal interest rate minus the rate of inflation (as discussed in the answer to #5). All of the other statements are thus incorrect.

9. Correct answer: a.

Discussion: Since the interest rate is 6%, only those investment projects earning a return greater than 6% will be worthwhile. Otherwise, an individual could just put money in the bank and earn 6%. Investment project A's return is 3% [($1,030-$1,000)/$1,000] × 100. Investment project B's return is 5% [($2,100 - $2,000)/$2,000]×100. Investment project C's return is 10% [($550-$500)/$500] × 100. Investment project D's return is 5% [($5,250-$5,000)/$5,000] × 100. Investment project E's return is 2% [($306-$300)/$300] × 100. Thus, since only investment project C has a return greater than 6%, it will be the only project that is worthwhile to invest in. All of the other projects earn a return less than 6%.

10. Correct answer: b.

Discussion: The Q-theory of investment, originated by James Tobin, a Nobel-prize winning economist, relates investment spending to stock prices. Statement a is a description of the neo-classical theory of investment. None of the other statements define the Q-theory of investment.

11. Correct answer: e.

Discussion: A firm can use its retained earnings to finance an investment project. It can also borrow from a bank, sell corporate bonds to the public (i.e. borrow from the public), and/or sell new shares (stock) in the firm to the public.

12. Correct answer: d.

Discussion: Statement d is not true because a rise in real interest rates reduces investment spending. Higher real interest rates reduce the present value of the earnings from a project. Thus, when a firm compares the benefits (earnings) from the project to the costs from undertaking the project, they may be more likely to find that the costs are greater than the benefits for higher real interest rates. Thus, the firm may be less likely to undertake the investment. So, higher real interest rates tend to reduce investment.

Statement a is true – higher prices typically lead to more investment. Statement b is true – if people expect the future dividends of stock to be high, the price of the stock will be high. In a sense, people are expecting to receive a greater sum of money in the future and thus are willing to pay more now (the present value), i.e. to pay a higher price for the stock today. Statement c is true – optimistic expectations about stock prices can raise stock prices today. That is, 'irrational exuberance' can cause stock prices to be elevated, even if there is no sound foundation for the optimistic expectations. Statement e is true and is an example of conducting a cost-benefit analysis. A firm compares the cost of a project today to the expected future benefits (earnings, payments) it will receive. However, it must calculate these benefits in present value terms and then compare these to the current costs. If the costs are less than the present value of the future benefits (earnings, payments), it is worthwhile for the firm to undertake the investment project.

13. Correct answer: c.

Discussion: The asset that is most liquid would be the one that is most quickly and easily convertible to cash. Money in a bank account satisfies this condition relative to the other options. Real estate and an antique car would have to be posted for sale and finding a buyer may take time. Money in an individual retirement account and in a pension fund will require some paper work for withdrawal and may involve penalties for early withdrawal.

14. Correct answer: e.

Discussion: Financial intermediaries provide all of the functions listed above. Examples of financial intermediaries are: commercial banks, savings and loans, investment banks, insurance companies, mutual fund companies, etc.

15. Correct answer: d.

Discussion: Bank runs occurred in the early 1930s (and even before then). A bank run is when a bank's customers (depositors) run to the bank and ask to withdrawal all of their money. Since banks do not, by law, have to keep all of a depositors' money on hand, customers found that they could not retrieve all of their money. This, of course, caused people to panic. Sometimes, bank runs are referred to as bank panics. Bank runs can reek financial havoc on depositors and an economy, in general. Thus, the government established deposit insurance so that customers could be sure that up to $100,000 worth of their money was protected even if the bank failed.

Statement a is not correct; the savings and loan crisis of the 1990s was in part due to the deregulation of the savings and loan industry coupled with the deposit insurance scheme provided by the government. Statement b is not correct; deposits are insured up to $100,000. Statement c is not correct; savings and loan institutions were unprofitable and many went bankrupt during the inflationary era of the 1970s. Statement e is not correct; banks are legally permitted to keep less than 100% of depositor's money on hand.

16. Correct answer: e.

Discussion: The behavior of investment spending is such that it changes over time. From 1970 to 2002, the share of investment as a component of GDP rose from 11% to 20%. So b is true. GDP can also rise and fall during very short periods of time, so that d is also true. Since these are true a must be false. Consumption is the largest component of GDP so c is false.

VIII. ANSWER KEY: ESSAY QUESTIONS

1. First of all, it is the real interest rate that influences investment spending and not necessarily the nominal interest rate. For example, compare two cases: (1) a nominal interest rate of 15% when the inflation rate is 10%; and (2) a nominal interest rate of 8% when inflation is 2%. In case (1), the real interest rate is 5% and in case (2), the real interest rate is 6%. Thus, even though in case (1), the nominal interest rate is higher, the real cost of borrowing is lower. Thus, the real interest rate is a better indicator of the true cost of borrowing funds for investment spending.

   At higher real interest rates, the opportunity cost of funding an investment project increases. In other words, the real rate of return necessary to be earned by the investment project must pass a higher hurdle in order for it to be considered more worthwhile than taking those funds and placing them in a bank or other interest bearing asset. For example, a firm may consider opening up a new factory or developing a new line of products. However, if the expected real payoff from funding such an investment is not as high as what could be earned by the firm simply investing those funds into an interest-bearing financial asset, then the firm may be inclined not to fund the investment project. Thus, higher real interest rates are typically associated with lower levels of investment spending. If higher real interest rates lead to lower levels of investment spending and lower levels of investment spending, through the multiplier, lead to lower levels of output (at least in the short run), then higher interest rates may be associated with lower levels of output (i.e. a stagnating economy). From the previous chapter, a reduction in investment spending of say $10 billion, caused by higher real interest rates, would lead to a reduction in output of say $20 billion if the multiplier is 2. Now, if the $20 billion decline in output influences investment spending as well, then investment spending may decline further (even without a change in real interest rates). That is, investment spending may decline by $2 billion more, and thus lead to a further drop in output of $4 billion (2 X $2 billion). This is an example of the multiplier-accelerator model at work.

2. basic principle of finance is that diversification reduces risk. For example, suppose you have $5,000 to invest. It may be less risky for you to invest $1,000 in five different financial assets than to invest all $5,000 into one financial asset. The reason why is that you spread out the risk of losing money (downside risk) on your $5,000, particularly if the returns on the $1,000 investments that you make are negatively correlated. Negative correlation means that when one return is low, the other is likely to be high. (If the returns were positively correlated, when one return is low, the other would be low as well. Of course, the reverse is true -- if one return is high, the other would be likely to be high). Since you can eliminate the downside risk of having both assets give low returns when they are

positively correlated, it may make more sense to place your money into assets that are negatively correlated. The same is true of banks who profit by making loans to different customers. They can reduce the risk of losing money by lending to a variety of different investment projects with different risk/return levels. If the bank is able to reduce the risk of losing money on loans it makes, it also reduces risk to its depositors of being able to pay them their money should they wish to withdrawal it.

Take It to the Net

We invite you to visit the O'Sullivan/Sheffrin page on the Prentice Hall Web site at:
http://www.prenhall.com/osullivan/
for this chapter's World Wide Web exercise.

CHAPTER 13
MONEY AND THE BANKING SYSTEM

I. OVERVIEW

In this chapter, you will learn what money is and what the functions of money are. You will learn about different measures of money. You will learn how the banking system works and how banks can create money through making loans to businesses and households. You will learn that the U.S. banking system operates under a fractional reserve system and it is this system that enables banks, through loan creation, to influence the money supply. You will be introduced to another multiplier concept – the money multiplier. You will learn about the Federal Reserve, our nation's central bank. You will also learn about the structure of the Federal Reserve System and what its primary functions are. You will learn that one of the main functions of a central bank is to act as a lender of last resort, particularly during times when financial stability may be threatened.

II. CHECKLIST

By the end of this chapter, you should be able to:

- Define money.
- Explain the three properties of money.
- Describe a barter system.
- Explain how money solves the problem of a "double coincidence of wants."
- Compare and contrast M1 and M2.
- Define assets, liabilities, and owner's equity.
- List some items that would be considered an asset of a bank; list some items that would be considered a liability of a bank.
- Define required reserves and excess reserves.
- Discuss how banks make loans, i.e. discuss the process of money creation.
- Explain how the creation of a loan by one bank can lead to a multiple expansion in the money supply.
- Define the money multiplier and use it to compute changes in the money supply.
- Explain why the money multiplier may be smaller than the simple formula suggests.
- Discuss the primary functions of the Federal Reserve.
- Define the Board of Governors and the Federal Open Market Committee.
- Discuss the role of the Chairman of the Federal Reserve System.
- Discuss the role of the Federal Reserve during financial crises.

III. KEY TERMS

Money: Anything that is regularly used in exchange.

Medium of exchange: The property of money that exchanges are made through the use of money.

Unit of account: The property of money that prices are quoted in terms of money.

Store of value: The property of money that it preserves value until it is used in an exchange.

Double coincidence of wants: The problem in a system of barter that one person may not have what the other desires.

Barter: Trading goods directly for goods.

Commodity money: A monetary system in which the actual money is a commodity, such as gold or silver.

Gold standard: A monetary system in which gold backs up paper money

Fiat money: A monetary system in which money has no intrinsic backing.

M1: The sum of currency in the hands of the public, demand deposits, other checkable deposits, and travelers' checks.

M2: M1 plus other assets, including deposits in savings and loans and money market mutual funds.

Balance sheet: An account for a bank that shows the sources of its funds (liabilities) as well as the uses for the funds (assets).

Liabilities: The sources of funds for a bank, including deposits of a financial intermediary.

Assets: The uses of the funds of a bank, including loans and reserves.

Owners' equity: The funds provided to a bank by its owners.

Reserves; The fraction of banks' deposits set aside in either vault cash or as deposits at the Federal Reserve.

Required reserves: The fraction of banks' deposits that banks are legally required to hold in their vaults or as deposits at the Fed.

Excess reserves: Any additional reserves that a bank holds above required reserves.

Reserve ratio: The ratio of reserves to deposits.

Money multiplier: An initial deposit leads to a multiple expansion of deposits. In the simplified case increase in deposits = (initial deposit). (1/reserve ratio).

Central bank: A banker's bank; an official bank that controls the supply of money in a country.

Lender of last resort: A central bank is the lender of last resort, the last place, all others having failed, from which banks in emergency situations can obtain loans.

Federal Reserve Banks: One of 12 regional banks that are an official part of the Federal Reserve System.

Board of Governors of the Federal Reserve: The seven-person governing body of the Federal Reserve system in Washington, DC.

Federal Open Market Committee (FOMC): The group that decides on monetary policy; it consists of the 7 members of the Board of Governors plus 5 of 12 regional bank presidents on a rotating basis.

IV. PERFORMANCE ENHANCING TIPS (PETS)

PET #1

When you withdraw money from your checking account to hold as cash, you have not increased the money supply. You have simply converted one form of money into another form.

Remember that the most liquid components of money are coin and currency and demand deposits (checking account balances). That is, both are components of the money supply. Thus, when you withdraw money from your checking account as cash, you have simply exchanged one form of money for another. The reverse also holds. If you deposit $100 in cash into your checking account, you have not decreased the money supply.

PET #2

Money and income do not measure the same thing in economics. Money is what you hold as cash and in your checking account and income is what you earn.

For example, you may earn $1,000 a week and keep $700 a week in your checking account and $100 as cash. The remaining $200 you may put into, e.g, a mutual fund or stock fund. The cash money and that in your checking account is "money" and is what you primarily use to make payments with. At any given point in time, the amount of money you have may not correspond to the amount of income you earn.

PET #3

The required reserve ratio is the ratio (or fraction or percentage) of demand deposits that a bank must legally hold on reserve, either in its vault or with the Federal Reserve Bank.

PET #4

The required reserve ratio applies to a bank's demand deposits and not to its total reserves.

Suppose a bank has $250,000 in reserves and $1,000,000 in demand deposits. If the required reserve ratio is 10%, then the bank must by law hold $100,000 as required reserves. Since the bank is currently holding $250,000 in reserves, the other $150,000 are referred to as "excess reserves." Do not make the mistake of applying the required reserve ratio to the bank's total reserves. That is, it is not correct to conclude that the bank's required reserves are 10% of $250,000 or $25,000.

PET #5

When a bank makes a loan, it effectively gives the borrower a check or checking account for the amount of the loan. Thus, loans add to the money supply.

170   Chapter 13

V.   PRACTICE EXAM: MULTIPLE CHOICE QUESTIONS

1. The defining property of money is that:
a) it is accepted as a means of payment.
b) it is easy to carry around.
c) its value depends on gold.
d) it can be saved.
e) it is countable.

2. Which one of the following is NOT true of money?
a) it serves as a store of value.
b) it serves as a unit of account.
c) it serves as a medium of exchange.
d) it is equal to income.
e) all of the above are true.

3. Suppose after the semester ends, you take a trip to the Bahamas. Upon arriving at the island, you make a stop at one of the markets and notice that everyone is carrying around jars full of little turtles. And, you notice the person in line in front of you just paid for a bottle of rum with 6 turtles. Someone else just bought a straw hat for two turtles. Thinking back to your economics class (as painful as that may be), you would conclude that:
a) this is a barter economy.
b) Egad, those little turtles are serving the function of money!
c) turtles are valueless.
d) turtle soup is a delicacy.
e) there is a problem of double coincidence of wants.

4. Mr. Potatohead has recently obtained a bank card from Idaho National Bank. Excited about the concept of using a little plastic card to get money from a machine, he quickly runs down to the nearest Automatic Teller Machine and withdraws $1000. This action has:
a) increased the money supply by $1000.
b) reduced the money supply by $1000.
c) reduced the bank's required reserves by $100 assuming the required reserve ratio is 10%.
d) not changed the money supply.
e) (c) and (d).

5. Which one of the following would lead to a change in the total money supply?
a) a customer's cash withdrawal from an ATM.
b) a bank loan to a customer.
c) interest payments by the Treasury on its debt.
d) depositing a paycheck in a bank.
e) none of the above.

6. Which one of the following statements is true?
a) approximately one-fourth of M1 is checking account balances (demand deposits plus other checkable deposits).
b) M2 is a narrower definition of money than M1.
c) M2 is used by economists to measure the amount of money that is regularly used in transactions.
d) inflation reduces the purchasing power of a given sum of money.
e) in dollar terms, M1 is greater than M2.

7. Which one of the following would NOT be considered an asset of a bank?
a) a loan to a corporation.
b) required reserves.
c) holdings of treasury securities.
d) deposits of its customers.
e) all of the above.

8. Which one of the following statements is true?
a) demand deposits are assets of a bank.
b) assets + liabilities = owner's equity.
c) a bank's reserves can either be kept in a bank's vault or held on deposit with a Federal Reserve bank.
d) if a bank is holding $500 as required reserves and has $2,000 in deposits, then the required reserve ratio must be 40%.
e) liabilities generate income for a bank.

9. By law, banks are required:
a) to hold 100% of customer deposits on reserve.
b) to hold a fraction of their reserves at the Federal Reserve bank.
c) to hold a fraction of demand deposits on reserve.
d) to lend out no more than the amount of their required reserves.
e) keep their discount rate at 5% or less.

10. The money multiplier is:
a) 1/required reserve ratio.
b) 1/(1-required reserve ratio).
c) 1/marginal propensity to save.
d) 1/excess reserves.
e) required reserves/demand deposits.

11. Suppose that while vacationing in Monaco, you won 25,000 French francs which is the equivalent of $5,000. When you return to the U.S., you deposit the $5,000 into your checking account. The effect is to (assuming the required reserve ratio is 20%):
a) increase your bank's liabilities by $5,000.
b) increase your bank's excess reserves by $4,000.
c) lead to a multiple expansion in the money supply (checking account balances) by $25,000.
d) increase your bank's required reserves by $1,000.
e) all of the above.

12. The money multiplier will be smaller when:
a) bank customers prefer to hold a bigger amount of their money as cash (instead of in their checking account).
b) banks prefer to lend out 95% of their excess reserves instead of 100%.
c) when the marginal propensity to save declines.
d) when the marginal propensity to consume increases.
e) (a) and (b).

13. The group responsible for deciding on monetary policy is:
a) the Federal Open Market Committee.
b) the Board of Governors.
c) the Federal Advisory Council.
d) the group of 12 Federal Reserve Bank presidents.
e) the Federal Monetary Control committee.

14. The purpose of having governors of the Federal Reserve serve fourteen-year terms is to:
a) ensure that the governors become well-experienced at policymaking.
b) insulate the governors' policy decisions from the influence of presidential elections and politics.
c) promote unity of opinion from shared time together.
d) establish long-standing ties with high-level officials of other nations' central banks.
e) ensure that price stability is achieved.

15. Which one of the following statements is true?
a) in the United States, the money multiplier is between 8-10.
b) one of the main roles of a central bank is to act as a lender of last resort.
c) in the United States, there are 10 Federal Reserve banks.
d) the Federal Open Market Committee (FOMC) consists of 15 members.
e) in countries where central banks that are independent of the Treasury, inflation rates are typically higher.

Money and the Banking System   173

VI. PRACTICE EXAM: ESSAY QUESTIONS

1. Suppose the banking system's required reserve ratio is 25% and that an elderly customer who has kept all of their savings, totaling $8,000, under a mattress has finally decided to deposit it in the bank. Explain the effects this action has on the bank's balance sheet and the money supply.

2. How does a country's preference for holding cash (as opposed to checking accounts) affect the size of the money multiplier?

VII. ANSWER KEY: MULTIPLE CHOICE QUESTIONS

1. Correct answer: a.

Discussion: Money is anything that is generally accepted as a means of payment. In other words, it is used to carry out transactions or economic exchanges. At one time, gold served as money since it was accepted as a means of payment. In some foreign countries, U.S. dollars fulfill the role of "money" since they are accepted as a means of payment.

While money is typically easy to carry around, it is not the defining property of money. Today, money's value does not depend on gold -- our money is thus referred to as "fiat" money. While money can be saved (the store of value function), that is not the defining characteristic of it. Also, while money is countable, it is not the defining characteristic of it.

2. Correct answer: d.

Discussion: See PET #2 above.

Statement a means that money can be saved (stored) and used to make future transactions (i.e. paying for college education, etc). Statement b means that money serves as a measuring rod for the value of goods and services. That is, if we had to compare the value of an apple to an orange, we could compare their values by expressing them in terms of a common denominator -- money or the dollar. Suppose an apple costs $0.35 and an orange costs $0.50, money has thus served as a unit of account. We would say that an orange is more valuable than an apple. Statement c means that money is used to pay for transactions -- buying food, paying rent, going to the movies, etc.

3. Correct answer: b.

Discussion: This is an example where turtles are serving as the medium of exchange. That is, they are accepted by the seller as a method of payment and used by the buyer as a method of payment.

A barter economy is one in which there is no "money." That is, there is no commodity that is universally accepted as a means of payment. In a barter economy, a double coincidence of wants problem exists. Money would help to eliminate the problem. The fact that turtles are used as a means of payment means that turtles must be valuable, not valueless. In this case, turtle soup may be a delicacy since eating turtle soup would be like eating money. However, statement d is more of a "for fun" answer than the correct answer.

4. Correct answer: e.

Discussion: Mr. Potatohead has simply converted one form of money (demand deposits) to another form (cash). Since both demand deposits and cash are part of the money supply, the money supply has not changed. (See PET #1 for review). However, since Mr. Potatohead as withdrawn $1,000 from the bank, the bank finds that its demand deposits decline by $1,000. With a required reserve ratio of 10%, the bank is now permitted to hold $100 less as required reserves (10% of $1,000).

5. Correct answer: b.

Discussion: When a bank makes a loan to a customer, it effectively gives the customer a check or checking account for the amount of the loan. This action increases the money supply.

Statement a is incorrect because a customer's cash withdrawal from an ATM simply converts one form of money (demand deposits) to another (cash). There is not change in the money supply from this action. Statement c is not correct. Interest payments by the Treasury on its debt simply transfer money from government bank accounts to the bank accounts of holders of the Treasury's debt (households, businesses, etc). Statement d is not correct. If you deposit a paycheck into your bank account, your "money supply" will increase but the "money supply" in the bank account of the business that pays you will decrease by the same amount. On net, there is no change in the money supply, just a transfer of ownership.

6. Correct answer: d.

Discussion: Inflation reduces the purchasing power of a given sum of money. For example, if you had $100 stowed away in your wallet for emergencies, the purchasing power of it would decline with inflation. That is, you could buy fewer goods and services with that $100 if inflation has occurred. If the inflation rate was 7% over the year, you would now need $107 to buy the same goods and services you could have bought in the previous year. Alternatively, with $100, you would be able to purchase the equivalent of $93.45 ($100/1.07) now.

Statement a is not true; about one-half (50%) of M1 is checking account balances (demand deposits plus other checkable deposits) based on the data provided for January 2004. Statement b is not true; M2 is a broader definition of money than M1. Statement c is not true; M1 is used by economists to measure the amount of money that is regularly used in transactions. Remember that M2 includes money held in money market mutual funds and other investments that may be used to pay for transactions, but typically not regular transactions. Statement e is not true; M2 is greater than M1 since it is a broader definition of money. In fact, M2 is nearly 5 times the amount of M1.

7. Correct answer: d.

Discussion: Demand deposits are liabilities of a bank. They are owed to customers (on demand). That is, demand deposits (checking accounts) are an item that a bank doesn't own. Assets are items of value that a bank owns -- just like assets are items of value that we own. Thus, loans to households and businesses are an asset of a bank since the loans are items that are owed to the bank (by its customers). A bank's reserves are also an asset since they are owned by the bank (not owed by the bank). A bank's reserves are like a checking account for the bank. A bank's holdings of treasury securities (or even stock) is an asset since they are owned by the bank (not owed by the bank).

8. Correct answer: c.

Discussion: A bank's reserves can be kept either in a bank's vault or held on deposit with a Federal Reserve bank (which is referred to as a reserve account with the Fed).

Statement a is not correct. Demand deposits are a liability of a bank. Statement b is not correct. Assets minus liabilities equal owner's equity (net worth). Statement d is not correct. If the bank is holding $500 as required reserves and has $2,000 in demand deposits, the required reserve ratio must be 25% ($500/$2,000). Statement e is not correct. Assets generate income for a bank. Liabilities are items that a bank owes.

9. Correct answer: c.

Discussion: The required reserve ratio is the fraction or percentage of demand deposits that the bank is legally obligated to hold on reserve. (See PET #3 and #4 for review).

Statement a is not correct. The U.S. banking system operates under a fractional reserve system which means that banks are legally permitted to hold only a fraction (i.e. less than 100%) of their deposits as reserves. Statement b is not correct; by law, banks must hold a fraction of their demand deposits as required reserves, not a fraction of their reserves. Statement d is not correct; banks can lend out the maximum amount of their excess reserves (an amount which typically exceeds their required reserves). By law, they cannot lend out any of their required reserves. Statement e is not correct; their is no stipulation on what interest rate banks are permitted to charge on loans to customers.

10. Correct answer: a.

Discussion: None necessary.

11. Correct answer: e.

Discussion: Your deposit of $5,000 into the bank increases the liabilities of the bank. That is, your checking account balance has increased by $5,000 which means that the bank is responsible to pay you, on demand, your $5,000 should you wish to withdraw it. Since the required reserve ratio is 20%, the bank is legally obligated to hold 20% of $5,000 as required reserves, i.e. $1,000. The remaining $4,000 of your deposits, the bank is permitted to lend out (or use in other ways). The $4,000 is referred to as excess reserves. If the bank lends out the $4,000 in excess reserves, the money supply will increase by $4,000 which will in turn end up in some other bank whose excess reserves will increase by $3,600. This bank will in turn lend out the $3,600. This process continues until the money supply will ultimately expand by [1/0.20] X $5,000 = $25,000.

12. Correct answer: e.

Discussion: The money multiplier process assumes that banks lend out all of their excess reserves and that customers do not choose to hold any of the newly created money as cash (currency) but prefer to keep it in their checking accounts. If customers prefer to hold a larger amount of their money as cash instead of in their checking accounts, banks will have fewer demand deposits and thus fewer reserves and thus a reduced ability to extend loans to customers. Remember that a bank's excess reserves serve as the base from which it is able to make loans. Thus, the money multiplier process will not go as far. Furthermore, if banks prefer to lend out a smaller amount of their excess reserves, then they will not be creating as many loans and thereby not allowing the money multiplier process to go as far.

The marginal propensity to save and consume have not been related to the money multiplier process.

176 Chapter 13

13. Correct answer: a.

Discussion: The Federal Open Market Committee (FOMC) consists of the seven governors of the Board of the Federal Reserve and five Federal Reserve Bank presidents. Four of the Federal Reserve bank presidents spend two-year rotating positions on the FOMC while the president of the New York Fed has a permanent seat on the FOMC.

14. Correct answer: b.

Discussion: The central bank of the U.S. was designed to be independent of the government so that it would not conduct policy in a way that was driven by politics or who was running for president of the U.S. Some research shows that central banks that have greater independence from their governments and their presidents are able to achieve lower rates of inflation.

15. Correct answer: b.

Discussion: One of the main roles of a central bank is to act as a lender of last resort. This helps promote financial stability, particularly during war times and stock market crashes. Thus, statement b is true.

Statement a is not true since the money multiplier for the United States is 2-3. Statement c is not true since the United States has 12 Federal Reserve banks. Statement d is not true since the Federal Open Market Committee consists of 12 members (5 Federal Reserve Bank presidents plus the 7 governors of the Federal Reserve System). Statement e is not true; countries where central banks are independent of the Treasury typically have *lower* rates of inflation.

VIII. ANSWER KEY: ESSAY QUESTIONS

1. When the elderly customer deposits the $8,000 cash into the bank, the bank will find that it now has $8,000 more in demand deposits and $8,000 more in reserves. However, the $8,000 in reserves must be broken up into two components -- required reserves and excess reserves. Since the required reserve ratio is 25%, the bank must by law hold 25% of $8,000 as required reserves. Thus, the bank must hold $2,000 as required reserves. The remaining $6,000 are referred to as "excess reserves" and are what the bank is permitted to lend out (or use in other ways). Since the money multiplier is 1/required reserve ratio, the value of it is 1/0.25 = 4. Thus, the potential maximum increase in the checking account balance money supply is 4 X $8,000 = $32,000. Since $8,000 of the $32,000 was simply the transfer of cash to a checking account, the banking system will, in effect, be able to generate $24,000 ($32,000 - $8,000) in loans. Another way to calculate the loan expansion part of the money multiplier process is to use the formula [1/required reserve ratio] X (initial change in excess reserves) which in this case would be 4 X $6,000 = $24,000.

2. The simple money multiplier formula, 1/required reserve ratio, used in the textbook assumes that all money generated through bank loans is ultimately re-deposited in other banks. Nobody holds any of it as cash. If the public preferred to hold some of the loan as cash, then the money multiplier would be smaller than based on the simple formula. The public's preference for holding money as cash instead of in checking accounts reduces the reserves of the banking system and thereby reduces their reserves and their ability to make loans.

Take It to the Net

We invite you to visit the O'Sullivan/Sheffrin page on the Prentice Hall Web site at:
http://www.prenhall.com/osullivan/
for this chapter's World Wide Web exercise.

CHAPTER 14
MONETARY POLICY IN THE SHORT RUN

I. OVERVIEW

In this chapter, you will learn how the Fed, through monetary policy, is able to influence interest rates thus aggregate spending and thus output (GDP). The context in which you will examine monetary policy is the short run in which prices are temporarily fixed. In this setting, monetary policy actions are not directed at inflation nor do monetary policy actions affect inflation. You will learn that monetary policy works through its effects on interest rates and exchange rates, which, in turn determine spending in an economy. You will use a supply and demand model of the money market to see how changes in money supply and money demand influence the price of money, i.e. the interest rate. You will learn how monetary policy affects the price of bonds. You will also learn about the relationship between interest rates and the price of bonds. You will also see that through monetary policy's effect on the exchange rate, net exports can be affected. You will learn about the limits to monetary policy and the problems associated with ensuring that monetary policy has its desired effects.

II. CHECKLIST

By the end of this chapter, you should be able to:

- Explain what is meant by 'the money market.'
- Give three reasons for why people hold or demand money.
- Explain why money demand is negatively sloped when graphed against the interest rate.
- Explain how the price level and GDP (national income) affect money demand.
- Explain how the Fed can influence the money supply through open market operations.
- Define open market purchases and sales of government bonds by the Fed.
- Illustrate the effect of open market purchases of government bonds by the Fed on the interest rate and the quantity of money using a diagram of money demand and money supply.
- Illustrate the effect of open market sales of government bonds by the Fed on the interest rate and the quantity of money using a diagram of money demand and money supply.
- Define the required reserve ratio and explain how changes in it can affect the money supply.
- Define the discount rate and explain how changes in it can affect the money supply.
- Define the federal funds rate.
- Illustrate the effects of changes in reserve requirements and changes in the discount rate using a diagram of money demand and money supply.
- Explain why higher interest rates reduce the price of bonds and vice-versa.
- Explain how lower (higher) interest rates affect investment spending and output.

- ❏ Use a schematic diagram to illustrate how the three monetary policy actions work to influence investment spending and net exports and GDP.
- ❏ Use a short run aggregate supply and aggregate demand diagram to illustrate how monetary policy actions influence aggregate demand, the price level, and GDP.
- ❏ Define 'depreciation' and 'appreciation' and explain how they affect net exports.
- ❏ Discuss the effects of monetary policy on the exchange rate and net exports and explain whether the effects work to enhance or offset the interest rate and investment spending effects.
- ❏ Give examples of expansionary and contractionary monetary policy.
- ❏ Define 'inside lags' and compare and contrast them for monetary policy and fiscal policy.
- ❏ Give some examples of inside lags as related to monetary policy.
- ❏ Define 'outside lags' and what it means for monetary policy making.
- ❏ Give some examples of outside lags as related to monetary policy.
- ❏ Describe which interest rates, short or long-term, the Fed has the most influence over.
- ❏ Describe which interest rate investment spending is more likely to react to.
- ❏ Explain how the Fed's actions can impact long-term interest rates.

III. KEY TERMS

Money market: The market for money in which the amount supplied and the amount demanded meet to determine the nominal interest.

Transactions demand for money: The demand for money based on the desire to facilitate transactions.

Illiquid: Not easily transferable to money.

Liquidity demand for money: The demand for money that represents the needs and desires individuals or firms can fill on short notice without incurring excessive costs.

Speculative demand for money: The demand for money that reflects holding money over short periods is less risky than holding stocks or bonds.

Open market purchase: The Fed's purchase of government bonds, which increases the money supply.

Open market sale: The Fed's sales of government bonds to the public, which decreases the money supply.

Discount rate: The interest rate at which banks can borrow from the Fed.

Federal funds market: The market in which banks borrow and lend reserves to and from one another.

Federal funds rate: The interest rate on reserves that banks lend each other.

Exchange rate: The rate at which currencies trade for one another in the market.

Depreciation of a currency: A decrease in the value of a currency.

Appreciation of a currency: An increase in the value of a currency.

180 Chapter 14

IV. PERFORMANCE ENHANCING TIPS (PETS)

PET #1

As real income (or real GDP) increases, the demand for money increases. As real income (or real GDP) decreases, the demand for money decreases.

Sometimes this point is confusing to students who will state "If I make more money (i.e. earn more income), I won't demand as much of it. Thus, the PET #1 seems backwards." The proper way to think about the relationship between money and income is this: at higher income levels, people typically make more transactions and thus need to have more money on hand (as cash or in checking accounts). That is, at higher income levels, people typically demand more money, not less (and vice-versa).

For example, consider what your average checking account balance is right now and how much you hold in your wallet. Also, consider what your income level is right now. Given that you are a student, your income is probably pretty low. Since your income is low, you probably don't buy steak and lobster every week, or go out to expensive restaurants very frequently, or take trips very frequently, or buy expensive clothing. Thus, your checking account balance plus what you hold as cash is probably low, too. However, after you graduate and start earning the big bucks, you will probably begin to undertake more transactions (money is fun to spend when you have it!). You may start buying more expensive clothing and buying it more frequently. You may decide to take some weekend visits to the beach or to some far away island. Maybe you'll even start taking tennis lessons and buying expensive art to decorate your apartment. This just means that you will need to hold more money in your checking account and in your wallet. So, we'd say that your demand for money has increased as your income has gone up.

PET #2

Factors relevant to the demand for money will cause the demand for money to shift. Changes in the interest rate will cause a movement along the money demand curve.

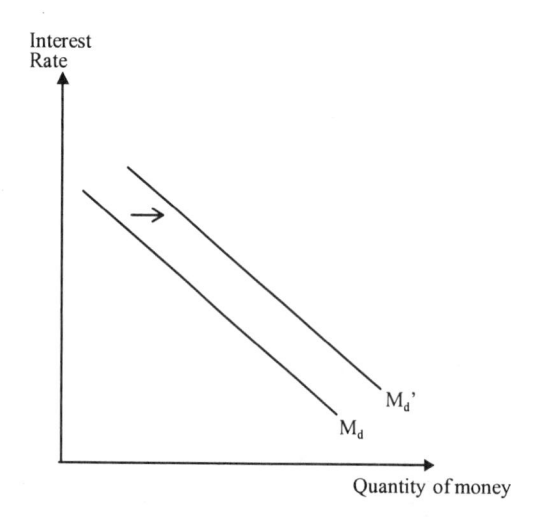

Your book suggests several other factors besides the interest rate that affect the demand for money. They are the price level and real GDP (real national income). As the price level rises, the demand for money increases since economic transactions become more expensive and people need more money to carry out those transactions (vice-versa for a decrease in the price level). This would be represented by a rightward shift in the demand curve above. Secondly, as PET #1 above suggests, changes in real GDP (real national income) also affect the demand for money. An increase in real national income will increase the demand for money (shift right) and vice-versa.

Changes in the interest rate are represented as movements along the money demand curve. Higher interest rates reduce the quantity of money demanded and lower interest rates raise the quantity of money demanded.

This is just an application of PET #1 from Chapter 1 of the study guide.

PET #3

Bonds are sold with a fixed promised payment that determines, together with the price of the bond, the effective interest rate on the bond. The promised payment relative to the price of the bond (minus 1) is the effective interest rate.

For example, suppose a bond has a promised payment of $1,100 next year. The promised payment is fixed (will not change) although the price at which the bond sells may. Suppose you buy the bond today for $1,000 and receive $1,100 next year, your return will be 10% = [($1,100/$1,000) - 1]. Now, suppose interest rates are currently 5% and the bond continues to pay $1,100 next year. You should be willing to pay $1,100/1.05 = $1,048 for the bond. In other words, if you pay $1,048 for the bond and get back $1,100 in a year, you will be earning a return of 5% [($1,100/$1,048) - 1] which is comparable to what you could earn if you put your $1,048 into some other interest bearing asset. As you can see, lower interest rates increase the price of bonds. The price of the bond increases by enough to produce a rate of return comparable to the going interest rate given the amount of the promised payment attached to the bond.

The reverse is also true. Suppose that the interest rate increases to 20%. Now, if you wanted to buy a bond with a promised payment of $1,100 next year, you should be willing to buy it for $917 ($1,100/1.20). This is because when you pay $917 for the bond and get back $1,100 next year, you will earn a 20% [($1,100/$917) - 1] return on your investment which is comparable to what you could earn if you put your money into another interest-bearing asset today for one year (since the interest rate is now 20%). As you can see, when interest rates rise, the price of bonds decrease. The price of the bond falls by enough to produce a rate of return comparable to the going interest rate given the amount of the promised payment attached to the bond.

PET #4

An increase in the money supply (expansionary monetary policy) can occur through:

- *an open market purchase of government bonds*
- *a reduction in the required reserve ratio (reserve requirements)*
- *a cut in the discount rate*

A decrease in the money supply (contractionary monetary policy) can occur through:

- *an open market sale of government bonds*
- *an increase in the required reserve ratio (reserve requirements)*
- *an increase in the discount rate*

PET #5

Investment spending is spending by businesses on plant and equipment. Investment spending declines when interest rates increase (because the cost of borrowing increases) and increases when interest rates decline (because the cost of borrowing decreases).

PET #6

Net exports increase when a currency depreciates and decrease when a currency appreciates.

Remember that net exports are exports minus imports. Since changes in currency values affect both exports and imports, net exports are affected. This is because a depreciation of a country's currency makes the goods it sells to foreigners less expensive and the goods it buys from foreigners more expensive. Thus, a depreciation increases a country's exports and reduces a country's imports. Since net exports equal exports minus imports, a depreciation will serve to raise net exports.

For example, suppose the U.S. dollar depreciates. The depreciation will make U.S. goods less expensive to foreigners. Foreigners will thus buy more goods from the United States. So, U.S. exports will rise. On the other hand, the dollar depreciation will make foreign goods more expensive to U.S. citizens. U.S. citizens will thus buy fewer goods from foreign countries. So, U.S. imports will decline. Taken together, this means that a depreciation of the dollar will increase net exports of the United States.

An appreciation of a currency works exactly the opposite of what is described above.

V. PRACTICE EXAM: MULTIPLE CHOICE QUESTIONS

1. Which one of the following statements is NOT true of money?
a) it is a component of wealth.
b) people hold money primarily to conduct transactions.
c) the opportunity cost of holding money is foregone interest earnings on other financial assets.
d) as interest rates rise, the quantity of money demanded increases.
e) all of the above are true.

2. Which one of the following would explain the liquidity motive for holding money?
a) stock prices are very variable and their rate of return risky compared to money.
b) bond prices are very variable and their rate of return risky compared to money.
c) a need to pay for an unexpected, big expense -- like when your car breaks down.
d) a need to pay for daily transactions like lunch.
e) it takes time to go to the bank and withdrawal cash from your checking account.

3. Which one of the following is a reason for holding money?
a) emergency need for money.
b) to pay for groceries, clothing, entertainment, and more.
c) to avoid risks associated with the stock market.
d) to avoid risks associated with the bond market.
e) all of the above.

4. Which one of the following statements is correct?
a) an increase in the price level will increase money demand and lower interest rates.
b) a decrease in the price level will increase money demand and lower interest rates.
c) an increase in real income (GDP) will increase money demand and raise interest rates.
d) a decrease in real income (GDP) will increase money demand and raise interest rates.
e) an increase in real income (GDP) will decrease money demand and lower interest rates.

5. Which one of the following statements is correct?
a) an increase in the money supply will shift the money supply curve to the right, lower interest rates, and reduce investment spending.
b) an increase in the money supply will shift the money supply curve to the right, lower interest rates, and raise output.
c) a decrease in the money supply will shift the money supply curve to the left, lower interest rates, and raise output.
d) a decrease in money demand will lower interest rates and raise investment spending.
e) (b) and (d).

184   Chapter 14

6. Which one of the following is NOT an example of expansionary monetary policy?
a) a cut in the discount rate.
b) a cut in the required reserve ratio.
c) an open market sale of government bonds by the Fed.
d) a cut in taxes.
e) (c) and (d).

7. Which one of the following statements is correct?
a) an open market purchase will raise interest rates.
b) a reduction in the required reserve ratio will lower interest rates.
c) a reduction in the discount rate will raise interest rates.
d) a cut in the tax rate will lower interest rates.
e) (a) and (b).

8. Which one of the following statements is true?
a) a cut in the required reserve ratio will raise investment spending and net exports.
b) an increase in the discount rate will cause other interest rates to rise and the dollar to depreciate.
c) an open market sale raises interest rates and investment spending.
d) an open market purchase will cause an appreciation of the dollar.
e) an increase in the required reserve ratio will increase the money supply and reduce interest rates.

9. If the Fed decreases the money supply, in the short run:
a) investment spending and output (GDP) will fall.
b) investment spending and output (GDP) will rise.
c) investment spending will fall and output (GDP) will rise.
d) investment spending will rise and output (GDP) will fall.
e) investment spending will not respond to changes in the money supply.

10. Which one of the following statements is true?
a) as interest rates increase, the price of bonds drop.
b) a bond priced at $100 with a promised payment of $105 next year implies an interest rate of 20% per year.
c) if the interest rate is 7.5% and a bond has a promised payment of $1,150 next year, the price of the bond must be $1,070.
d) as interest rates drop, the price of bonds drop.
e) (a) and (c).

11. An open market sale by the Fed will, in the short run:
   a) raise interest rates and increase (appreciate) the value of the U.S. dollar against foreign currencies.
   b) raise interest rates and decrease (depreciate) the value of the U.S. dollar against foreign currencies.
   c) decrease interest rates and increase (appreciate) the value of the U.S. dollar against foreign currencies.
   d) decrease interest rates and decrease (depreciate) the value of the U.S. dollar against foreign currencies.
   e) raise interest rates but have no effect on the value of the U.S. dollar against foreign currencies.

12. An open market purchase by the Fed will, in the short run:
   a) raise interest rates, increase (appreciate) the value of the U.S. dollar, and increase net exports.
   b) decrease interest rates, decrease (depreciate) the value of the U.S. dollar, and increase net exports.
   c) decrease interest rates, increase (appreciate) the value of the U.S. dollar, and decrease net exports.
   d) raise interest rates, decrease (depreciate) the value of the U.S. dollar, and increase net exports.
   e) decrease interest rates, decrease (depreciate) the value of the U.S. dollar, and decrease net exports.

13. Which one of the following statements is true?
   a) a cut in the discount rate will increase investment spending and net exports in the short run.
   b) an open market sale will increase investment spending and net exports in the short run.
   c) an increase in the required reserve ratio will increase investment spending and reduce net exports in the short run.
   d) contractionary monetary policy will reduce investment spending but raise exports and leave an undetermined affect on output.
   e) none of the above.

14. Which one of the following statements is NOT true?
   a) stabilization policies are aimed at maintaining an output (GDP) level at potential (or full-employment).
   b) contractionary monetary policy is used when inflation is a threat.
   c) good policymaking depends on good forecasts.
   d) difficulty with recognizing what state the economy is in is an example of an inside lag in policymaking.
   e) lags in implementing policy are referred to as outside lags.

15. Which one of the following statements is true?
   a) outside lags mean that a policy may take effect after the economy has recovered from its problems.
   b) a depreciation of the dollar will decrease U.S. exports and increase U.S. imports.
   c) monetary policy has a longer inside lag than fiscal policy.
   d) the Fed directly influences long-term interest rates through policy actions and indirectly influences short–term interest rate through affecting expectations.
   e) none of the above are true.

16. Which one of the following statements is true?
a) the federal funds rate is the interest rate that the Fed charges on loans to private banks.
b) the federal funds rate in the interest rate private banks charge on overnight loans to each other.
c) firms and households typically borrow at short-term interest rates.
d) changes in the discount rate are interpreted by the financial market as a signal about what the Fed's policy will be in the future.
e) (b) and (d).

17. An open market purchase of government bonds by the Fed will:
a) reduce aggregate demand and lead to a lower price level and output level.
b) reduce aggregate demand and lead to a higher price level and lower output level.
c) raise aggregate demand and lead to a higher price level and output level.
d) raise aggregate demand and lead to a higher price level with no effect on output.
e) increase aggregate supply and lead to a lower price level and higher output level.

18. Which one of the following statements is true?
a) an increase in the required reserve ratio will shift aggregate demand to the left.
b) an increase in the discount rate will shift the aggregate supply curve to the left.
c) an open market sale will shift aggregate demand to the right.
d) an open market purchase will shift aggregate demand to the left.
e) a reduction in the required reserve ratio will shift aggregate supply to the right.

VI. PRACTICE EXAM: ESSAY QUESTIONS

1. Use the money supply/money demand model to demonstrate how an upturn in the business cycle might affect interest rates and investment spending. If the Fed wanted to keep interest rates at the level they were at before the upturn in the business cycle, what could the Fed do?

2. Suppose the Fed increases the money supply at the same time that the government reduces government spending. Use the short run aggregate supply and aggregate demand diagram to demonstrate the effects on spending and output. Be sure to discuss the international channel through which monetary policy works as well.

VII. ANSWER KEY: MULTIPLE CHOICE QUESTIONS

1. Correct answer: d.

Discussion: Statement d is incorrect because as interest rates rise, the quantity of money demand decreases. That is, there is a negative relationship between the quantity of money demanded and the interest rate. This is reflected in a money demand curve that is negatively sloped when graphed against the interest rate. While there are other reasons that people hold money (for liquidity and speculative reasons), the transactions motive is the primary motive for holding money. The opportunity cost of holding money is foregone interest earnings on other financial assets. Money held as cash earns no interest whereas money held in a checking account may earn some interest but the interest rate is very low compared to other financial assets in which money could be placed.

Money is one component of wealth. An individual's holdings of stock, bonds, real estate, art, gold, etc. are other components of wealth.

2. Correct answer: c.

Discussion: Money is the most liquid component of wealth. You can easily convert it to cash to pay for things or can write a check to pay for things. Obviously, money is held to pay for daily transactions (the transactions motive as implied in Statement d), but some money is held in order to cover unexpected expenses. In other words, you never know when you may need to pay for something quickly. This is the liquidity (or "precautionary") motive for holding money.

Statements a and b are examples of the speculative motive for holding money. Statement e is not an explanation of the liquidity motive.

3. Correct answer: e.

Discussion: There are three broad reasons for holding money – to pay for transactions, for liquidity, and for speculative reasons. Statement a is an example of a liquidity motive for holding or demanding money. Statement b is an example of a transactions motive for holding money. Statements c and d are examples of the speculative motive for holding money. Thus, all provide examples of a demand for money.

4. Correct answer: c.

Discussion: An increase in real income is a shift factor of money demand. At higher income levels, people undertake more transactions and thus demand more money. As the demand for money increases (shifts right) the interest rate rises, holding fixed the money supply.

Statement a is not correct; while an increase in the price level will increase money demand, interest rates will go up, not down. Statement b is not correct because a decrease in the price level will reduce money demand and reduce interest rates. Statement d is not correct because a decrease in real income will reduce money demand and reduce interest rates. Statement e is not correct because an increase in real income will increase money demand and raise interest rates.

5. Correct answer: e.

Discussion: An increase in money supply is represented by a rightward shift in the money supply curve. As the supply of money increases, the price of money (the interest rate) drops. As the interest rate drops, investment spending increases which leads to a multiple expansion in output. Thus, statement b is correct. A decrease in money demand will lower the price of money (the interest rate). At lower interest rates, investment spending (and consequently output) will increase. Thus, statement d is correct.

Statement a is not correct because investment spending will increase, not decrease. Statement c is not correct because a decrease in the money supply will raise, not lower, interest rates and thereby reduce investment spending and thus output.

6. Correct answer: e.

Discussion: Expansionary monetary policy is monetary policy actions that lead to an increase in the money supply, lower interest rates, a currency depreciation, and ultimately more spending. Statement c is a correct answer because an open market sale is an example of contractionary monetary policy, NOT expansionary monetary policy. Statement d is also a correct answer because a cut in taxes is NOT an example of expansionary monetary policy but instead, an example of expansionary fiscal policy. Thus, statement e is correct since both statements c and d are correct.

Statements a and b are both examples of expansionary monetary policy since they both can lead to an increase in the money supply, lower interest rates, a currency depreciation, and more spending.

7. Correct answer: b.

Discussion: A reduction in the required reserve ratio is one arm of monetary policy that can lead to an increase in the money supply. Since the reduction in the required reserve ratio increases the money supply, interest rates will decrease.

Statement a is incorrect because an open market purchase is an increase in the money supply which leads to lower interest rates, not higher interest rates. Statement c is not correct because a cut in the discount rate acts to increase the money supply and thereby lower interest rates, not raise them. Statement d is not correct because a tax cut is an example of fiscal policy and, at this point, is not assumed to have any effect on interest rates. Statement e cannot be correct because statement a is not correct.

8. Correct answer: a.

Discussion: Statement a is the correct answer since a cut in the required reserve ratio leads to an increase in the money supply and thus lower interest rates. The reduction interest rates raise investment spending. Since the policy also depreciates the currency, net exports also rise.

Statement b is not correct; although an increase in the discount rate will cause other interest rates to rise, it will not cause the dollar to depreciate. The policy will actually cause the dollar to appreciate. Statement c is not correct since an open market sale does not raise investment spending; it reduces it. Statement d is not correct since an open market purchase will cause the dollar to depreciate. Statement e is not correct because an increase in the required reserve ratio will decrease the money supply and raise interest rates.

9. Correct answer: a.

Discussion: A decrease in the money supply raises interest rates. The increase in interest rates raises the cost of borrowing and thus reduces investment spending (spending by businesses on plant and equipment). As investment spending declines, output (GDP) declines because there is less spending taking place in the economy.

Based on the answer above, none of the other statements are correct.

10. Correct answer: e.

Discussion: Interest rates and the price of bonds are negatively related. This means that as interest rates increase, the price of bonds drop and as interest rates drop, the price of bonds increase. Thus, statement a is correct. Statement c is also correct. Using the formula:

Price of bond = promised payment next year/(1+interest rate)

yields:

Price of bond = $1,150/1.075 = $1,070.

Statement b is not correct. Re-arranging the formula above to determine the interest rate would give 5% [($105/$100) - 1], not 20%. Statement d is not correct because statement a is correct.

11. Correct answer: a.

Discussion: An open market sale is a decrease in the money supply. As the money supply decreases, the price of money, the interest rate, increases. As the interest rate increases, foreigners demand more of U.S. financial assets since they offer a better rate of return. In order to buy U.S. assets, foreigners must give up their own currency for U.S. dollars. That is, the demand for dollars increases (and the supply of foreign currency increases). As the demand for dollars increases, the price of a dollar relative to foreign currency rises. In other words, the U.S. dollar appreciates against other currencies.

For this reason, statement b is not correct. Statements c and d cannot be correct since an open market sale increases interest rates, not decreases them. Statement e is not correct because monetary policy can influence the exchange rate.

12. Correct answer: b.

Discussion: Statement b is correct because an open market purchase of government bonds by the Fed will lead to an increase in the money supply. The increase in the money supply will decrease interest rates. This will cause the dollar to depreciate, too. As the dollar depreciates, exports will rise and imports will decline causing net exports to increase.

Since statement b is correct, none of the other possible combinations of outcomes offered in statements a, c, d, or e can be correct.

13. Correct answer: a.

Discussion: A cut in the discount rate leads to an increase in the money supply. An increase in the money supply reduces interest rates and raises investment spending. Also, the reduction in interest rates ultimately leads to a depreciation of the dollar. As the dollar depreciates, exports increase (because they become less expensive) and imports decrease (because they become more expensive). Thus, net exports increase as the dollar depreciates.

Statement b is not correct. An open market sale raises interest rates and reduces investment spending. Furthermore, an open market sale will appreciate the U.S. dollar and reduce net exports. Statement c is not correct. An increase in the required reserve ratio will reduce the money supply and raise interest rates, thereby reducing investment spending. The dollar will appreciate and net exports will decline. Statement d is not correct because contractionary monetary policy will appreciate the dollar and make U.S. exports more expensive. Thus, U.S. exports will decline (not increase).

14. Correct answer: e.

Discussion: Lags in implementing policy (fiscal or monetary) are referred to as inside lags. (Lags in recognizing what state the economy is in are also referred to as inside lags). Lags in policy implementation occurs because it takes time for policymakers to meet and decide on what to do. The inside lag in monetary policy is much shorter than for fiscal policy.

15. Correct answer: a.

Discussion: An outside lag is the lag or time it takes for the effects of a policy to be felt on the economy. Sometimes the outside lag is so long that the economy has recovered from its economic problems before the policy effects are felt. This is not good. If the economy has already recovered and the policy begins to take effect, the policy may now produce some undesirable and unintended consequences. For example, suppose the Fed enacted an expansionary monetary policy today because the economy was in a recession. Suppose that the effects on investment spending and GDP are not transmitted to the economy until a year later. By that time, however, the economy may be out of a recession and perhaps is growing rapidly by itself. The expansionary monetary policy might further the growth but exacerbate (increase) inflation. In this way, the policy has created some undesirable and unintended effects.

Statement b is not correct. A dollar depreciation will raise U.S. exports and reduce U.S. imports, not the other way around. Statement c is not correct. Monetary policymakers meet every six weeks and thus the inside lag is much shorter than for fiscal policy (where Congress has to meet and decide on fiscal policy). Statement d is not correct. The Fed directly influences *short-term* interest rates and indirectly influences long-term interest rates by affecting the financial market's expectations of whether the Fed will increase or decrease interest rates in the future.

16. Correct answer: e.

Discussion: Statement e is correct since both statements b and d are correct. Statement b is correct since the federal funds rate (contrary to the use of the word 'federal') is the interest rate that private banks charge on overnight loans to each other, i.e. on borrowing reserves from each other. Statement d is correct since changes in the discount rate are visible to the financial market and changes in it are often viewed as an indicator of what the Fed may do in the future.

Statement a is not correct. The discount rate is the interest rate that the Fed charges on loans to private banks. Statement c is not correct since firms and households typically borrow at long-term interest rates, not short-term interest rates.

17. Correct answer: c.

Discussion: An open market purchase of government bonds by the Fed is considered expansionary policy. An open market purchase reduces interest rates and depreciates the dollar. The drop in interest rates and the dollar depreciation lead to an increase in investment spending and net exports. Both of these are components of aggregate demand. Since both of these spending components increase, aggregate demand increases. An increase in aggregate demand when shifted out along the short-run aggregate supply curve will lead to a higher price level and an increase in output (GDP).

Given the discussion above, none of the other answers can be correct.

18. Correct answer: a.

Discussion: Statement a is correct since an increase in the required reserve ratio leads to a reduction in the money supply and a higher interest rate. The rise in the interest rate reduces investment spending. Also, the rise in the interest rate leads to an appreciation of the currency and consequently a decline in net exports. The reduction in investment spending and net exports means that businesses and foreigners are buying/demanding fewer goods and services. This is represented by a leftward shift in the aggregate demand curve.

Statement b is not correct; an increase in the discount rate would shift the aggregate demand curve (not aggregate supply) to the left for the same reasons as discussed above. Statement c is not correct; an open market sale of government bonds by the Fed will shift the aggregate demand curve to the left for the same reasons as discussed above. Statements a, b, and c are examples of contractionary monetary policy since they all cause a rise in interest rates and a reduction in spending. Statement d is not correct; an open market purchase (expansionary monetary policy) will shift the aggregate demand curve to the right, not to the left. Statement e is not correct; a reduction in the required reserve ratio will shift the aggregate demand curve (not aggregate supply) to the right.

VIII. ANSWER KEY: ESSAY QUESTIONS

1. An upturn in the business cycle means that output and income have increased. Money demand increases when income increases (primarily through the transactions motive). The increase in money demand is represented by a rightward shift in money demand as shown below.

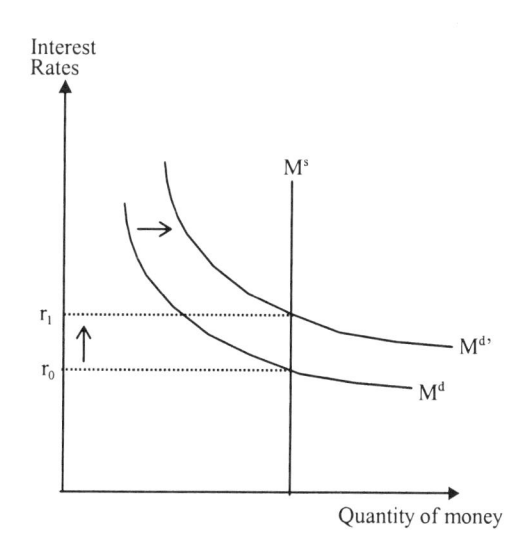

As money demand increases along a fixed supply of money, the price of money or the interest rate rises. The increase in the interest rate has a negative effect on spending. An increase in the interest rate raises the cost of borrowing and so businesses cut back on their purchases of plant and equipment (investment spending declines) and consumers, too, may cut back on their purchases of durable goods like automobiles and appliances. This translates into reduced aggregate spending which in turn reduces production and GDP. Thus, the upturn in the business cycle and output will be dampened to a degree because of rising interest rates.

If the Fed wanted to prevent the increase in interest rates, it could increase the money supply through an open market purchase, reduction in the required reserve ratio, and/or cut in the discount rate. This would serve to increase the money supply in response to the increased demand for money. This would be represented by a rightward shift in the money supply curve above (which you can draw in). Consequently, the interest rate could be prevented from rising and the dampening of the business cycle upturn curtailed.

2. An increase in the money supply is an expansionary monetary policy because, in the short run, the policy leads to an increase in spending and thus an expansion of production, output, and income. An increase in the money supply reduces interest rates and raises investment spending. Consumer spending may also increase. The increase in spending leads to a multiple expansion in GDP as businesses respond to the increased demand by producing more goods and services. Thus, production, output, and income increase. Furthermore, the lower interest rates lead to a depreciation of the U.S. dollar which in turn makes U.S-produced goods less expensive to foreigners who will then buy more of our goods. Thus, U.S. exports increase. On the other hand, the dollar depreciation makes foreign-produced goods more expensive to U.S. citizens who will then cut back their purchases of them and instead buy U.S. made equivalents. Thus, U.S. imports decrease. The increase in exports and decrease in imports means that there's more spending on U.S. made goods. That is, net exports increase.

The increase in investment spending (and possibly consumer spending) and net exports is represented by a rightward shift in the aggregate demand (AD) curve as shown in the graph below. The interest and exchange rate effects of the expansionary monetary policy, in the short run, reinforce each other and ultimately lead to an increase in spending and hence output (GDP).

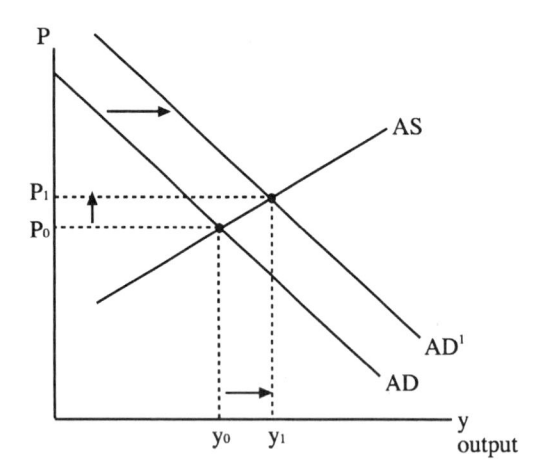

A decrease in government spending is a contractionary fiscal policy. A reduction in government spending on goods and services reduces production, output, and income, in the short run. This would be represented by a leftward shift in the aggregate demand (AD) curve as shown in the graph below. The graph shows that as spending declines, output declines, too.

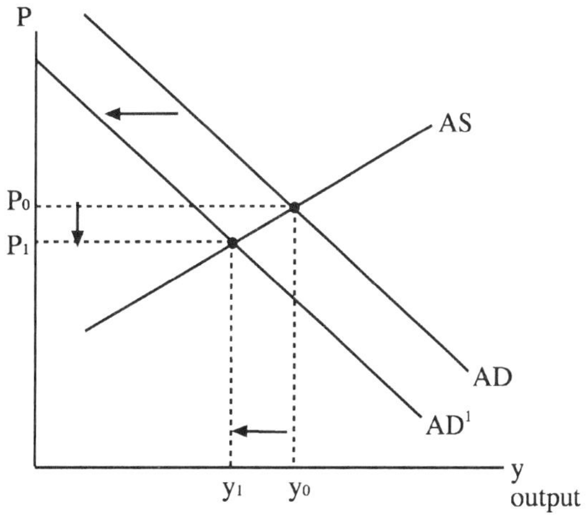

The discussion above reveals that the policies work in opposite directions. Expansionary monetary policy works to raise spending and output (GDP) whereas contractionary fiscal policy works to reduce spending and output (GDP), in the short run. Without knowing the magnitudes of the policy actions, it is difficult to predict whether on balance, output will rise or fall.

Take It to the Net

We invite you to visit the O'Sullivan/Sheffrin page on the Prentice Hall Web site at:

http://www.prenhall.com/osullivan/

for this chapter's World Wide Web exercise.

CHAPTER 15
FROM THE SHORT RUN TO THE LONG RUN

I. OVERVIEW

In this chapter, you will consider what happens as an economy moves from the short run to the long run. As you will see, the key distinction between the short run and long run is over the flexibility or adjustment of wages and prices to changes in market conditions. You will consider what would happen in an economy if it were operating below the full-employment level of output and policy action was not taken. You will also consider what would happen in an economy if it were operating above the full-employment level of output and no policy action was taken. You will see that when the economy is operating below the full-employment level of output, the price level will drop and output will rise toward the full-employment level. You will also see that when the economy is operating above the full-employment level of output, the price level will rise and output will decline back to the full-employment level of output. You will use aggregate demand and supply diagrams to illustrate these points. You will also consider how monetary and fiscal policy can be used to stabilize the economy and what potential problems arise with stabilization policies. You will learn about the liquidity trap and how it can hinder monetary policy from working. You will also learn about the political business cycle and how policy actions may be influenced by a politician's desire to be re-elected. You will learn about the effectiveness of monetary policy in the long run. You will see that according to the long run neutrality of money proposition, changes in the money supply leave no permanent effects on the level of output or real interest rates or real investment spending. You will revisit the concept of crowding out and learn how it is possible for an increase in government spending to crowd out investment spending, thus leaving no ultimate impact on aggregate demand. Lastly, you will review the historical development of economic ideas related to the short run (Keynesian economics) and the long run (Classical economics). You will see that these two different schools of thought stem from different assumptions about the speed with which wages and price adjust to changing market conditions.

II. CHECKLIST

By the end of this chapter, you should be able to:

❑ Explain what differentiates the short run from the long run in macroeconomics.
❑ Explain the relationship between wages and prices (the wage-price spiral).
❑ Explain why when output is above potential (and the unemployment rate below the natural rate), wages and prices increase.
❑ Explain why when output is below potential (and the unemployment rate below the natural rate), wages and prices decrease.
❑ Use short and long run aggregate supply curves with aggregate demand to show what happens when an economy is operating above or below its potential or full-employment level of output.

- Use aggregate demand and aggregate supply curves to discuss how monetary and fiscal policy might be used in cases where the economy is operating above or below its potential or full-employment level of output and is not expected to recover quickly on its own.
- Explain how lags in policymaking can interfere with good policymaking.
- Discuss the liquidity trap and how it impairs monetary policy.
- Explain what causes a political business cycle.
- Explain how, in an economy operating below the full-employment level of output, the drop in the price level helps to increase spending. Be sure to discuss the effects of the price level decline on the money market. Illustrate these points with an aggregate demand and aggregate supply diagram along with a money supply and money demand diagram.
- Explain why some economists and others believe that monetary and fiscal policy have no effect on the level of output in the long run.
- Define the long run neutrality of money proposition.
- Illustrate and explain why, in the long run, an increase in the money supply only leads to a higher price level, with no ultimate increase in output. Use an aggregate demand and supply diagram and money supply and money demand diagram.
- Explain why crowding out and crowding in occur and consider the implications for investment spending, total (aggregate) spending (demand), and the capital stock.
- Describe the main difference between Classical and Keynesian economics.
- Discuss where Friedman's sits on the difference between Classical and Keynesian economics.
- Define Say's Law.

III. KEY TERMS

Wage–price spiral: Changes in wages and prices causing more changes in wages and prices.

Aggregate demand curve: The relationship between the level of prices and the quantity of real GDP demanded.

Short-run aggregate supply curve: A relatively flat horizontal supply curve. It reflects the idea that prices do not change very much in the short run and that firms adjust production to meet demand.

Long-run aggregate supply curve: A vertical aggregate supply curve. It reflects the idea that in the long run, output is determined solely by the factors of production.

Liquidity trap: A situation in which interest rates are so low, they can no longer fall.

Political business cycle: The effects on the economy of using monetary or fiscal policy to stimulate the economy before an election to improve reelection prospects.

Long-run neutrality of money: An increase in the supply of money has no effect on real interest rates, investment, or output in the long run.

Crowding out: The reduction in investment (or other component of GDP) in the long run caused by an increase in government spending.

IV. PERFORMANCE ENHANCING TIPS (PETS)

PET #1

The short run aggregate supply curve is very flat and shifts up when wages (or other input prices) increase and shifts down when wages (or other input prices) decrease.

PET #2

The long run aggregate supply curve is vertical and is positioned at the potential (or full-employment) level of output. Increases in the capital stock, labor force, productivity of the labor force, and technology will cause the long run aggregate supply curve to shift to the right. Decreases in the capital stock, labor force, productivity of the labor force, and technology will cause the long run aggregate supply curve to shift to the left.

PET #3

Monetary and fiscal policy are policy tools that influence spending and thus aggregate demand. Changes in monetary and fiscal policy will thus, in the short run, cause aggregate demand to shift (without any change in aggregate supply).

PET #4

In the short run, increases in the money supply raise the level of output and raise the price level slightly. In the long run, increases in the money supply raise only the price level, with no effect on output. In the short run, decreases in the money supply reduce the level of output and have a negligible effect on the price level. In the long run, decreases in the money supply lower only the price level, with no effect on output.

Panel A below shows the short run and long run effects of an increase in the money. Panel B shows the short run and long run effects of a decrease in the money supply.

Panel A: Increase in the Money Supply

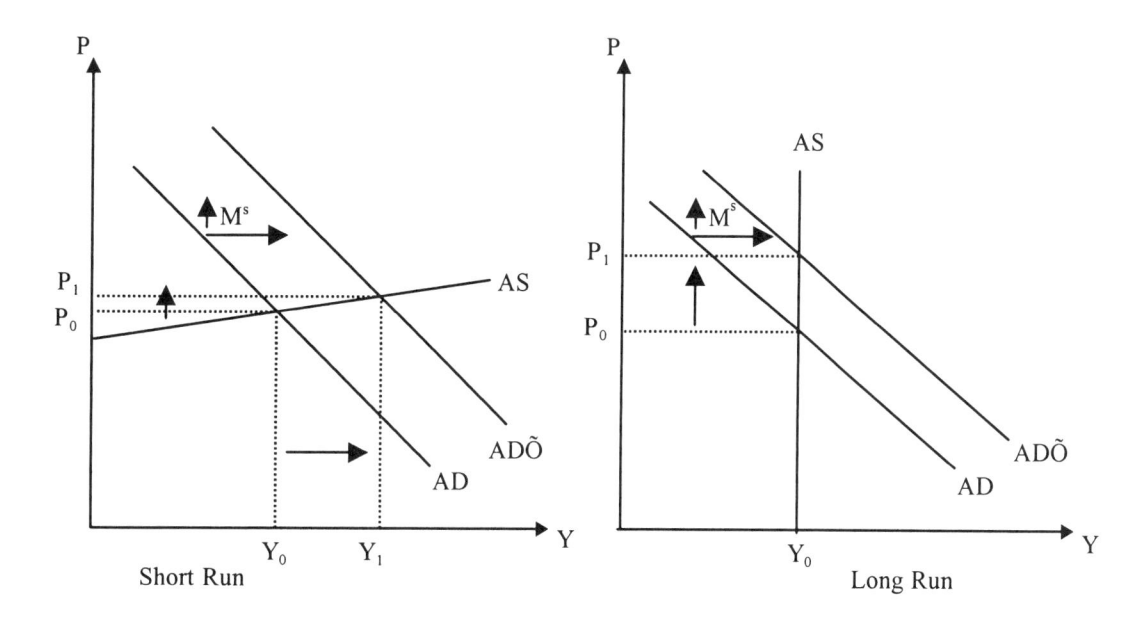

P₁
P₀
M^s
AS
AD'
AD
Y₀ Y₁
Short Run

P₁
P₀
AS
M^s
AD'
AD
Y₀
Long Run

Panel B: Decrease in the Money Supply

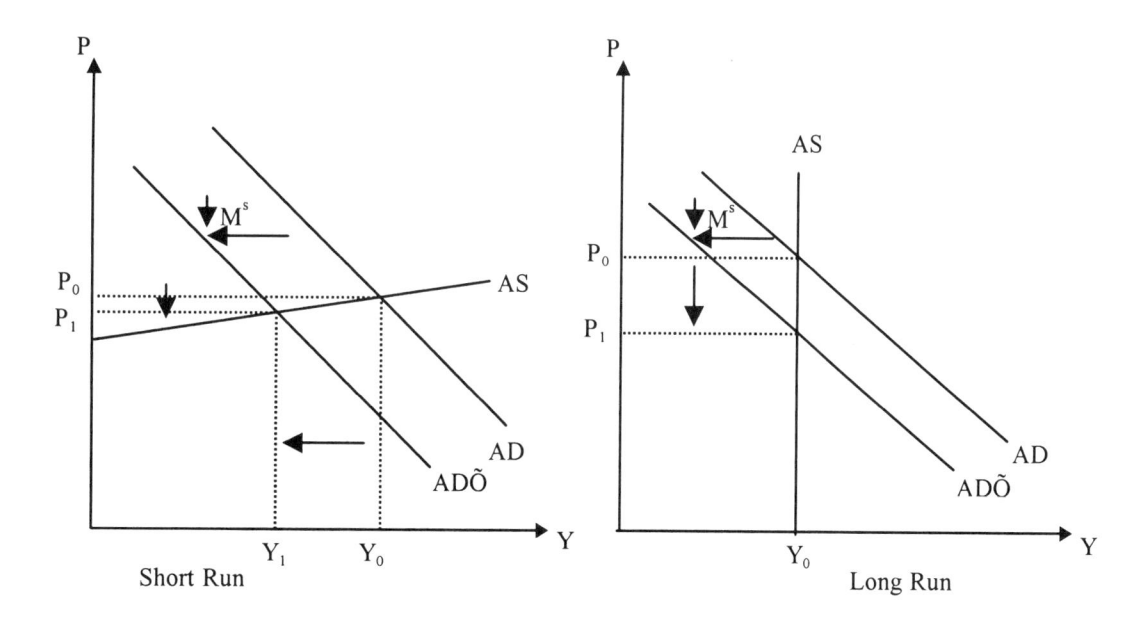

P₀
P₁
M^s
AS
AD
AD'
Y₁ Y₀
Short Run

P₀
P₁
AS
M^s
AD
AD'
Y₀
Long Run

V. PRACTICE EXAM: MULTIPLE CHOICE QUESTIONS

1. Which one of the following statements is NOT true?
   a) short run economics refers to a time period over which wages and prices do not adjust.
   b) the long run aggregate supply curve is vertical at the full-employment (or potential) level of output.
   c) when the economy is operating below the full-employment (or potential) level of output, wages and prices will in the long run decline.
   d) Keynes was skeptical that an economy operating far from the full-employment level of output would return to full-employment on its own.
   e) Friedman believes that a policy may be necessary to push an economy toward the full-employment level of output when it is operating below the full-employment level of output.

2. Suppose an economy is currently operating above its potential level of output. One consequence would be:
   a) an increase in wages and a leftward shift in the short run aggregate supply curve.
   b) a reduction in the price level.
   c) an increase in investment spending.
   d) a leftward shift in aggregate demand as the price level rises.
   e) an unemployment rate above the natural rate of unemployment.

3. Consider an economy that is currently operating below its potential level of output. Which one of the following statements is correct?
   a) the economy will eventually return to the potential level of output and a lower price level without a policy intervention.
   b) an open market sale may help to push the economy to the potential level of output more quickly than letting the economy adjust by itself.
   c) wages and prices will spiral upward.
   d) interest rates will decline and investment spending will increase.
   e) (a) and (d).

4. Consider an economy that is currently operating above the potential level of output. Which one of the following statements is correct?
   a) the unemployment rate is below the natural rate of unemployment.
   b) firms will find it difficult to hire and retain workers.
   c) firms may be willing to pay higher wages to workers.
   d) the price level will rise.
   e) all of the above.

5. Which one of the following statements is true of the adjustment process?
a) when output is above its potential level, wages will fall.
b) when output is above its potential level, interest rates will fall.
c) when output is below its potential level, investment spending will rise.
d) when output is below its potential level, the demand for money will increase.
e) (c) and (d).

6. If output is above its potential level, then:
a) money demand will shift to the left and the interest rate will rise.
b) money demand will shift to the right and the interest rate will fall.
c) money demand will shift to the left and the interest rate will fall.
d) money demand will shift to the right and the interest rate will rise.
e) none of the above.

7. If output is above its potential level, then:
a) prices will rise and money demand will shift to the left.
b) investment spending and the level of output will decline.
c) interest rates will increase and money demand will shift to the left.
d) wages will rise and interest rates will decrease.
e) money demand will shift to the right and wages will fall.

8. The long run neutrality of money means that changes in the money supply:
a) have no long run effect on real interest rates, investment, or output.
b) have no long run effect on prices.
c) cause crowding out.
d) do not shift aggregate demand.
e) shift aggregate demand and aggregate supply be equal and offsetting amounts.

9. In the long run, an open market sale will:
a) increase prices and increase output.
b) increase output and increase prices.
c) decrease prices and increase output.
d) decrease output and decrease prices.
e) decrease prices and have no effect on output.

10. In the long run, crowding out occurs because:
a) decreases in the money supply raise interest rates and reduce investment spending.
b) increases in government spending raise the price level and interest rates and reduce investment spending.
c) when the economy is at the potential level of output, increases in government spending necessarily require reductions in other spending in the economy.
d) increases in the money supply raise the price level and reduce spending by households and businesses.
e) (b) and (c).

11. Which one of the following statements is true of the political business cycle?
a) politicians have an incentive to decrease the money supply about a year or so before an election.
b) incumbent presidents have an incentive to enact contractionary policies prior to the election and expansionary policies after the election.
c) President Carter attempted to stimulate the economy prior to his election in an effort to make voters feel good so that he would be re-elected.
d) the political business cycle implies that the unemployment rate will decline prior to an election and rise after an election.
e) expansionary monetary and fiscal policies are always favored by politicians.

12. Which one of the following statements is true of the liquidity trap?
a) It describes a situation in which interest rates are so low, they can no longer fall.
b) It describes a situation in which interest rates are so high, they can no longer rise.
c) The adjustment process works efficiently and smoothly.
d) The adjustment process does not work.
e) (a) and (d).

VI. PRACTICE EXAM: ESSAY QUESTIONS

1a. Suppose that the price of oil increases. Use short run aggregate supply and aggregate demand to explain the short run and long run effects of this event. Assume the economy is currently operating at the potential level of output.

1b. Now, considering your answer to part (a), what policy or policies would you advocate or would you advocate any policy intervention at all? Explain. Be sure to relate your answer to the speed of adjustment of the economy.

2. The long run neutrality of money proposition implies that activist monetary policy has no lasting effects on the level of output. If this is true, is there any role for the Fed in the economy?

VII. ANSWER KEY: MULTIPLE CHOICE QUESTIONS

1. Correct answer: e.

Discussion: Statement e is not true because Milton Friedman believed that an economy is self-correcting meaning that, e.g. when an economy is in a recession operating below the full-employment level of output, it will recover on its own without the need for policy. Keynes disagreed. He argued that there may be situations when the economy is in a recession or depression and so policy for recovery may be necessary.

Statement a is correct; short run economics refers to a period of time during which wages and prices are sticky, not flexible, and therefore do not have time to adjust to market demand or supply conditions. Statement b is correct. The long run aggregate supply curve is used to represent the behavior of the supply-side of the economy in the long run when wages and prices are flexible and have had time to adjust to economic disturbances. In the long run, the potential level of output is determined by supply-side factors like the size (and age) of the capital stock, the size and productivity of the labor force, and the state of technology. The potential level of output is not determined or influenced by the price level. A vertical aggregate supply curve represents this independence of potential output from the price level. Statement c is correct; when the economy is operating below the potential level of output, there is an excess supply of labor (unemployment above the natural rate). The excess supply of labor exerts downward pressure on wages. As wages drop, the cost of production drops, and thus the prices at which output sells drop. Statement d is correct since Keynes believed that an economy may not be self-correcting.

2. Correct answer: a.

Discussion: An economy that is operating above its potential level of output is operating beyond its capacity. That is, there will be shortages of labor (and capital). The shortage of labor means that wages will rise. Since wages are an input cost of production and they have increased, the short run aggregate supply curve will shift leftward.

Given the answer above, statement b is not correct. The price level will rise in the short run, since wage costs have increased. Statement c is not correct. The increase in the price level will increase the demand for money which will in turn raise interest rates. The increase in interest rates will reduce investment spending, not increase it. Statement d is not correct. As the price level rises, there will be a leftward movement along the aggregate demand curve, not a shift in it. Statement e is not correct. If the economy is operating above potential, the unemployment rate must be below the natural rate of unemployment.

3. Correct answer: e.

Discussion: If the economy is operating below the potential level of output, wages and prices will decline. As prices decline, the demand for money will decline (shift left) and the interest rate will fall. As the interest rate falls, the level of investment spending (and perhaps consumer spending on durables) will rise. The increased spending will in turn lead to increased production which will move the economy back up to its potential level of output. Thus, statements a and d are both correct.

Statement b is not correct. An economy that is operating below potential, if anything, needs a stimulative or expansionary policy action, not a contractionary one. An open market sale is a contractionary monetary policy since it decreases the money supply. This would move the economy further away from the potential level of output. Statement c is not correct. As mentioned above, wages and prices will spiral downward, not upward.

4. Correct answer: e.

Discussion: Statements a-d are all true of an economy operating above the full-employment level of output. Sometimes it is said that an economy in this situation is "overheated." In any case, when an economy is operating above the full-employment level of output, demand for goods and services exceeds the long run supply. This would be illustrated with a short run aggregate supply and aggregate demand curve intersecting at an output level above the long run (full-employment) level of output (which is marked by the long run aggregate supply curve). In this situation, the unemployment rate will be less than the natural rate of unemployment. That is, there will be an excess demand for labor (workers) and firms will find it difficult to hire and retain workers. This will cause the wage rate to rise. Since labor costs are a major portion of production costs, the increase in wages will lead to higher prices for goods and services and thus a higher overall price level. Thus, the price level will increase, too.

5. Correct answer: c.

Discussion: When output is below its potential level, wages and prices spiral downward. As prices drop, the price level drops as well. As the price level drops, the demand for money declines (shifts left). As the demand for money declines, the interest rate drops. As the interest rate drops, investment spending increases. Thus, statement c is correct.

Statement a is not correct. When output is above potential, wages will rise (due to labor shortages). Statement b is not correct. When output is above potential, prices will rise which will in turn increase the demand for money causing interest rates to rise, not fall. Statement d is not correct. The discussion above indicates that money demand will decrease, not increase.

6. Correct answer: d.

Discussion: When output is above its potential level, wages and therefore prices rise. As the price level rises, the demand for money increases. This is represented by a rightward shift in the money demand curve. The increased demand for money leads to a rise in interest rates.

Based on the above discussion, none of the other answers can be correct.

7. Correct answer: b.

Discussion: This question is an application of question (6) above. If output is above its potential level, wages and prices will rise. The increase in the price level will lead to an increase in the demand for money which will in turn cause interest rates to rise. As interest rates rise, investment spending declines. As investment spending declines, the economy responds by producing less output. Thus, output declines as well.

Statements a and c are not correct because money demand will shift to the right. Statement d is not correct because interest rates will increase, not decrease. Statement e is not correct because wages will rise, not fall.

8. Correct answer: a.

Discussion: The long run neutrality of money proposition means that monetary policy is, in the long run, ineffective at altering "real variables" which are variables like the real interest rate (nominal interest rate minus inflation rate), investment, output, and even employment. However, this is not to say that monetary policy can't affect the price level in the long run. It can and does.

9. Correct answer: e.

Discussion: An open market sale is contractionary monetary policy, i.e. a decrease in the money supply. The decrease in the money supply shifts the aggregate demand curve to the left. As the aggregate demand curve shifts left along the long run aggregate supply curve, the price level drops but there is no final change in the level of output the economy produces. This is an example of the long run neutrality of money proposition.

Statements a, b, and c can be ruled out because contractionary policy in either the short or long run does not increase the level of output. Statement d is not correct because in the long run, the level of output is unaffected by monetary policy.

10. Correct answer: e.

Discussion: Crowding out refers to what happens to private sector spending (most notably investment spending, but consumption as well) when the government increases its spending on goods and services. Increases in government spending, in the long run, move the economy above potential and thus lead to higher wages and prices. As prices rise, the price level increases and the demand for money increases. As the demand for money increases, interest rates rise and thus investment (and consumer spending on durables) declines. This is the crowding out effect. On net, government spending crowds out investment and consumer spending by an amount equal to the increase in government spending leaving no change on total spending and thus on output. Thus, statement b is correct. Statement c is also correct. When the economy is at potential, it is physically unable to produce any more output in response to increased spending. Thus, the increase in government spending comes at the expense of a reduction in spending by businesses (investment spending) and by households (consumption spending).

Statements a and d are not correct because crowding out is not used in reference to changes in the money supply.

11. Correct answer: d.

Discussion: The political business cycle means that incumbent politicians have an incentive to enact expansionary policies prior to the election and contractionary policies after the election. This is because the unemployment rate will tend to go down prior to an election (causing people to vote for the incumbent) and rise after an election (when they can't do anything about it).

Based on the reasoning above, statements a and b are not correct. Statement c is not correct because President Carter enacted contractionary policies prior to re-election. Statement e is not correct. Politicians do not always favor expansionary policies -- incumbent may prefer them prior to an election -- but contractionary policies may be favored in cases where inflation is high.

204 Chapter 15

12. Correct answer: e.

Discussion: A liquidity trap describes a situation in which interest rates are so low then can no longer fall. This was one of the reasons why Keynes expressed doubts about whether a country could recover from a major recession. When the economy is experiencing a liquidity trap, the adjustment process no longer works. So from this description both a and d are correct so that e is the correct or best answer. Also from the above explanation, b and c cannot be correct.

VIII. ANSWER KEY: ESSAY QUESTIONS

1a. Oil is indirectly an input into the production of most goods and services. Thus, when the price of oil increases, the cost of production rises. This is represented by an upward shift in the short run aggregate supply curve as drawn below. The economy moves from point A to point B.

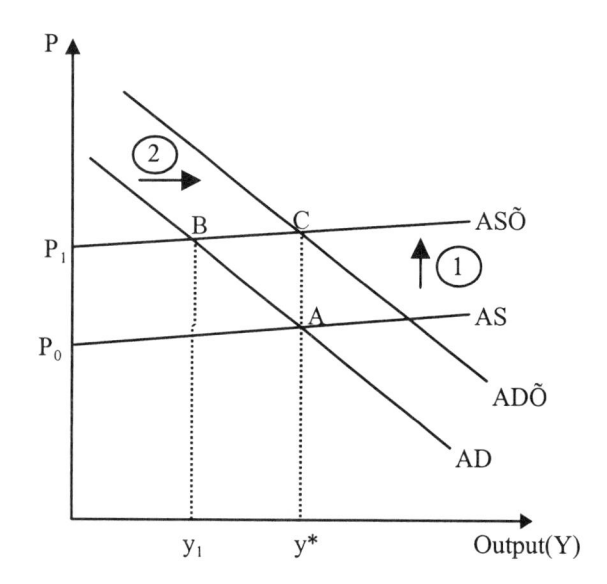

In the short run, the effect of the oil price increase is to raise the price level (create inflation) and reduce output below its potential level (compare point B to point A). This combination of outcomes is sometimes referred to as "stagflation" since not only does inflation occur but the economy (output and income) stagnate. In this situation, the economy is likely to experience a surplus of labor since unemployment will increase. Thus, wages and prices will begin to fall.

The decline in wages and prices will enable the economy, in the long run, to return to the potential level of output (y*). The fall in prices will reduce the price level which will in turn reduce the demand for money. As the demand for money declines, the interest rate will fall which will in turn stimulate investment spending (and spending on consumer durables). Businesses will respond to the increased level of spending by producing more output and hiring more workers. The spending stimulus and consequent increase in output is shown as a movement along the AD curve from point B back to point A.

1b. If I believed that the speed of adjustment, i.e. the length of time it took the economy to move from point B to back to point A was relatively short, say under one year, I would be inclined to argue that no policy intervention should take place to assist the economy's return to the potential level of output. I would argue that the economy will naturally, and rather quickly, readjust. Moreover, if the lags in policy (either fiscal or monetary) are long and/or I have my doubts about the forecasting accuracy on which policy is based, I'd argue even more ardently in favor of a "do nothing" approach. Also, if the oil price increase reduced output (compare output levels at point A to point B) by a "trivial" amount (say 0.5%), I would be inclined to argue that the reduction in output is not significant enough to warrant policy intervention.

On the other hand, if the speed of adjustment from point B back to point A was relatively slow, I would argue that perhaps some expansionary policy intervention is warranted. In this case, the Fed could increase the money supply so as to stimulate spending (investment and consumer durables) and thus production and output, or fiscal policy could be undertaken by raising government spending or transfers or lowering taxes. This would be represented by a rightward shift in aggregate demand along the AS' curve, as shown above. The result would be that output would return to its potential level, y^*, where AS' and AD' intersect. However, the price level would remain at its post-oil-price increase level. (Compare the price level at point C to that at point A). Thus, there is a cost to acting now: the price level will remain higher than if we had let the economy self-adjust and not intervened at all.

2. There are several arguments that can be made in favor of a role for activist monetary policy. The long run neutrality of money proposition does not imply that monetary policy is ineffective in the short run (as discussed in essay 1 above) nor does it imply that monetary policy is ineffective at influencing inflation. The long run neutrality of money proposition only says that output cannot be influenced by monetary policy in the long run. Money, (i.e. monetary policy) can, in the short run, influence output, and money can, in the long run, influence the price level.

If the aim of the Fed is to keep the price level stable, it may need to actively use monetary policy. For example, if the economy is operating above potential, the price level will rise. To prevent this, the Fed could step in with contractionary monetary policy and thereby remove the price (and wage) pressures from the economy. On the other hand, if the economy is operating below potential, the price level will drop. If the Fed is satisfied with the current rate of inflation and doesn't see any reason for the economy to suffer (i.e. unemployment would, in this case, be above the natural rate), the Fed could step in with expansionary monetary policy (as in the example given in the answer to 1b above). Output would return to its potential level (which assumes that the Fed can influence output in the short run) without any increase in the price level relative to its starting point.

After you read the next chapter, your answer may be different.

Take It to the Net

We invite you to visit the O'Sullivan/Sheffrin page on the Prentice Hall Web site at:
http://www.prenhall.com/osullivan/
for this chapter's World Wide Web exercise.

CHAPTER 16
THE DYNAMICS OF INFLATION AND UNEMPLOYMENT

I. OVERVIEW

In this chapter, you will learn about the role expectations of future inflation play in preferences for holding money, wage setting, real interest rates, and the determination of inflation and unemployment. You will use an expectations Phillips curve to explore the relationship between the unemployment rate relative to the natural rate of unemployment and unanticipated inflation. You will learn about the factors that may lead to changes in the natural rate of unemployment. You will learn how expectations of future inflation can be influenced by the stance of monetary policy and the commitment of central bankers to maintaining low inflation. You will learn that central banks that are credibly committed to low inflation often have an easier time securing low inflation. You will also be introduced to the concept of the velocity of money using the equation of exchange. You will learn what role the rate of money growth, velocity growth, and growth in real GDP have in determining the rate of inflation. You will learn what role the budget deficit plays and how it is financed in determining inflation. You will learn that countries which experience hyperinflation are typically countries that run large budget deficits which are financed by printing money. You will use the real-nominal principle throughout the chapter.

II. CHECKLIST

By the end of this chapter, you should be able to:

❑ Discuss how expectations of inflation affect individual and business decision-making.
❑ Explain why countries with higher money growth rates typically have higher nominal interest rates.
❑ Recite the real-nominal principle and explain money illusion.
❑ Explain how money growth that exceeds the public's expected rate of inflation will increase money demand and the real interest rate, and vice-versa.
❑ Define the expectations Phillips curve.
❑ Discuss what happens to inflation when the unemployment rate is above the natural rate and when it is below the natural rate.
❑ Discuss the two broad classes of theories about how the public forms its expectations of inflation.
❑ Discuss the experience of the United States with inflation and unemployment during the 1980s.
❑ Define the natural rate of unemployment and explain what might cause shifts in it.
❑ Explain how central bankers can influence expectations of inflation.
❑ Explain how a central bank that is committed to fighting inflation may deter rational wage setters from demanding excessive wage increases.
❑ Discuss the empirical evidence regarding the relationship between central bank independence and the rate of inflation.

The Dynamics of Inflation and Unemployment 207

- ❑ Define the velocity of money.
- ❑ Set out the equation of exchange (or the quantity equation). Also, express it in terms of growth rates (i.e. percentage changes).
- ❑ Use the equation of exchange to predict inflation or velocity given information on the other variables in the equation.
- ❑ Define hyperinflation.
- ❑ Discuss the major cause of hyperinflation.
- ❑ Discuss the behavior of money demand and velocity during hyperinflation.
- ❑ Define monetarism or what it means to be a monetarist.

III. KEY TERMS

Nominal wages: Wages expressed in current dollars.

Real wages: Nominal or dollar wages adjusted for changes in purchasing power.

Money illusion: Confusion of real and nominal magnitudes.

Expectations of inflation: The beliefs held by the public about the likely path of inflation for the future.

Expectations Phillips curve: The relationship that describes the links between inflation and unemployment, taking into account expectations of inflation.

Rational expectations: The economic theory that analyzes how people form expectations in such a manner that, on average, they forecast the future correctly.

Quantity equation: The equation that links money, velocity, prices and real output. In symbols, we have $M \cdot V = P \cdot y$.

Velocity of money: Nominal GDP divided by the money supply. It is also the rate at which money turns over during the year.

Hyperinflation: An inflation rate exceeding 50% per month.

quantity equation: An equation that links the growth rates of money, velocity, prices, and real output.

Monetarists: Economists who emphasize the role of money in determining nominal income and inflation.

Seignorage: Revenue raised through money creation.

IV. PERFORMANCE ENHANCING TIPS (PETS)

PET #1

The unanticipated rate of inflation is the difference between the actual rate of inflation and the expected rate of inflation. Unanticipated inflation will be greater than zero when the unemployment rate is less than the natural rate of unemployment. Unanticipated inflation will be less than zero when the unemployment rate is greater than the natural rate of unemployment.

For example, suppose that the natural rate of unemployment is 5% and the actual unemployment rate is 4.6%. Then, the actual inflation rate will exceed the rate of inflation that was expected. That is, the public may have expected inflation to be 6% when it turns out that inflation is actually 7.5%.

For another example, suppose that the actual unemployment rate is 8%. Since the actual unemployment rate is above the natural unemployment rate, the actual inflation rate will be less than the rate that was expected by the public. That is, the public may have expected 4% inflation when the actual inflation rate turns out to be 3%.

PET #2

Given any three values for the variables in the equation of exchange (quantity equation), the fourth variable's value can be determined.

The growth version of the equation of exchange is:

$$\%\Delta \text{ Money} + \%\Delta \text{ Velocity} = \%\Delta \text{ price level} + \%\Delta \text{ real GDP}$$

Suppose you are told that the inflation rate is currently 3% per year and the Fed is happy to maintain this rate of inflation but would like to achieve a 4% growth rate in real GDP per year. Furthermore, you are told that the percentage change in velocity is 1% per year. What money growth rate would be consistent with the Fed's commitment to 3% inflation and 4% growth in output?

The equation above can be solved for %Δ Money as:

$$\begin{aligned}\%\Delta \text{ Money} &= \%\Delta \text{ price level} + \%\Delta \text{ real GDP} - \%\Delta \text{ Velocity} \\ &= 3\% + 4\% - 1\% \\ &= 6\%\end{aligned}$$

PET #3

In the long run, the rate of inflation will equal the growth rate of money, holding other factors constant.

This is just a special case of PET #2 above where other factors constant mean that velocity and real GDP are not growing (percentage change = 0). So, if the money supply is growing at 3% a year, other factors constant, the rate of inflation will also be 3% per year.

PET #4

When expected inflation exceeds the rate of growth of the money supply, money demand will be increasing more than money supply will be increasing. Thus, nominal and real interest rates will rise. When expected inflation is less than the rate of growth of the money supply, money demand will be increasing more than money supply will be increasing. Thus, nominal and real interest rates will fall.

Remember from the previous chapter that increases in the price level act to increase the demand for money (and vice-versa). Similarly, when the price level is expected to increase (i.e. expected inflation is greater than zero), the demand for money will increase and at a rate equal to the expected inflation rate. Using a money supply/money demand diagram, you would represent this with a rightward shift in money demand. If expected inflation exceeds the rate of growth of the money supply, then the rightward shift in money demand will be greater than the rightward shift in money supply. As a consequence, the nominal interest rate will increase. With expectations of inflation unchanged, the real interest rate rises, too. The reverse is true when the expected rate of inflation is less than the growth rate of the money supply.

PET #5

Central banks that are credibly committed to maintaining a stable price level and low inflation reduce the expected rate of inflation held by the private sector.

The consequences of a central bank's commitment to price level stability and low inflation are that workers and unions are less likely to press for excessive wage demands, long-term real interest rates are likely to be lower (which is good news for people who must borrow to purchase a new home, car, appliances, etc. and for businesses who must borrow to finance investment), and businesses are less likely to raise their price in anticipation that all prices will be going up in the future.

PET #6

If the price level is increasing by a factor of X every month, then over a year, the price level will have increased by a factor of X^{12}.

For example, if a candy bar and soda cost $1 today and the price level is increasing three-fold every month (300%), then at the end of the month, the candy bar and soda will cost $1 X 3 = $3. At the end of the next month, the candy bar and soda will costs $3 X 3 = $9, and so on. Thus, at the end of the year, the candy bar and soda will cost $1 X 3^{12} = $1 X 531,441 = $531,441!

Alternatively, if you had $1 today and prices were increasing three-fold every month (300%), then your $1 would be worth $1/3 = $0.33 at the end of the month. At the end of the next month, the $1 would be worth $0.33/3 = $(1/3)/3 = $0.11, and so on. Thus, at the end of the year, the $1 would be worth $1/3^{12}$ = 1/531,441 = $0.0000018!

V. PRACTICE EXAM: MULTIPLE CHOICE QUESTIONS

1. If nominal wages increase by 6% while the inflation rate is 6%, then:
a) workers may suffer money illusion believing their real wages have increased 6%.
b) real wages have increased by 0%.
c) real wages have increased by 12%.
d) real wages have increased by 1%.
e) (a) and (b).

210 Chapter 16

2. Which one of the following statements is true?
a) the expected real rate of interest = nominal rate + expected rate of inflation.
b) money illusion is the confusion of nominal and real magnitudes.
c) if two countries had the same real rate of interest but one had a higher inflation rate, it would have a lower nominal interest rate.
d) if money demand and money supply each grow by 3% per year, the real interest rate will rise by 3% per year.
e) Milton Friedman is the father of the rational expectations school of thought.

3. If the public currently expected the inflation rate to be 8% and the Fed increased the money supply by 5%, then:
a) real interest rates would increase in the short run.
b) money demand would decline by 8%.
c) money demand would decline by 5%.
d) money demand would increase by 8%.
e) (a) and (d).

4. If the Fed increased the money supply by 10% and the public expected inflation to be 6%, then:
a) the nominal and real interest rates will drop in the short run.
b) in the long run, inflation will be 10%, other factors constant.
c) real GDP will rise and unemployment will fall in the short run.
d) in the long run, the real interest rate will remain constant.
e) all of the above.

5. The expectations Phillips curve shows:
a) that if the actual unemployment rate is below the natural rate of unemployment, inflation will be higher than anticipated.
b) that the unemployment rate varies with anticipated inflation.
c) can be used to calculate the misery index.
d) that the natural rate of unemployment can be defined as the unemployment rate associated with a zero percent inflation rate.
e) that there is a permanent, negative relationship between the inflation rate and the unemployment rate.

6. Which one of the following statements is true?
a) rule of thumb expectations and rational expectations produce very different forecasts for inflation when the economy is stable and there are no major policy changes.
b) rational expectations forecasts take into consideration the anticipated effects of policy changes.
c) Alan Greenspan was responsible for ridding the economy of double-digit inflation in the early 1980s.
d) the natural rate of unemployment today is estimated to be more than it was during the 1980s.
e) a decrease in the length of time that unemployment insurance is offered to unemployed workers will raise the natural rate of unemployment.

7. Which one of the following is a factor that could cause the natural rate of unemployment to change?
a) unexpected changes in the productivity of workers.
b) a prolonged recession which causes some workers' skills to become outdated.
c) a change in the power of labor unions.
d) a change in the dollar amount of unemployment compensation that is granted.
e) all of the above.

8. Which one of the following statements is NOT true?
a) central bankers, through monetary policy, can influence expectations of inflation.
b) a central bank that is committed to fighting inflation will be more likely to do nothing when the unemployment rate rises above the natural rate (i.e. economy goes into a recession).
c) if people believe the Fed prefers to use expansionary monetary policy during economic downturns, they will be more inclined to push for higher nominal wages.
d) a central bank that whose sole goal is to keep the inflation rate low is more likely to use monetary policy to help stabilize output.
e) none of the above are true.

9. Empirical evidence shows that:
a) inflation rates in the United States in the late 1990s increased as the unemployment rate fell below the natural rate of unemployment.
b) countries with hyperinflation typically have very slow money growth rates.
c) countries in which central banks are more independent (autonomous) tend to have lower rates of inflation.
d) countries in which central banks are more independent (autonomous) tend to have higher GDP growth rates.
e) (c) and (d).

10. The velocity of money:
a) is equal to the supply of money divided by nominal GDP.
b) will be high when people hold onto money for a long period of time.
c) has ranged between 14 and 19 since the late 1950s for the U.S. using the M2 money supply.
d) is equal to the (price level X real GDP)/ money supply.
e) is the cause of hyperinflation.

11. Which one of the following statements is true?
a) if the growth rate in velocity is 3%, the inflation rate is 9%, and the money growth rate is 4%, then output must be growing at -2%.
b) if the monthly inflation rate is 14%, purchasing power will be cut in half in 5 months.
c) if prices are rising by a factor of 5 each month, then $1 today will be worth $0.20 at the end of the month.
d) if prices are rising by a factor of 2 each month, then something that costs $5 today will cost $20,480 at the end of the year.
e) all of the above are true.

12. Which one of the following statements is true?
a) hyperinflation is defined to be inflation in excess of 50% a year.
b) if prices increased by a factor of 3 each year, at the end of a year, an item that costs $1 would now cost $300.
c) if prices increased by a factor of 3 each year, at the end of a year, $1 would now be worth $0.33.
d) if prices increased by a factor of 3 each year, at the end of two years, an item that costs $1 would now cost $9.
e) c and d.

13. Which one of the following statements is NOT true?
a) hyperinflation typically occurs where governments print money to pay for their budget deficits.
b) countries that have a limited ability to collect taxes, yet run government deficits, typically have hyperinflation.
c) if a government finances its budget deficit by borrowing from the public, the money supply will increase.
d) a monetarist believes that in the long run, inflation is caused by growth in the money supply.
e) the theory of rational expectations suggests that a credible Fed can deter wage increases.

VI. PRACTICE EXAM: ESSAY QUESTIONS

1. Suppose the Fed decreases the money supply in order to contain inflationary pressures in the economy. How does the policy work on short and long-term interest rates and how might the credibility of the Fed's commitment to fighting inflation affect long-term interest rates?

2. Explain what causes hyperinflation and what happens during episodes of hyperinflation.

VII. ANSWER KEY: MULTIPLE CHOICE QUESTIONS

1. Correct answer: e.

Discussion: If nominal wages increase by 6% while the inflation rate is 6%, then workers may suffer money illusion believing their real wages have increased 6%. That is, workers may not take into account the effects of inflation on their wage increase. If this happens, they may believe that the purchasing power of their wages has increased by 6% when, in fact, it has not changed at all since the price level has increased by 6%, too. That is, workers' real wages have not increased at all. Thus, only statements a and b are correct.

2. Correct answer: b.

Discussion: Money illusion occurs when an increase in, e.g. the nominal wage rate, is perceived as an increase in the real wage. In fact, an increase in the nominal wage rate only makes a worker better off if the nominal wage increase is bigger in percentage terms than the inflation rate. In this case, the real wage rate would rise. However, if the percentage increase in the nominal wage is equal to the inflation rate, then there is no change in the purchasing power of the worker's wage and thus the worker is no better off than before, despite the increased nominal wage. (The same is true for savers. They should consider their real return, not their nominal return).

Statement a is not correct. The expected real interest rate = nominal interest rate minus the expected rate of inflation. Statement c is not correct. If two countries had the same real rate of interest but one had a higher inflation rate, it would have a higher, not lower nominal interest rate. For example, if both countries had a real rate of interest of 5% and inflation was 5% in country A and 20% in country B, the nominal interest rate in country A would be 10% and that in country B would be 25%. Statement d is not correct. If money demand and money supply each grow by 3% per year, the real interest rate will not change. Statement e is not correct. Milton Friedman is the "father" of monetarism and Robert Lucas is the "father" of rational expectations.

3. Correct answer: e.

Discussion: If the public expected the inflation rate to be 8%, they would want to hold 8% in cash and/or checking account balances. That is, money demand would increase by 8%. But, money supply is not growing as fast as money demand. This would be represented by a bigger shift rightward in money demand than the rightward shift in money supply. Thus, the nominal (and real) interest rate would increase in the short run. (See PET #4 for review).

Statements b and c cannot be correct because money demand will increase, not decrease.

4. Correct answer: e.

Discussion: This question is the reverse of question (2). In this case, the money supply will shift rightward by more than money demand will shift rightward (compare 10% to 6%). Thus, the nominal and real interest rates will drop in the short run. As the real interest rate drops, spending by businesses on plant and equipment (investment) will increase and lead to an increase in real GDP. As real GDP rises, the unemployment rate will fall. This all happens in the short run. In the long run, money is neutral and so the real interest rate will return to its initial level, i.e. it remains constant in the long run. However, the 10% increase in the money supply, other factors constant, will create a 10% inflation rate.

5. Correct answer: a.

Discussion: The expectations Phillips curve shows the relationship between the unemployment rate (relative to the natural rate of unemployment) and the unanticipated rate of inflation. The relationship is negative, i.e. if the unemployment rate is below the natural rate, say 4.7% compared to 6%), then the actual inflation rate may exceed the expected inflation rate (e.g. 10% compared to an expected rate of 8%). Thus, when the unemployment rate is below the natural rate of unemployment, unanticipated inflation is greater than zero. In this example, the unanticipated rate of inflation (actual minus expected) would be 2%.

Statement b is not true since the expectations Phillips curve shows that unemployment varies with the unanticipated rate of inflation. Statement c is not correct. Moreover, you have not been introduced to the misery index (sum of inflation plus unemployment). Statement d is not correct. The expectations Phillips curve shows the natural rate of unemployment is defined where unanticipated inflation is zero, i.e. where the anticipated inflation rate is equal to the actual inflation rate. Statement e is not correct. The expectations Phillips curve will show that there is NO permanent relationship between the inflation rate and the unemployment rate. In fact, the view is that an economy will eventually always return to its natural rate of unemployment regardless of a inflation rate.

6. Correct answer: b.

Discussion: Statement b is true because rational expectations forecasts are 'forward-looking' and in that sense, take into consideration the effects of any policy changes on future outcomes. Rule-of-thumb forecasts are much more simple and are based on the past. For example, a rule of thumb forecast for inflation might be that the expected or anticipated inflation rate will be what is has averaged over the past five years.

Statement a is not true; rule of thumb expectations and rational expectations produce *similar* forecasts for inflation in an environment where the economy is stable and there are no major policy changes. Statement c is not true since it was Paul Volcker, not Alan Greenspan, who was responsible for ridding the economy of double-digit inflation in the early 1980s by severely reducing the money supply and raising interest rates. Consequently, his policies led to a major recession. Statement d is not true since the natural rate of unemployment today is estimated to be *less*, not more, that it was during the 1980s. Statement e is not true; a decrease in the length of time that unemployment insurance is offered will make it more likely that an unemployed worker will accept a job earlier, rather than later. This will serve to *reduce*, not raise, the natural rate of unemployment.

7. Correct answer: e.

Discussion: All of the above changes could cause changes in a nation's natural rate of unemployment. Europe used to have a lower natural rate of unemployment than the United States but since the 1970s, the natural rate of unemployment in Europe has exceeded that in the United States. The change in Europe's natural rate is attributed to statements c and d. Other explanations for changes in the natural rate of unemployment are offered in statements a and b.

8. Correct answer: d.

Discussion: Statement d is not true. A central bank whose sole goal is to keep the inflation rate low is less likely, not more likely, to use monetary policy to help stabilize output. That is, the central bank will be more likely to "do nothing" even if output fell below its potential level.

9. Correct answer: c.

Discussion: Empirical evidence has found a negative relationship between central bank independence and inflation rates. That is, countries with higher degrees of central bank independence typically have lower rates of inflation. Germany, Switzerland, and even the U.S. are good cases in point.

Empirical evidence does not suggest that a higher degree of central bank independence is associated with higher GDP growth rates. Thus, statement d is not true. Statement a is not true. In fact, the U.S. experienced declines in the inflation rate as the unemployment rate fell below the natural rate of unemployment. Statement b is not true. Countries with excessively high money growth rates (typically countries with big budget deficits that must be financed by "printing money") have hyperinflation. Bolivia and Argentina have provided some good, recent cases in point.

10. Correct answer: d.

Discussion: The velocity of money is defined as nominal GDP (which is equal to the price level X real GDP) divided by the money supply. Thus, statement d is correct and statement a is not correct. Statement b is not correct because the velocity of money is low, not high, when people hold onto money for a long period of time. Statement c is not correct. For the U.S. the M2 velocity of money has ranged between 1.4 and 1.9, not 14 and 19. Velocity numbers in the double digits are typically indications of hyperinflation. Statement e is not correct. The velocity of money does not cause hyperinflation. However, hyperinflation may cause the velocity of money to increase significantly.

11. Correct answer: e.

Discussion: Statement a requires that you apply the growth version of the equation of exchange (see PET #2 for review). In this case, output growth is equal to money growth (4%) + velocity growth (3%) minus the inflation rate (9%) = -2%. Statement b requires that you apply the Rule of 70 (from previous chapters). In this case, since inflation is stated on a monthly basis, the rule of 70 implies that purchasing power will be cut in half (inflation will double) in 70/14 = 5 months. Statement c is correct. If prices are rising by a factor of 5 each month, then $1 today will be worth 1/5 = $0.20 at the end of the month. Statement d is also correct. If prices are rising by a factor of 2 each month, then over the course of the year, prices will have increased by a factor of 212 = 4,096. If something costs $5 today, then it will cost $5 X 4,096 = $20,480 at the end of the year! That shows the power of compounding!

12. Correct answer: e.

Discussion: Statement c is correct. If prices increased by a factor of 3 each year, then $1 would now be worth less than $1. It would be worth $1/3 which is $0.33. Statement d is also correct. If prices increased by a factor of 3 each year, at the end of *two* years, an item would cost $1 x 3 x 3 which is $9.

Thus, statement b is not correct. At the end of one year, an item that cost $1 would now cost $3. Statement a is not true since hyperinflation is defined as an inflation rate in excess of 50% *per month*. Annualized, this means that hyperinflation occurs when a country experiences an annualized rate of inflation of 13,000 % = $(1 + 0.50)^{12}$.

13. Correct answer: c.

Discussion: Statement c is not true because a government that finances its budget deficit by borrowing from the public will not alter the money supply. It is only when the government prints money to pay for its deficit that an increase in the money supply occurs. All of the other statements are true.

VIII. ANSWER KEY: ESSAY QUESTIONS

1. A decrease in the money supply initiated by the Fed is aimed at reducing spending in the economy and thereby taking pressure off of prices throughout the economy and thus at reducing the inflation rate. The way it works is that the contraction in the money supply temporarily causes the nominal interest rate to rise (while inflation remains at its current level). Consequently, the real interest rate rises, too. Short term interest rates (nominal and real) will rise.

   What happens to long term interest rates depends on how the Fed's actions influences the expectations of the private sector. This is because long term interest rates carry a premium (are higher) for higher expected rates of inflation. If the private sector believes that the Fed will bring down the inflation rate into the future (and keep it down), expectations of future inflation will be reduced and nominal long-term interest rates may not rise by as much as nominal short term interest rates rise following the open market sale. In fact, it is possible that nominal long term interest rates could decline even though nominal short term interest rates rise. However, if the private sector does not believe that the Fed is committed to securing and maintaining a low rate of inflation for the economy, expectations of future inflation may not change at all and thus nominal long-term interest rate may rise (and possibly even more than nominal short-term interest rates rise).

2. The most common cause of hyperinflation is a government budget deficit that is financed by the government printing money to pay for it. Most industrialized countries finance their government budget through tax revenues. Any shortfall between government expenditures and tax revenues (budget deficit) is financed by selling government bonds (IOUs) to households and businesses and not by printing money. The problem with financing a government budget deficit by printing money is that the money supply expands (by a multiple) of the amount of money printed. The equation of exchange (quantity equation) in growth rates shows the link between the growth rate of the money supply and the inflation rate which is one for one, assuming that the growth rate in velocity is zero and the growth rate in output is zero. That is, a country whose money supply grows by 25% per year will have an inflation rate of 25% per year. When a country continually runs a budget deficit and finances it by printing money, the private sector begins to expect higher inflation which they in turn build into their negotiations for wages. This wage pressure also adds to inflation. Before too long, the rate of inflation begins to spiral up. This is a situation of hyperinflation.

During hyperinflationary episodes, money loses its value (its purchasing power) very rapidly. For example, if inflation were 20% per month, $1 today would be worth $0.11 at the end of the year $[1/(1.20)^{12}]$. Alternatively, an item that cost $1 today would cost $8.92 at the end of the year. With hyperinflation, because prices are rising so rapidly, people tend to spend it just as rapidly (before prices rise even more). Thus, during hyperinflation the velocity of money is typically very high (double digits).

Take It to the Net

We invite you to visit the O'Sullivan/Sheffrin page on the Prentice Hall Web site at:
http://www.prenhall.com/osullivan/
for this chapter's World Wide Web exercise.

CHAPTER 17
CURRENT ISSUES IN MACROECONOMIC POLICY

I. OVERVIEW

In this chapter, you will learn about three debates in macroeconomic policy: (1) Should the federal government balance its budget? (2) Should the Federal Reserve target the inflation rate? and (3) Should consumption be taxed instead of income? As you will see, the answers to these questions depend on several, often conflicting, considerations. In answering the first question, you will consider whether deficits lead to inflation. You will consider whether government debt presents future generations with a tax burden and slower economic growth. You will consider whether financing deficits with borrowing rather than through higher taxes will lead to more government spending. You will also consider whether and under what circumstances a deficit might be good for an economy. You will also learn about how a balanced budget amendment might work. In answering the second question, you will revisit the costs of inflation. You will then consider the debate over whether the Fed should have a single objective – to target inflation only – or whether it should have some flexibility in achieving both inflation and employment (and output) goals. You will also consider what would be an appropriate level of inflation for the Fed to target. You will hear critics' views on the use of monetary policy to stabilize the economy. You will also consider whether the Fed or Congress should set the inflation target, if there were one. Lastly, in answering the third question, you will consider the economic consequences of replacing an income tax with a consumption tax. You will consider whether consumption taxes lead to more or less savings. You will consider the "fairness" of consumption taxes. You will also consider whether there are other means besides a consumption tax that can be used to increase savings.

II. CHECKLIST

- ❏ Explain the relationship between deficits, surpluses, and debt.
- ❏ Discuss the projections for the U.S. federal budget and its implications for the U.S. government debt to GDP ratio.
- ❏ Explain why projections by the CBO were wrong regarding the deficits the federal government has experienced since 2001.
- ❏ Explain why some economists argue that surpluses in the Social Security fund should not be included in calculating the federal budget balance.
- ❏ Explain the two methods of financing a government budget deficit.
- ❏ Explain what 'monetizing the deficit' means and why countries might rely on this method to finance their deficits.
- ❏ Discuss the macroeconomic effects of monetizing government deficits.
- ❏ Explain why national debt may be a burden on future generations.
- ❏ Explain how saving promotes capital formation.
- ❏ Discuss the relationship between government deficits, private saving, and investment.

- ❑ Explain how a government deficit competes with (or 'crowds out') private investment and reduces real incomes and real wages.
- ❑ Explain Ricardian equivalence and the implications it carries for saving and investment in economies that run government deficits.
- ❑ Discuss Nobel laureate James Buchanan's views on government deficits.
- ❑ Discuss the circumstances under which a government deficit can be good for a country.
- ❑ Explain the relationship between the government deficit and recessions.
- ❑ Discuss the pros and cons of a balanced budget amendment.
- ❑ Discuss the costs of inflation.
- ❑ Discuss the merits and criticisms of focusing monetary policy exclusively on inflation.
- ❑ Discuss problems associated with using monetary policy to stabilize the economy.
- ❑ Discuss what inflation rate target should be set and who should set it.
- ❑ Explain why the U.S. tax system penalizes saving.
- ❑ Define consumption taxes and discuss the key feature.
- ❑ List some of the ways to reduce the amount of taxes paid on saving.
- ❑ Discuss whether consumption taxes will increase savings.
- ❑ Explain what is meant by double taxation.
- ❑ Explain how a consumption tax works for people with different income, consumption, and saving levels.
- ❑ Explain whether you think a consumption tax is fair or not.
- ❑ Define capital gains.
- ❑ Consider the incentive effects of an income tax, a consumption tax, and an income tax that exempts paying taxes on income earned from savings (interest, dividends, rents, and capital gains).

III. KEY TERMS

Government debt: The total of all past government deficits.

Deficit: The excess of total expenditures over total revenues.

Surplus: The excess of total revenues over total expenditures.

Government expenditure: Spending on goods and services plus transfer payments.

Monetizing the deficit: Purchases by a central bank of newly issued government bonds.

Ricardian equivalence: The proposition that it does not matter whether government expenditure is financed by taxes or by debt.

Consumption taxes: Taxes based on the consumption, not the income, of individuals.

Capital gains: Profits investors earn when they sell stocks, bonds, real estate, or other assets.

IV. PERFORMANCE ENHANCING TIPS (PETS)

PET #1

A government's budget balance is the difference between the tax revenues it collects and the expenditures on goods, services, transfer payments, and interest on the national debt it makes. A budget deficit adds to the national debt whereas a budget surplus reduces the national debt.

When tax revenues are greater than government expenditures, the government's budget is in a surplus and the stock of national debt will decline. When tax revenues are less than government expenditures, the government's budget is in a deficit and the stock of national debt will rise. When tax revenues equal government expenditures, the government's budget is in balance and the stock of national debt will not change.

For example, if the government runs a budget deficit of $25 billion this year and last year's debt level was $100 billion, this year's debt level will rise to $125 billion. If the government runs a budget surplus of $25 billion this year and last year's debt was $100 billion, this year's debt level will drop to $75 billion.

PET #2

When a government is unable to finance its budget deficit by selling bonds to businesses, households, and foreign citizens because nobody is willing to buy the bonds, the central bank is forced to buy the bonds. When the central bank purchases government securities issued directly by the Treasury, the money supply increases. This is called 'monetizing the deficit' which is to say "the government prints money to pay for its budget deficit."

Notice the similarity of the effects of a central bank purchase of government bonds (or government securities) directly from the government and an open market purchase of government bonds from the private sector (discussed in the chapter on Money, Banking, and the Federal Reserve System). The central bank purchase is similar to an open market purchase except that the central bank is purchasing bonds, not from the private sector, but from the government. The central bank pays for the bonds by issuing a check to the government. Thus, the government's checking account balance rises which also means that the nation's money supply increases. When the money supply increases, particularly by large amounts, the effect can be to create high rates of inflation.

PET #3

The deficit and debt as a percentage of GDP are calculated as:

(Deficit/GDP) X 100
(Debt/GDP) X 100

Sometimes, the deficit and debt are stated as a percentage of GDP in order to remove the "shock value" of the sheer numbers (and perhaps lead to a more balanced discussion of the potential economic

Chapter 17

problems attributed to the deficit). For example, a government deficit of $200,000,000,000 ($200 billion) doesn't seem nearly as shocking as, say, a government deficit that is, e.g. 2.3% of GDP. The same is true for the national debt.

PET #4

Ricardian Equivalence implies that consumption expenditures (i.e. household spending) will be crowded out (reduced) by an amount equal to the increase in government budget deficit. Thus, investment expenditures are not crowded out.

The reduction in consumption expenditures means that at the same time households increase their savings. The increase is saving is by an amount equal to the increase in the government budget deficit. The rise in saving is what prevents business spending (investment) from being crowded out. In other words, the pool of saving available to fund government and business borrowing rises so that business borrowing to finance investment is not crowded out (reduced) by the amount of government borrowing.

PET #5

Consumption taxes may be considered an economic growth policy in the case that consumption taxes lead to increased savings. With more saving available, there is a bigger pool of funds from which businesses can borrow to pay for purchases of new plant and equipment. That is, businesses are able to make more capital investments. With more investments being made, a country's capital stock grows. With a bigger capital stock, the productivity, and therefore real wages of workers increase. In addition, with a bigger capital stock, more output (GDP) can be produced.

V. PRACTICE EXAM: MULTIPLE CHOICE QUESTIONS

1. Suppose you are given the following information:

1990 -- government debt is $5,000 billion
1990 -- government deficit is $200 billion
1991 -- government deficit is $150 billion
1992 -- government surplus is $80 billion

At the end of 1992, government debt will be:

a) $270 billion.
b) $5,430 billion.
c) $5,350 billion.
d) $350 billion.
e) $5,270 billion.

2. Which one of the following statements is true:
a) it is certain that the U.S. will run budget surpluses over the next decade.
b) some economists argue that Social Security should be part of the government budget since it represents a payment the government is obligated to make.
c) forecasts of the government's budget position are based on an assumption that the U.S. economy will grow without recession.
d) it is typical for the debt to GDP ratio to decrease during wars.
e) it is forecasted that the debt to GDP ratio will decline as society ages since Social Security and Medicare payments will decline as death rates increase.

3. Which one of the following is a method for funding a government deficit?
a) government can borrow from households and businesses.
b) government can borrow from foreigners.
c) government can borrow from the central bank.
d) government can increase taxes.
e) all of the above.

4. Monetization of the budget deficit:
a) leads to increases in the money supply.
b) helps to bring down the rate of inflation.
c) occurs when the Treasury sells government bonds to commercial banks.
d) helps stabilize the economy.
e) is commonly practiced in industrialized countries.

5. Which one of the following has NOT been considered as a burden associated with government debt?
a) a reduction in the capital stock.
b) a reduction in real wages and real incomes.
c) lower taxes for future generations.
d) a reduction in investment.
e) debt servicing.

6. Ricardian equivalence means that:
a) a society should be indifferent between the central bank purchasing government debt and the public purchasing government debt.
b) budget deficits and budget surpluses are equivalent in terms of their effect on the saving and investment.
c) investment spending is crowded out by an amount equal to the increase in the budget deficit.
d) saving rises by an amount equal to the budget deficit.
e) (c) and (d).

7. Suppose you believe in Ricardian equivalence. You would assert that:

a) a budget deficit of $10 billion will generate $10 billion more worth of saving.
b) a budget deficit of $10 billion will reduce consumption spending by $10 billion.
c) a budget deficit will create capital deepening.
d) a budget deficit imposes a burden on the current generation.
e) (a), (b), and (d).

8. Government deficits:
a) may decrease during recessions because of "automatic stabilizers."
b) may decrease during recessions as expansionary fiscal policy is used.
c) may worsen the economy during recessions.
d) may help avoid the need for large tax increases during times of war.
e) none of the above are true.

9. A balanced budget amendment:
a) could limit the use of fiscal policy during recessions.
b) may not be enforceable because the government could always impose mandates or requirements on businesses to carry out actions where the balanced budget amendment restricts the government.
c) may not really create a balanced budget because Congress will find loopholes and other ways of presenting the appearance of a balanced budget when in fact there is not one.
d) may lead to legal challenges by various interested parties.
e) all of the above.

10. Which one of the following is a cost of inflation?
a) menu costs associated with firms having to change posted prices.
b) costs associated with time and resources devoted to reducing the effects of inflation on the purchasing power of money.
c) distortions in calculating taxes because inflation may not be factored in.
d) redistribution of money from lenders to borrowers.
e) all of the above.

11. Which one of the following is NOT a reason for having the Fed be committed to focus monetary policy on inflation only?
a) in the long run, monetary policy has not lasting effects on employment so it is best to focus only on inflation.
b) if the Fed is focuses on unemployment, too, it will distract the Fed from its mission to keep the inflation rate down.
c) the Fed's credibility regarding policy will be enhanced and so the private sector will be more responsive to changes in monetary policy.
d) having a single goal will help keep the Fed free from making policy based on politics.
e) long-term interest rates will become less sensitive to changes in short-term rates.

12. Which one of the following statements is true?
a) monetary policy can be more quickly enacted than fiscal policy.
b) critics of nominal GDP targeting argue that Fed policy to stabilize inflation has done more harm than good.
c) one alternative suggested to inflation-targeting is for the Fed to target nominal GDP.
d) nominal GDP targeting gives the Fed flexibility in pursuing inflation and output goals.
e) all of the above.

13. Consumption taxes:
a) will increase saving.
b) may or may not increase saving.
c) would be equivalent to an income tax system in which all saving was exempted from taxes.
d) are a form of double taxation.
e) (b) and (c).

14. Which one of the following statements is true?
a) a policy to give less financial aid for college to people who have saved more for college will encourage saving.
b) Capital gains on the sale of stocks, bonds, real estate, and other assets are exempt from taxes.
c) in the United States, citizens pay taxes on income from salary and wages but not on income earned from interest and dividends.
d) corporate income is taxed twice.
e) the United States is a high saving country.

15. The surpluses that existed when President Bush took office turned into deficits because:
a) The tax substantial tax cuts passed during his first term.
b) The recession in 2001 reduced tax revenues.
c) Increased spending on the war in Iraq.
d) Increased spending on the war in Afghanistan.
e) All of the above

VI. PRACTICE EXAM: ESSAY QUESTIONS

1. Discuss the pros and cons of mandating that the Federal Reserve have zero inflation as its one and only policy goal.

2. Explain under what circumstances a consumption tax could lead to faster economic growth.

224 Chapter 17

VII. ANSWER KEY: MULTIPLE CHOICE QUESTIONS

1. Correct answer: e.

Discussion: Debt at the end of 1992 will be based on the deficits and surpluses and the starting level of debt. Deficits add to the debt and surpluses reduce the debt. Thus, the debt will increase by (+$200 + $150 - $80) = $270 billion. Since the starting level of debt was $5,000 billion in 1990. Debt at the end of 1992 will be $5,270 billion.

Based on the answer above, none of the other statements can be correct.

2. Correct answer: c.

Discussion: When the Congressional Budget Office prepares its forecast of the federal government's budget balance (deficit or surplus), it uses several assumptions. One of those assumptions is that real GDP will continue to grow, uninterrupted by recession.

Statement a is not true since it is not certain that the United States will continue to run budget surpluses. The budget surpluses have only been forecasted and have not yet materialized. A major economic crisis or downturn could lead to an unforecasted budget deficit. Statement b is not true since some economists have argued that Social Security should not be part of the government's budget precisely because Social Security is an obligated payment. Social security is not viewed as a program that should be cut or downsized. Statement d is not true since it is typical for the debt to GDP ratio to increase, not decrease, during wars. Statement e is not true since it is forecasted that the debt to GDP ratio will increase as society ages because Medicare and social security expenses paid by the government are likely to increase.

3. Correct answer: e.

Discussion: Statements a-d are all examples of methods the government can utilize to pay for government spending.

4. Correct answer: a.

Discussion: Monetization of the debt occurs when a government covers its budget deficit by selling bonds to the central bank. (See PET #2). When the central bank, in effect, pays for the government's deficit spending, it gives money to the government that was not in circulation to begin with. Thus, monetization of the debt increases the money supply. Increases in the money supply also create inflation. Some economies that monetize bigger and bigger government deficits will experience hyperinflation. Thus, statement b is not correct.

Statement c is not correct since monetization of the debt occurs when the government sells bonds to the central bank, not commercial banks. Statement d is not correct since monetization of the debt may destabilize the economy, particularly if it generates hyperinflation. Statement e is not correct since industrialized countries typically refrain from monetizing government debt. Developing countries are more apt to rely on debt monetization.

5. Correct answer: c.

Discussion: Higher, not lower, taxes are considered to be a burden that future generations will encounter as they will be the ones that must pay interest on government debt issued in previous years to pay for deficits.

Statements a and d are burdens of government deficits. Bonds issued by the government to pay for a budget deficit compete with bonds issued by corporations to pay for their purchases of new plant and equipment (capital). They compete in the sense that savers now have the option of using their saving to buy not only corporate bonds but government bonds as well. For example, if private saving was $100 billion and there were no government bonds, all $100 billion would be used to buy corporate bonds (i.e. loan saving to corporations) allowing corporations $100 billion to use to buy new plant and equipment. If now there are government bonds issued as well, not all $100 billion will necessarily go to corporations since of the $100 billion may be used to purchase government bonds (i.e. lend to the government). Consequently, corporations cannot fund as much investment and thereby add to the capital stock and/or replace worn out capital. Thus, as investment declines, the capital stock may eventually deteriorate. Statement b is also a burden of a government deficit and is related to statements a and d. With reduced investment in plant and equipment, the productivity of workers may decline and thereby lead to a decline in their real incomes and wages. Statement e is a burden of the government deficit since debt servicing means that interest on the national debt must be paid for. The way it is paid for is through taxes on households and businesses.

6. Correct answer: d.

Discussion: The proposition of Ricardian equivalence means that households increase their saving by an amount equal to the budget deficit. They do this because they anticipate that the interest payments on the debt (debt service) arising from the current budget deficit will be paid for by higher taxes in the future. Thus, in order be able to pay for the higher taxes, households increase their saving today (in an amount equal to the budget deficit). The increase in saving also means that households must cut back on consumption. So, there is a burden on the current generation -- they must reduce their consumption expenditures. Consumption expenditures are thus "crowded out."

Statements a and b are not correct. They do not define or describe Ricardian Equivalence. Statement c is not correct. Ricardian equivalence means that there is no crowding out associated with the increased budget deficit. That is, investment spending does not decline when the government runs a budget deficit; however, consumption spending does decline. Statement e is not correct because statement c is not correct.

7. Correct answer: e.

Discussion: As discussed in the answer to question (6) above and in PET #5 of this chapter, a budget deficit of $10 billion will raise saving by $10 billion. If saving increases by $10 billion, consumption must decrease by $10 billion. Thus, statements a and b are correct. Statement d is correct; the burden on the current generation is the reduction in consumption expenditures that they must make in order to save enough to pay for the future taxes they anticipate paying to service the debt.

Statement c is not correct. Capital deepening occurs if the level of net investment (gross investment spending minus depreciation) increases. Ricardian equivalence only suggests that the level of gross investment spending will not be reduced as a result of the budget deficit. It does not say anything about net investment or even whether net investment will increase.

8. Correct answer: d.

Discussion: By allowing a government to run budget deficits and not mandating that it balance its budget, crisis events can be funded more smoothly. For example, if the United States entered into a war which causes government spending to increase dramatically, a balanced budget amendment would require that taxes be increased during war times to help fund the increase in government spending. A temporary increase in taxes may present an economic hardship for families and businesses. Families and businesses may instead find it easier to help pay for the war through more modest tax increases spread out over a period of time instead of in the year the excess spending is incurred.

Statements a and b are not correct since government deficits are likely to increase for two reasons during a recession. First, automatic stabilizers, which increase spending on unemployment compensation, and the like as the economy goes into a recession, will elevate government spending. Also, as incomes decline during a recession, tax revenues collected by the government will decline. Both of these effects will increase the budget deficit during a recession. Second, during a recession, policymakers (Congress) may decide to cut taxes or increase government spending (i.e. use fiscal policy) to help lift the economy out of a recession. Fiscal policy, too, may thus create a budget deficit during a recession. Statement c is not correct based on the discussion of statements a and b. That is, government deficits can actually serve to help reduce the magnitude of the recession. Thus, government deficits may actually help to stabilize the economy. Statement e is not correct since statement d is correct.

9. Correct answer: e.

Discussion: Without escape clauses, having to balance the budget could limit the use of fiscal policy during recessions. Automatic stabilizers act to increase the budget deficit during recessions. If the effects of the automatic stabilizers on the budget position must be offset so as to keep the budget in balance, the government may find itself having to raise taxes or cut government spending in order to keep the budget balanced. These actions could actually worsen the recession. If the objective of a balanced budget amendment is to limit the tax and spend nature of the government, a balanced budget amendment could still prove to be unenforceable. In effect, the government could balance its budget, say be reducing government spending on, e.g. research and development, but then mandate companies to place a certain some of money into a research and development fund for national uses. Loopholes are always discovered as a way to get around a law politicians may not like to deal with. Thus, some government spending programs may be taken "off budget" meaning that they will not show up as a government expense. In that way, the government's budget will be easier to balance. A balanced budget amendment might also invite legal challenges, particularly by groups most affected by the balancing budget act. If the government decides to balance the budget by raising taxes 100% on alcohol and tobacco and reducing government spending on the space program, you can bet that the affected parties will show up in Washington to fight the changes. Thus, all of the above statements are correct.

10. Correct answer: e.

Discussion: All of the statements imply costs of inflation.

11. Correct answer: e.

Discussion: Statement e is the correct answer because it is NOT correct. If the Fed is committed to pursuing an inflation goal only (as opposed to inflation and unemployment (and relatedly, output) goals, long-term interest rates will become *more* sensitive to changes in short-term interest rates, not less sensitive. This is considered desirable because, for monetary policy to have a bigger impact on the economy (spending and thus inflation), it must affect the rates at which consumers and businesses borrow. Since most people borrow money at long-term interest rates as opposed to short-term interest rates, it would be best if monetary policy could alter long-term interest rates. However, in practice, the Fed only has direct control over short-term interest rates (notably, the federal funds rate). Thus, anything the Fed can do to give it more control over long-term interest rates would be desirable. If the Fed were to focus only on inflation, it would be likely to achieve more control over long-term interest rates through its ability to influence short-term interest rates.

Statements (a) – (d) are all reasons for why some argue that the Fed should be charged with pursuing only one goal – the goal of low inflation.

12. Correct answer: e.

Discussion: All the statements are true.

13. Correct answer: e.

Discussion: A consumption tax may or may not increase saving. Thus, statement b is true. While a consumption tax makes consumption more expensive and consequently may reduce consumption and lead to more saving, a consumption tax could also, by inducing more saving, and therefore more wealth over time, lead to the need to save less. Thus, statement b is correct. Statement c is also correct since any income that is not consumed, is saved. For example, suppose you earn $40,000 a year. To make it simple, you use $30,000 to fund consumption. Let the consumption tax rate be 20%. Thus, you will pay $6,000 in consumption taxes. Of your $40,000 income, you will have $4,000 to put toward saving. Now, suppose there is an income tax but saving is exempted from taxes. This means that the income tax you would pay to the government would be based on your income less saving. That is, your income tax will be based on $36,000, not $40,000. Now, if the government set the income tax rate at 16.7%, you would pay $6,000 in income taxes (0.167 X $36,000) just like under the consumption tax. Notice that the amount of your income left for consumption will be $30,000. So, you are still able to save the same amount -- $4,000, and consume the same amount -- $30,000. Thus, an income tax that exempts saving can be made equivalent to a consumption tax.

Statement a is not correct since the effect of a consumption tax on saving is not certain as the discussion above illustrates. Statement d is not correct since a consumption tax will help to avoid the incidence of double taxation that arises when income earned through saving or dividends is taxed twice.

14. Correct answer: d.

Discussion: In the United States, corporate income is taxed twice. Corporations must pay taxes on the income they earn and then when they distribute their income to their shareholders through dividend payments, the shareholders must pay tax again since this is treated as income.

Statement a is not true. If colleges provide less financial add to people who have saved more for college, it will *discourage* people from saving for college. Statement b is not true. Capital gains (increases in the price of an asset that an individual earns (or 'gains') when they sell the asset that they purchased at a lower price, are taxed in the United States. Statement c is not true since citizens pay taxes on income earned not only through working (salary and wages) but on income earned through saving. That is, citizens also pay taxes on income earned from interest and dividends they may earn on assets they hold. Statement e is not true since the United States is a low saving country.

15. Correct answer: e.

Discussion: All the statements are true.

VIII. ANSWER KEY: ESSAY QUESTIONS

1. Inflation is costly to society for many reasons so a policy to rid the economy of inflation by mandating that the Fed adopt zero% inflation as its only goal seems worthwhile. However, there may be other reasons to believe that tying the hands of the Fed to this one goal may not be sensible. Inflation increases the cost to businesses of having to changed posted prices -- businesses may have to reprint brochures, catalogs, and menus as inflation increases. Shoe-leather costs are also generated with inflation. These are costs that individuals and businesses may encounter as they search for ways to avoid the effects of inflation on their income, saving, and spending. Inflation may also lead to distortions in our tax system if it is based on nominal and not inflation-adjusted income. Inflation also harms individuals living on fixed incomes -- incomes that do not increase or keep pace with inflation. Inflation that is unanticipated may also harm lenders and benefit borrowers. For these reasons, mandating that the Fed achieve zero percent rate of inflation makes sense.

    However, remember that if the Fed is committed to bringing inflation down and holding it at zero percent, it may need to "engineer" a recession to get the desired reduction in inflation. Contractionary monetary policies which temporarily reduce spending (aggregate demand) will help bring down inflation but will likely temporarily lead to increased unemployment. It has also been argued that achieving a 0% inflation rate could present some problems. First, with 0% inflation, were there to be non-policy induced decline in aggregate demand, deflation would result. However, since wages are not likely to be cut during episodes of deflation, firms will lay off workers instead. Thus, it may be better for the Fed to work toward achieving a small positive rate of inflation on the order of 2-3% instead of a 0% rate. Additionally, since it is well known that the inflation rate, as currently measured, overestimates the true rate of inflation by 0.5-1.5 percentage points, a goal of 0% inflation could actually produce a true rate of inflation of -0.5% to -1.5%. That is, a policy goal of 0% inflation could actually generate deflation. Deflation imposes costs of its own on the economy, just as does inflation.

    Finally, mandating that the Fed take price stability as its only goal means that the Fed may not be permitted to undertake expansionary policies were the economy to find itself in a recession. Some economists believe that the recessionary effects of such policies will be much smaller when the Fed is mandated to achieve 0% inflation because policy actions taken by the Fed will be viewed as more credible. Policy credibility for an institution like the U.S. central bank (the Fed) could generate spillover benefits in financial markets in the United States and around the world.

    As you can see, there is not agreement on whether a mandate to force the Fed to take on 0% inflation as its one and only goal is sensible.

2. A consumption tax is expected to lead to faster economic growth if the tax increases the level of saving in the economy and the increased saving is used to fund investments in the capital stock, including technology. For purposes of discussion, let's say that our current income tax system is replaced with a consumption tax system that keeps tax revenues of the government the same. Let's also assume that the level of government spending remains the same. Thus, public or government saving does not change. Now, let's assume that the consumption tax increases the level of private

saving. The increased level of saving means that there is a larger pool of funds that businesses can borrow from to pay for purchases of new plant, equipment, and technology. Consequently, a consumption tax is likely to indirectly lead to a higher level of investment in an economy. A higher level of investment is then expected to promote faster economic growth. Increased investment means that businesses will be working with more up-to-date equipment and technology and that businesses may also be able to expand production through opening up more new factories. More output and at a faster rate can now be produced with the existing labor force than before. The new investments actually help to make the labor force more productive. Thus, alongside the faster economic growth comes higher real incomes and real wages.

A consumption tax may not generate the scenario above if the consumption tax leads to lower saving or an unchanged level of saving. Additionally, if the government increases spending on non-investment related projects and tax revenues remain the same under the new tax system, then saving available from which businesses can fund investment may decline. That is, the increase in government spending could crowd out private investment. This would hurt economic growth.

Take It to the Net

We invite you to visit the O'Sullivan/Sheffrin page on the Prentice Hall Web site at:
http://www.prenhall.com/osullivan/
for this chapter's World Wide Web exercise.

PART 6: THE INTERNATIONAL ECONOMY

CHAPTER 18
INTERNATIONAL TRADE AND PUBLIC POLICY

I. OVERVIEW

In this chapter, you will learn why trade can be mutually beneficial to countries. You will re-encounter the principle of opportunity cost and use it to determine comparative advantage. You will learn that free trade can lower the price that consumers would pay for goods compared to the prices they would pay if they did not trade (autarky). You will also learn that there are resource movements from one industry to another associated with moving from a position of no trade (autarky) to a position of free trade. These resource movements mean that free trade will, in the short run, create employment losses and factory closings in some industries but expansion in others. You will learn about policies that restrict trade -- tariffs, bans on imports, quotas, and voluntary export restraints. You will learn that protectionist trade policies are typically designed to protect job losses in specific industries. However, protectionist trade policies impose costs on consumers. Thus, you will see that protectionism creates some winners and losers within a country. You will learn that protectionist trade policies initiated by one country may invite retaliation by a trading partner. You will learn about the rationale for protectionist trade policies and criticisms of these arguments. You will learn about some recent trade policy debates over foreign producers "dumping" their products in the U.S., over the impact of trade agreements on the environment, and about whether free trade causes income inequality. You will also learn about some recent trade agreements.

II. CHECKLIST

By the end of this chapter, you should be able to:

- Explain the benefits from specialization and trade as compared to autarky.
- Use an output table to calculate the opportunity costs of production in two countries for two different types of goods and determine in which good a country has a comparative advantage.
- Draw a production possibilities curve using information from an output table. Explain what the different points on the production possibilities curve represent.
- Explain what determines the range of terms of trade that would be mutually beneficial to two countries.
- Draw a consumption possibilities curve using information about the terms of trade. Explain what the different points on the consumption possibilities curve represent.
- Describe the employment effects of free trade.
- Explain who the winners and losers are from free trade.
- List the different types of protectionist trade policies.
- Explain how the different protectionist trade policies work and their effects on import prices.

- Compare and contrast the effects of an import ban to an import quota on equilibrium price and quantity using demand and supply curves.
- Compare and contrast an import quota to a tariff.
- Explain how the threat of retaliation by one country can persuade another country to loosen its protectionist policies.
- Explain why import restrictions might lead to smuggling.
- Define the Smoot-Hawley Tariff Bill.
- Discuss some arguments (or rationales) for protectionist trade policies.
- Describe the practice of dumping and predatory dumping (pricing).
- Explain why some firms might dump their products in other countries.
- Discuss why trade policy and environmental issues have become linked.
- Explain how trade might cause income inequality to widen.
- Discuss some recent trade agreements.

III. KEY TERMS

Production possibilities curve: A curve showing the combinations of two goods that can be produced by an economy, assuming that all resources are fully employed.

Autarky: A situation in which each country is self-sufficient, so there is no trade.

Comparative advantage: The ability of one person or nation to produce a good at an opportunity cost that is lower than the opportunity cost of another person or nation.

Absolute advantage: The ability of one person or nation to produce a good at a lower absolute cost than another person or nation.

Terms of trade: The rate at which two goods will be exchanged.

Consumption possibilities curve: A curve showing the combinations of two goods that can be consumed when a nation specializes in a particular good and trades with another nation.

Voluntary export restraint (VER): A scheme under which an exporting country voluntarily decreases its exports.

Import quota: A limit on the amount of a good that can be imported.

Import licenses: Rights, issued by a government, to import goods.

Tariff: A tax on an imported good.

Learning by doing: Knowledge gained during production that increases productivity.

Infant industries: Industries that are at an early stage of development.

232 Chapter 19

General Agreement on Tariffs and Trade (GATT): An international agreement that has lowered trade barriers between the United States and other nations.

World Trade Organization (WTO): An organization that oversees GATT and other international trade agreements.

Dumping: A situation in which the price a firm charges in a foreign market is lower than either the price it charges in its home market or the production cost.

Price discrimination: The process under which a firm divides consumers into two or more groups and picks a different price for each group.

Predatory pricing: A pricing scheme under which a firm decreases its price to drive a rival out of business, and increases the price when the other firm disappears.

IV. PERFORMANCE ENHANCING TIPS (PETS)

PET #1

In autarky, a country is constrained to consume what it produces. With trade, a country is able to consume a bundle of goods different from what it produces. Trade permits consumption beyond the production possibilities frontier and thus makes a country potentially better off.

PET #2

Opportunity cost calculations used to determine comparative advantage should be based on a per unit comparison.

(This is a review of PET #1 from Chapter 3.) Suppose you are given the following information:

	Country A	Country B
Wood products per hour	10	8
High-tech products per hour	15	4

The information in the table tells you that Country A can produce 10 units of wood products in one hour (with its resources) and 15 units of high-tech products in one hour. Country B can produce 8 units of wood products in one hour (with its resources) and 4 units of high-tech products in one hour. How can this information be used to determine which country has a comparative advantage in wood production and which country has a comparative advantage in high-tech production?

The easiest way to compute comparative advantage is to determine what the opportunity cost of production is for each good for each country, on a per unit basis. To do this, you must first answer how much Country A must give up if it were to specialize in the production of wood. For every additional hour of effort devoted to producing wood products, Country A would give up the production of 15 units of high-tech products. (Of course, it is then able to produce 10 more units of wood products.) On a per unit basis, Country A must give up 1.5 units of high-tech products for each 1 unit of wood products = (15 high-tech products/hour)/(10 wood products/hour) = 1.5 high-tech products/1 wood product. You would read this as "for Country A, the opportunity cost of 1 wood product is 1.5 high-tech products." For Country B, for every additional hour of effort devoted to producing wood products, it must give up 4 units of high-tech products. (Of course, it is then able to produce 8 more units of wood products.) On a per unit basis, Country B must give up 0.5 units of high-tech products for each 1 unit of wood products = (4 high-tech products/hour)/(8 wood products/hour). You would read this as "for Country B, the opportunity cost of 1 wood product is 0.5 high-tech products." Thus, Country B has the lower opportunity cost of producing wood products since it has to give up fewer high-tech products.

Since Country B has the lower opportunity cost of wood production, it should specialize in wood production. (Wood production is "less costly" in Country B than in Country A). If this is true, then it must also be true that Country A has the lower opportunity cost of high-tech production and thus should specialize in producing high-tech goods.

Let's see if this is true using the numbers from the table above. For Country A, the opportunity cost of producing more high-tech products is that for every additional hour of producing high-tech products, it must give up producing 10 units of wood products. (Of course, it is then able to produce 15 more units of high-tech products). On a per unit basis, Country A must give up 0.67 wood products for every 1 high-tech product = (10 wood products/hour)/(15 high-tech products per hour). You would read this as "for Country A, the opportunity cost of 1 high-tech product is 0.67 wood products." For Country B, the opportunity cost of producing more high-tech products is that, for every additional hour of producing high-tech products, it must give up producing 8 units of wood products. (Of course, it is then able to produce 4 more units of high-tech products.) On a per unit basis, Country B must give up 2 wood products for every one unit of high-tech products = (8 wood products/hour)/(4 high-tech products/hour). Thus, Country A has the lower opportunity cost of producing high-tech products since it has to give up fewer wood products. (High-tech production is "less costly" in Country A than in Country B.)

PET #3

Opportunity cost calculations used to determine comparative advantage are also used to determine a range for the terms of trade that would create mutually beneficial exchanges between two countries.

In PET #2 above, the opportunity cost in Country A of producing wood products is 1.5 high-tech products (i.e., 1.5 high-tech products/1 wood product). In Country B, the opportunity cost of producing wood products is 0.5 high-tech products (i.e., 0.5 high-tech products/1 wood product). Thus, the terms of trade range that would be beneficial to both countries must be between 0.5 high tech/1 wood product and 1.5 high-tech products/1 wood product.

For example, a mutually beneficial terms of trade might be 1 high-tech product/1 wood product. Country A would only have to give up (trade) 1 high-tech product in return for 1 wood product if it trades. If Country A produces for itself, it will have to cut production by 1.5 high-tech products to get back 1 wood product. The extra 0.5 high-tech product the country "saves" can then be used to buy more from the foreign country. Thus, Country A gains from trade. On the other hand, Country B would give up (trade) 1 wood product to Country A and get in return 1 high-tech product. If Country B produces for itself, it will only get back 0.5 high-tech products by reducing wood production by 1 unit. Thus, Country B gains, as well.

PET #4

Trade protection reduces the total supply of a good in a country. The reduced supply will increase the price a country pays for the protected good.

Your textbook mentions different types of trade protection -- import bans, import quotas, voluntary export restraints, and tariffs -- all of which act to raise the price of the goods and services that a country imports from other countries. Protectionist trade policies effectively reduce the total supply of a good (where the total supply comes from domestic production plus foreign imports) by restricting the amount of foreign imports. Thus, in terms of supply and demand analysis, protectionist trade policies shift the supply curve to the left. A leftward shift in the supply curve raises the price of a good. (See the box in PET #7 in Chapter 4 for review.)

V. PRACTICE EXAM: MULTIPLE CHOICE QUESTIONS

1. Use the table below to answer the question. Assume that each country can use its resources to produce either stuffed animals or pineapples.

	Country A	Country B
Stuffed Toys (per day)	200	300
Pineapples (per day)	400	900

   a) Country B has a comparative advantage in the production of both goods.

   b) Country A has a comparative advantage in the production of stuffed toys and Country B has a comparative advantage in the production of pineapples.

   c) Country B has a comparative advantage in the production of stuffed toys and Country A has a comparative advantage in the production of pineapples.

   d) Country A has a comparative advantage in the production of both goods.

   e) neither country has a comparative advantage in the production of stuffed toys.

2. Suppose the opportunity cost of producing one unit of lumber in Canada is 3 units of auto parts and that the opportunity cost of producing one unit of lumber in Japan is 6 units of auto parts. If the terms of trade are one unit of lumber for 8 auto parts, then:

   a) Canada and Japan will be able to engage in mutually beneficial trade.

   b) Japan will benefit from trade but Canada will not.

   c) Canada will benefit from trade but Japan will not.

   d) Canada will specialize in the production of auto parts.

   e) (a) and (d).

3. Use the graph below to complete the following question.

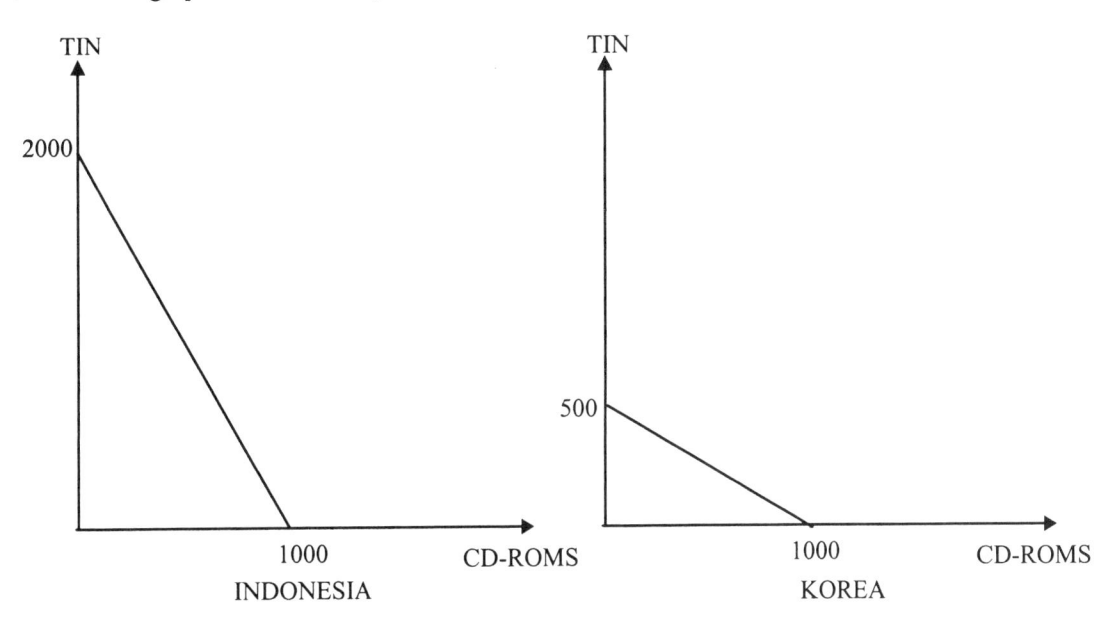

   a) Indonesia will specialize in tin production.
   b) a terms of trade of 250 units of tin for 100 CD ROMs will lead to greater consumption possibilities for Indonesia than its consumption possibilities in autarky.
   c) a mutually beneficial terms of trade would be 1.5 units of tin for 1.0 units of CD ROMs.
   d) if trade occurs, workers in the CD ROM industry in Korea will become unemployed.
   e) (a) and (c).

4. Which one of the following is NOT an example of a protectionist trade policy?
   a) ban on imports.
   b) voluntary export restraint.
   c) tariff.
   d) import quota.
   e) all of the above are protectionist trade policies.

5. Which one of the following trade policies would create the biggest increase in the price of the protected good?
   a) an import ban.
   b) a voluntary export restraint.
   c) an import quota.
   d) a tariff.
   e) a WTO license.

6. Which one of the following would NOT be a result of a tariff imposed by the U.S. on footwear imported from Brazil?
a) U.S. footwear firms will be winners.
b) employment in the U.S. footwear industry will be higher than compared to a situation of free trade.
c) the price that U.S. consumers pay for footwear produced in the U.S. will be lower than compared to a situation of free trade.
d) U.S. citizens should prefer a tariff on footwear to an import quota.
e) all of the above would result from the tariff on Brazilian footwear.

7. Which one of the following statements is true?
a) under an import quota, if the government sells import licenses to importers, then importers may not make money from the quota.
b) Japan's agreement to a voluntary export restraint on its automobile exports to the U.S. resulted in a decrease in the price of U.S.-made automobiles.
c) the threat of retaliation may persuade a country to impose harsher protectionist trade policies on its trading partners.
d) the Smoot-Hawley Tariff bill was designed to gradually lead to the removal of tariffs around the world.
e) the NAFTA agreement turned a U.S. trade surplus with Mexico into a U.S. trade deficit.

8. Which one of the following would NOT be a likely result of protectionist trade policies?
a) retaliation.
b) smuggling.
c) consumers paying a higher price for the protected good.
d) unemployment in the protected industry.
e) inefficient production.

9. Which one of the following statements is true?
a) protectionist trade policies often obtain Congressional approval because of the lobbying efforts of a limited group of people most likely to benefit from the protection.
b) the infant industry argument for trade protection is that it promotes learning by doing and thus can enable a new industry to be able to compete with other producers from around the world.
c) a problem with granting trade protection to an infant industry is that the protection is not likely to be removed as the industry matures.
d) by protecting infant industries from foreign competition, trade protection may lead to inefficient production by the protected industries.
e) all of the above are true.

10. Which one of the following is a problem with a government subsidizing an industry in the hope of establishing a world-wide monopoly?

a) the taxpayers ultimately pay for the government subsidy.

b) there is no guarantee that country will be able to profit from securing the monopoly.

c) another country may also grant a subsidy to the same industry.

d) the government may end up subsidizing an industry in which there are not economies of scale.

e) all of the above are problems.

11. Which one of the following statements is NOT true?

a) dumping occurs when a firm charges a price in a foreign market that is below its cost of production.

b) dumping is illegal under international trade agreements.

c) predatory dumping is an attempt to drive competitors out of the industry so that the dumping firm can gain monopoly status.

d) countries are permitted to restrict imports from other countries if the production methods used by other countries cause harm to the environment.

e) the wages of skilled labor in the U.S. have risen relative to the wages of unskilled labor as world trade has increased.

VI. PRACTICE EXAM: ESSAY QUESTIONS

1. Suppose the U.S. initially has no trade restrictions on imports of copper. Explain how a tariff on copper creates winners and losers within the U.S. Where might resources (labor and capital) move after the tariff is imposed? Be sure to address the government's use of the tax revenues earned by the tariff. Use demand and supply analysis to show the effects of the tariff.

2. Discuss some of the arguments made in favor of trade protection.

VII. ANSWER KEY: MULTIPLE CHOICE QUESTIONS

1. Correct answer: b.

Discussion: Country A's opportunity cost of producing 1 stuffed toy is 2 pineapples (i.e., 400 pineapples per day/200 stuffed toys per day = 2 pineapples/1 stuffed toy). That is, in order to produce 1 more stuffed toy, Country A would have to take resources out of pineapple production and put them into stuffed toy production. Thus, pineapple production would decrease by 2 units. Country B's opportunity cost of producing 1 stuffed toy is 3 pineapples (i.e., 900 pineapples per day/300 stuffed toys per day = 3 pineapples/1 stuffed toy). That is, in order to produce 1 more stuffed toy, Country B would have to take resources out of pineapple production and put them into stuffed toy production. Thus, pineapple production would decrease by 3 units in Country B. Thus, it "costs" less to produce stuffed toys in Country A (in terms of what must be given up) than it does in Country B. Since Country A has the comparative advantage in stuffed toy production, Country B must have a comparative advantage in pineapple production. To assure yourself that this is true, you can invert the ratios above so that Country A must give up producing 1/2 stuffed toy in order to produce 1 more pineapple whereas Country B must give up producing 1/3 stuffed toy in order to produce 1 more pineapple. Thus, pineapple production is less "costly" (in terms of what must be given up) in Country B than in Country A.

Based on the above discussion, none of the other statements are correct.

2. Correct answer: c.

Discussion: A mutually beneficial terms of trade must be between 3 auto parts/1 unit of lumber and 6 auto parts/1 unit of lumber. Since Canada's opportunity cost of producing lumber is less than Japan's opportunity cost of producing lumber, Canada has a comparative advantage in lumber production and thus should trade lumber for auto parts. Japan should do the reverse. At a terms of trade of 8 auto parts/1 unit of lumber, Canada will benefit since in autarky, she could only exchange one unit of lumber for 3 auto parts; with trade she would get 5 **more** auto parts per unit of lumber. However, at a terms of trade of 8 auto parts/1 unit of lumber, Japan will not benefit since in autarky, she would have to give up 6 auto parts in order to produce one unit of lumber whereas with trade, she would have to give up 2 **more** auto parts in order to purchase lumber from Canada. Thus, Japan would be worse off with trade than producing lumber for herself. (See PET #3 above for review.)

Statement a is not correct. For trade to benefit both countries, the terms of trade must range between 3 auto parts/1 unit of lumber and 6 auto parts/1 unit of lumber. Otherwise, one country will gain and the other country will lose. Statement b is not correct based on the discussion above. Statement d is not correct because Canada will specialize in lumber production. Statement e is not correct because neither statement a or d are correct.

3. Correct answer: e.

Discussion: The slope of the production possibilities curve gives the opportunity cost of producing tin (or CD ROMs). The slope of the production possibilities curve for Indonesia shows that the production of 1 CD ROM "costs" 2 units of tin. For Korea, the opportunity cost of producing 1 CD ROM is 0.5 units of tin. Since CD ROMs incur a lower opportunity cost in Korea than Indonesia, Korea will specialize in and export CD ROMs while Indonesia will specialize in and export tin. Thus, statement a is correct. Since the terms of trade are between 0.5 units of tin/1 CD ROM and 2 units of tin/1 CD ROM, trade can be mutually beneficial. Thus, statement c is correct.

Statement b is not correct. Statement b implies a terms of trade of 2.5 units of tin/1 CD ROM. While this terms of trade would be beneficial to Korea, it would not be beneficial to Indonesia. (See PET #3 above for review.) Statement d is not correct. Since Korea will specialize in CD ROM production, labor and capital will have to move to the CD ROM industry. Thus, workers will become, at least temporarily, unemployed in the tin industry, not in the CD ROM industry.

4. Correct answer: e.

Discussion: None necessary.

5. Correct answer: a.

Discussion: An import ban completely eliminates any imports of the good. For example, an import ban on cigarettes imposed by the U.S. would mean that no cigarettes produced in foreign countries would be permitted into the U.S. Thus, the total supply of cigarettes available to the U.S. market would be reduced. In this case, the total supply of cigarettes available to the U.S. market would have to come solely from U.S. production of cigarettes. The import ban would thus be represented by a leftward shift in the supply curve where the new supply curve would now be that attributed to domestic production only. Since this policy is the most restrictive on imports, the increase in the price of cigarettes will be the biggest of any of the policies.

Statement b, c, and d are not correct. An import quota and a voluntary export restraint do not drive imports to zero but instead simply restrict the amount of imports to sum number (greater than zero). A tariff is a tax on the price of the imported good and also acts to reduce the supply of the imported good, but not to zero. Statement e is not correct. There is no such thing as a WTO license.

6. Correct answer: c.

Discussion: Statement c is not correct. A tariff on footwear from Brazil will raise the price to U.S. consumers of footwear, regardless of whether the footwear is produced in Brazil or the U.S.

Statement a is correct. U.S. footwear firms will be winners in the sense that they will be able to get a higher price for the footwear that they sell to U.S. consumers. Statement b is correct. In free trade, there would be less production of footwear by U.S. producers and more by foreign producers. Thus, under free trade, employment in the U.S. footwear industry would be lower than when footwear is subject to a tariff, which is to say employment in the U.S. footwear industry would be higher with the tariff than in free trade. Statement d is correct. A tariff raises the price of the protected good (footwear in this case) less than does an import quota. Moreover, the government collects tariff revenue that the government could then use to fund government programs that benefit consumers (or to even give them tax refunds!).

7. Correct answer: a.

Discussion: When the government establishes an import quota, it gives licenses to importers which dictate how much of a good they are permitted to import. Naturally, importers are aware that they can profit by having an import license because they can buy the good from the foreign Country At the unrestricted price and sell in the home Country At the quota-induced price which is higher. However, if importers have to pay for the import licenses, then some of the profit that they expect to make from the import quota will be "eaten up" by the cost of the import license. That is, paying for the import license is a cost that an importer would have to consider in determining how profitable it would be to have the license.

Statement b is not true. Japan's agreement to a voluntary export restraint (VER) on its automobile exports to the U.S. resulted in a higher, not lower price of U.S.-made automobiles. U.S. consumers paid approximately $660 more for a U.S.-made automobile after the VER. Statement c is not true. The threat of retaliation may persuade a country to impose less harsh (i.e., less restrictive) protectionist trade policies on its trading partners, not harsher policies. Statement d is not correct. The Smoot-Hawley Tariff bill raised U.S. tariffs by an average of 59% and is pointed to as a policy that may have worsened the U.S. depression of the 1930s. Statement e is not correct. The devaluation of the peso is much more likely to have turned the U.S. trade surplus with Mexico into a U.S. trade deficit. The devaluation of the peso effectively made Mexican products much cheaper than U.S.-made products.

8. Correct answer: d.

Discussion: Protectionist trade policies are "protectionist" because they protect workers in the domestic industry from job losses that might occur were the industry left open to foreign competition. Thus, protectionist trade policies typically (at least in the short run) enhance employment in the protected industry.

All of the others may be a result of protectionist trade policies.

9. Correct answer: e.

Discussion: None necessary.

10. Correct answer: e.

Discussion: When a government subsidizes an industry, it gives money to the industry. The money the government has to give to the industry is ultimately provided by taxpayers. There is no guarantee that a country will be able to profit from securing a monopoly in a particular industry since other governments, may have, at the same time, chosen to subsidize the same industry. In this case, one or both countries may end up earning losses. The government also may choose to subsidize an industry thinking that the industry has large economies of scale (low average cost of production at very large levels of output) and thus is much more likely to exist as a monopoly (single producer). However, if it turns out that the industry is actually able to exist with more than one producer, the government-subsidized industry may find itself having to compete with producers from other firms around the world. In this case, monopoly profits anticipated by the government may not materialize.

11. Correct answer: d.

Discussion: Statement d is not true. Countries are NOT permitted to restrict imports from other countries if the production methods used by other countries cause harm to the environment. For example, suppose that Chile produces aluminum using a method that creates a lot of air pollution (more than what would be permitted under U.S. standards). Under World Trade Organization (WTO) laws, the U.S. would not be permitted to restrict the importation of Chilean aluminum into the U.S. even though the production methods used by Chilean producers would be outlawed in the U.S.

VIII. ANSWER KEY: ESSAY QUESTIONS

1. First of all, one might wonder why the U.S. decided to institute a tariff on a previously freely traded good. There are a few explanations. One explanation might be that the U.S. imposed the tariff as a retaliatory action to its trading partner's decision to impose a tariff on a U.S. good(s). The retaliation may be used as a device to prompt the trading partner to remove their tariff on a U.S. good(s). An alternative explanation might be that workers in the U.S. copper industry felt threatened by the competition from copper producers in foreign countries. Fearing that the competition might mean that U.S. copper producers would lose their market to foreign producers (and thus jobs and profits), workers/management in the U.S. copper industry may have lobbied Congress for trade protection.

When a tariff is introduced on foreign imports of copper, there will be winners and losers in the U.S. The winners will be the copper producers and workers in the copper industry. The price at which producers can sell copper will increase (as the graph below shows) and thus their profits may increase as well.

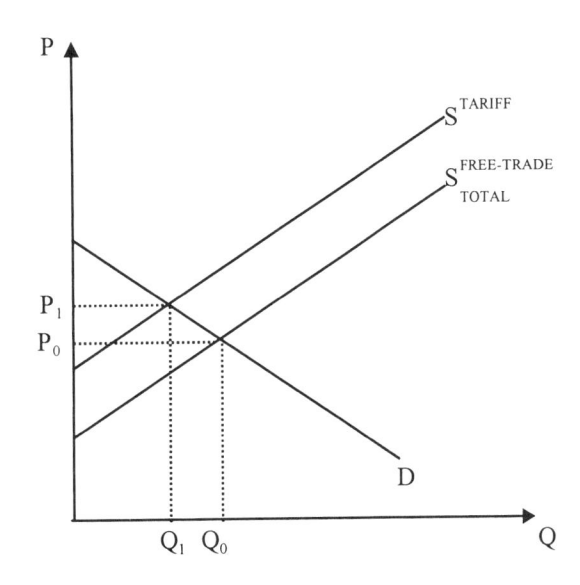

More workers and capital may now be needed in the copper industry, so resources may be taken out of other industries and moved into copper production. Thus, workers with skills in the copper industry will benefit. However, since the tariff raises the price of copper, users (buyers) of copper will lose.

Since the tariff generates tariff revenue for the government, the government may be able to use the revenue to offset some of the higher costs to copper users (i.e., subsidize copper users). Alternatively, the government may be able to use the tariff revenue to reduce income taxes on all workers, i.e., all workers might be given a tax refund. Or, the government could use the tariff revenue to help pay for other government programs that the citizens of the country feel are worth supporting.

2. There are several arguments made in favor of trade protection. One argument is that trade protection should be granted to industries that are just starting out -- so-called "infant industries." The argument is that the infant industries need protection from international competition in the early stages of development so that they become competitive themselves. Without the protection, the industry may not be successful, so the country loses out on establishing an industry that it may want. Another argument made in favor of trade protection is that trade protection "keeps jobs at home." Here, the argument is that without trade protection, the industry will be unable to compete against foreign competitors and so

the domestic industry will go out of business. Thus, by granting protection to a domestic industry, a government can prevent the industry from going out of business and thereby prevent any attendant job losses that would result. Another argument made in favor of protection is that monopoly profits may be obtained. In this case, protection would be granted to industries which are likely to survive as monopolies. By granting protection to a monopoly industry, the country becomes the sole producer of the industry output and may thus be able to extract monopoly profits from sales around the world. The government may encourage this if it is able to share in the profits with the producer. Another argument that can be made in favor of protection is that it can be used to get trading partners to loosen their trade restrictions. For example, a country may threaten to or actually impose stiff tariffs against a good or set of goods imported from another country to prompt the country to reduce its tariffs. The U.S. used this type of threat against Japan and was successful in getting Japan to loosen some of its trade restrictions against the U.S. Another argument made in favor of protection is that it will "level the playing field." This is a tit-for-tat application of protectionism. For example, if one country's government subsidizes a particular industry, then its production costs are unfairly low relative to the production costs of the same industry in other country that is not subsidizing the industry. Thus, to compete on a level ground, trade protection is considered to be a fair response.

This discussion provides arguments made in favor of trade protection. To be sure, there are many arguments that can be made against trade protection.

We invite you to visit the book's Companion Website at:
http://www.prenhall.com/osullivan/
for further exercises and practice quizzes.

CHAPTER 19
THE WORLD OF INTERNATIONAL FINANCE

I. OVERVIEW

In this chapter, you will learn how movements in the value of currencies affect economies around the world. You will use a supply and demand model to understand what causes the value of currencies to change. You will learn how to convert foreign currency prices to U.S. dollar equivalents using the exchange rate. You will also learn how to convert U.S. dollar prices to foreign currency equivalents using the exchange rate. You will learn how changes in interest rates and prices in the U.S. can lead to changes in the value of the dollar against other currencies. You will re-encounter the real-nominal principle which requires that you consider movements in the exchange rate after adjusting for inflation, i.e. movements in the real exchange rate. You will learn about the relationship between the real exchange rate and a country's net exports. You will learn about the law of one price and purchasing power parity. You will learn about current account, financial account, and capital account transactions and the relationship between them. You will learn about fixed exchange rate systems where countries agree to keep the value of their currencies fixed against others. You will learn that fixed exchange rate systems require intervention by governments (or central banks) in the market for foreign exchange. You will consider the pros and cons to a fixed versus a floating exchange rate system. You will learn a little of the history of the U.S. experience with different exchange rate systems. You will learn about European Union and the euro – the currency now used by many different European countries. You will learn about the Mexican financial crisis of 1994, the Asian financial crisis of 1997, and the Argentine Crisis of 2002.

II. CHECKLIST

By the end of this chapter, you should be able to:

❑ Explain a currency appreciation and depreciation.
❑ Explain how a currency appreciation or depreciation might affect exports and imports.
❑ Use an exchange rate to convert the foreign currency price of a good to an equivalent price in U.S. dollars (or another currency besides the U.S. dollar).
❑ Use an exchange rate to convert the U.S. dollar price of a good to an equivalent price in foreign currency.
❑ Use demand and supply analysis to show how changes in the demand and supply of a currency affect its price (the exchange rate).
❑ Explain how an increase in the prices and interest rates of a country may affect the price of its currency. Use demand and supply analysis to illustrate.
❑ Define and compute a real exchange rate.
❑ Define an appreciation and depreciation of the real exchange rate. Give a numerical example.
❑ Describe the law of one price.

- Describe purchasing power parity and its implications for the real exchange rate.
- Explain the relationship between inflation in one country relative to another and the exchange rate between the two countries.
- Define the current account, the financial account, and the capital account.
- Describe the types of transactions that give rise to a deficit and those that give rise to a surplus.
- Describe the relationship between the current account and the financial account assuming the capital account is zero.
- Explain why the balance of payments must sum to zero under a flexible exchange rate system.
- Explain how foreign exchange market intervention works to keep exchange rates stable.
- Describe what actions a country would have to take to keep its currency's value from increasing or decreasing.
- Explain what actions a government must take to keep its exchange rate fixed if it has a balance of payments deficit or surplus.
- Explain what actions besides foreign exchange market intervention a country may need to take in order to eliminate a persistent balance of payments deficit or surplus under a fixed exchange rate system.
- Discuss the U.S. experience with fixed and floating (flexible) exchange rates.

3 Discuss the Mexican financial crisis, the Asian financial crisis, and the Argentine financial crisis.

III. KEY TERMS

Exchange rate: The rate at which currencies trade for one another in the market.

Appreciation of a currency: An increase in the value of a currency.

Depreciation of a currency: A decrease in the value of a currency.

Real exchange rate: The market exchange rate adjusted for prices.

Multilateral real exchange rate: An index of the real exchange rate with a country's trading partners.

Law of one price: The theory that goods easily tradeable across countries, should sell at the same price, expressed in a common currency.

Purchasing power parity: Theory of exchange rates, stating that the exchange rate between two currencies is determined by the price levels in the two countries.

Current account: The sum of net exports (exports minus imports) plus income received from investments abroad plus net transfers from abroad.

Financial account: The value of a country's sales less purchases of assets. A sale of a domestic asset is a surplus item on the financial account, while a purchase of a foreign asset is a deficit item on the financial account.

Capital account: The value of capital transfers and transactions in nonproduced, non-financial assets in the international accounts.

Net international investment position: Domestic holdings of foreign assets minus foreign holdings of domestic assets.

Foreign exchange market intervention: The purchase or sale of currencies by governments to influence the market exchange rate.

Balance of payments surplus: Under a fixed exchange rate system, a situation in which the demand for a country's currency exceeds the supply of the currency at the current exchange rate.

Devaluation: A decrease in the exchange rate to which a currency is pegged in a fixed rate system.

Revaluation: An increase in the exchange rate in a fixed exchange system.

Balance of payments deficit: Under a fixed exchange rate system, a situation in which the supply of a country's currency exceeds the demand for the currency at the current exchange rate.

Fixed exchange rates: A system in which governments peg exchange rates.

Flexible exchange rates: A currency system in which exchange rates are determined by free markets.

Euro: The common currency in Europe.

IV. PERFORMANCE ENHANCING TIPS (PETS)

PET #1

The exchange rate is the price of one currency in terms of another. It can be thought of just like the price of any good or service.

Think about the price of any good or service, say a painting priced at $200, i.e. $200/painting. The item in the denominator is what is being priced. The same is true for an exchange rate. Suppose the exchange rate is expressed as 0.50 U.S. dollars/1 euro. In this case, the currency that is being priced is the euro. Its price is 50 cents. The inverse of this exchange rate would be 2 euros/$1 U.S. dollar. Now, the currency that is being priced is the dollar. One dollar is priced at (or costs) 2 euros.

If the price of a painting rises, we would say the painting has appreciated in value. If the price of a painting falls, we would say the painting has depreciated in value. The same is true for an exchange rate. If the exchange rate decreased from 0.50 U.S. dollars/1 euro to 0.40 U.S. dollars/1 euro, we would say that the euro has depreciated since it now worth 40 cents instead of 50 cents. If the euro has depreciated against the dollar, then it must be true that the U.S. dollar has appreciated. To see this, the inverse of 0.40 US dollars/1 euro is 2.5 euros/1 U.S. dollar. Thus, the dollar has appreciated in value since it is now worth 2.5 euros instead of 2 euros.

PET #2

You can think of the terms "U.S. assets" and "foreign assets" as referring largely to U.S. financial assets and to foreign financial assets.

Financial assets include stocks, mutual funds, corporate bonds, and government bonds (though your book also includes real estate). For example, suppose a U.S. resident purchases a Treasury bond issued by the British government. We would say that the U.S. resident has acquired a foreign asset. Alternatively, if a German resident purchases a U.S. corporate bond, we would say that the German resident has acquired a U.S. asset.

PET #3

A U.S. resident's purchase of a foreign asset means that the U.S. resident is lending his saving to the foreign country. A foreign resident's purchase of a U.S. asset means that the foreign resident is lending his saving to the United States. In the terminology of balance of payments accounting, aA U.S. resident's purchase of a foreign asset is also called an "increase in holdings abroad." A foreign resident's purchase of a U.S. asset is referred to as an "increase in foreign holdings in the United States."

PET #4

If %Δexchange rate = foreign inflation rate - U.S. inflation rate,

then, %Δreal exchange rate = 0.

(where exchange rate is expressed as foreign currency/U.S. dollar)

For example, suppose the exchange rate is 2 marks/U.S. dollar and rises to 2.2. The percentage change in the exchange rate is 10% [(2.2 - 2)/2) X 100]. If the German inflation rate is 12% and the U.S. inflation rate is 2%, the percentage change in the real exchange rate will be zero.

PET #5

*An increase in the net foreign assets of country A means that country A's net purchases of foreign assets is greater than foreigners' net purchases of the country A's assets. An increase in net foreign assets held by Country A also means that country A is on net lending to foreign countries; this also means that country A is running a **financial** account **deficit** (not surplus).*

*A decrease in the net foreign assets of Country A means that Country A's net purchases of foreign assets is less than foreigners' net purchases of Country A's assets. A decrease in net foreign assets held by Country A also means that Country A is running a **financial** account **surplus** (not deficit).*

For example, suppose that in 1995 country A's residents purchased $100 billion worth of foreign assets and sold $20 billion of foreign assets (which had been acquired in previous years). Country A's net purchases of foreign assets (purchases minus sales of foreign assets) will be $80 billion. If the residents of foreign countries purchase $150 billion worth of Country A's assets and sell $30 billion of Country A's assets (which had been acquired in previous years), foreign countries' net purchases of Country A's assets would be $120 billion (purchases minus sales of country A's assets). Now, since country A has, on net, purchased $80 billion of foreign assets and foreign countries have, on net, purchased $120 billion of country A's assets, we would say that there was a **decrease** in the **net** foreign assets of country A equal to $40 billion (80 - 120). We would also say that foreign countries are on net, lending to Country A, i.e. country A is on net borrowing from foreign countries. We would also say that country A has a financial account surplus.

PET #6

A current account deficit (surplus) of $X means that the financial account plus the capital account must be in a surplus (deficit) of $X. Since the capital account balance is negligible and so assumed to be zero in your textbook, we can say that a current account deficit (surplus) of $X means that the financial account must be in a surplus (deficit) of $X.

For example, suppose that Japan has a current account surplus of 50 billion yen against the United States. Japan's financial account must be in a deficit of 50 billion yen against the United States. The deficit on the Japanese financial account means that Japan's net acquisition (purchases less sales) of U.S. assets are greater than the United States' net acquisition (purchases less sales) of Japanese assets. In effect, this means that on net, Japan lends 50 billion yen to the U.S. That is, Japan is acquiring more U.S. assets than the U.S. is acquiring of Japanese assets – the U.S. net foreign asset position must be declining. (See PET #5 above).

Also, since Japan has a current account surplus of 50 billion yen with the U.S, then it must be the case that the U.S. has a current account deficit of 50 billion yen with Japan. The U.S. current account deficit of 50 billion yen is thus financed by Japan lending 50 billion yen to the U.S. through its financial account.

PET #7

If the price of a currency (i.e. the exchange rate) is fixed below its equilibrium value, there will be an excess demand for the currency. If the price of a currency is fixed above its equilibrium value, there will be an excess supply of the currency.

For example, suppose the exchange rate is $0.50/euro at which it is fixed. First of all, the currency that is being priced is the euro. Its price is $0.50. Thus, the demand and supply curves drawn below represent the demand and supply of euros.

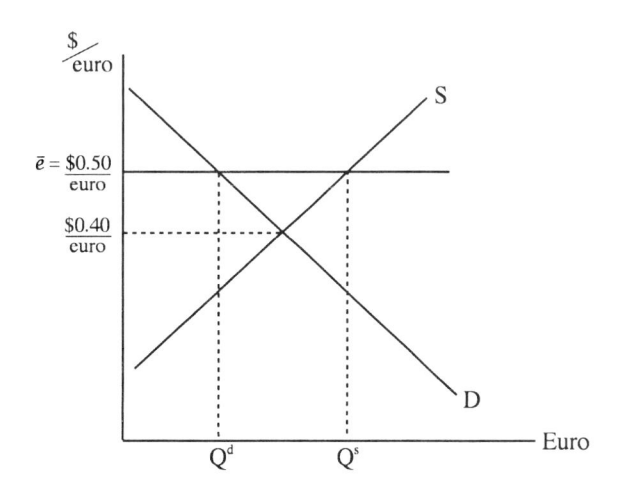

Since the equilibrium price of a euro is $0.40/euro, the quantity of euros supplied must exceed the quantity of euros demanded at the fixed rate. That is, there will be an excess supply of euros. This also means that there must be an excess demand for dollars.

The reverse happens when the exchange rate is fixed below the equilibrium price. If the exchange rate is fixed at $0.30/euros, the quantity of euros demanded will exceed the quantity of euros supplied. That is, there will be an excess demand for euros. This also means that there must be an excess supply of dollars.

PET #8

A country's balance of payments (BOP) is equal to the sum of the current account, the financial account, and the capital account:

BOP = current account + financial account + capital account

A country with a balance of payments deficit (BOP < 0) will be paying more in foreign currency for its purchases of goods, services, and assets than it is earning in foreign currency through its sales of goods, services, and assets. That is, it will be demanding more foreign currency than it is being supplied. Thus, a country with a balance of payments deficit will experience an excess demand for foreign currency (and correspondingly, an excess supply of its own currency).

A country with a balance of payments surplus (BOP > 0) will be paying less in foreign currency for its purchases of goods, services, and assets than it is earning in foreign currency through its sales of goods, services, and assets. That is, it will be demanding less foreign currency than it is being supplied. Thus, a country with a balance of payments surplus will experience an excess supply of foreign currency (and correspondingly, an excess demand for its own currency).

V. PRACTICE EXAM: MULTIPLE CHOICE QUESTIONS

1. Suppose the current franc/deutschemark rate is 4.1. If this rate changed to 3.80, we would say that:
a) the deutschemark has depreciated.
b) the franc is now worth fewer deutschemarks.
c) the demand for francs must have decreased.
d) the supply of deutschemarks must have decreased.
e) (b) and (c).

2. Suppose the price of a Swedish crystal vase is 80 Swedish krona and the current exchange rate is 6 Swedish krona per U.S. dollar. Which one of the following statements would be true?
a) an increase in Swedish interest rates will reduce the dollar price of the crystal vase.
b) an increase in U.S. interest rates will reduce the dollar price of the crystal vase.
c) the current dollar price of a Swedish crystal vase is $480.
d) if the price of a U.S. crystal vase is $30, then Swedish crystal vases cost more than U.S. crystal vases.
e) none of the above.

3. A decrease in interest rates in Japan will:
a) reduce the demand for yen.
b) cause a depreciation of the yen.
c) raise the demand for yen and appreciate the yen.
d) reduce the supply of yen and depreciate the yen.
e) (a) and (b).

4. Suppose that prices in Austria fall relative to those in the U.S. Which one of the following would be expected to happen?
a) the shilling/dollar exchange rate will fall.
b) the demand for shillings will fall.
c) the supply of dollars will fall.
d) Austria's net exports will increase.
e) (a) and (d).

5. Which one of the following statements is true?
a) the U.S. multilateral real exchange rate decreased during the early to mid 1980s.
b) the law of one price applies to goods like houses and haircuts which cannot be traded.
c) purchasing power parity calculations may provide a reasonable guide to setting an appropriate exchange rate for countries that have experienced hyperinflation.
d) an increase in the U.S. real exchange rate will be associated with an increase in U.S. net exports (U.S. exports minus U.S. imports).
e) all of the above are true.

6. Which one of the following items is NOT classified as a current account transaction?
a) exports.
b) imports.
c) purchases of foreign assets.
d) income earnings paid to foreign holders of U.S. assets.
e) net transfers.

7. Which one of the following transactions would give rise to a supply of foreign currency from the U.S perspective?
a) income earned by foreigners holding U.S. assets.
b) U.S. imports.
c) a foreigner's purchase of a U.S. asset.
d) U.S. aid to a foreign country.
e) none of the above.

8. Which one of the following transactions would give rise to a demand for foreign currency from the U.S perspective?
a) income earnings from U.S. investments in foreign countries.
b) sale of a U.S. telephone system to an Indonesian business.
c) a U.S. resident's purchases of a government bond issued by Switzerland.
d) sale of U.S. financial services to a Mexican government.
e) none of the above.

9. Which one of the following statements is true, assuming the capital account is zero?
a) if the U.S. has a financial account surplus, it will have a current account surplus, too.
b) if the U.S. has a financial account surplus, it will have a current account deficit.
c) a surplus on the U.S. current account generates an excess demand for foreign currency.
d) a surplus on the U.S. financial account generates an excess demand for foreign currency.
e) (b) and (d).

10. If the current yen/$ exchange rate is 135 and the U.S. government believed that the exchange rate was too high, the U.S. government:
a) might sell dollars to the private market.
b) might buy dollars from the private market.
c) might buy yen from the private market.
d) fix the exchange rate.
e) (a) and (c).

11. Which one of the following statements is true?
a) under fixed exchange rates, a persistent balance of payments deficit in country A means that country A's currency is in excess demand in the private market.
b) under fixed exchange rates, a country with a persistent balance of payments deficit may need to devalue its currency.
c) under floating exchange rates, a country with a current account deficit necessarily has a financial account deficit of the same amount, too.
d) under fixed exchange rates, a country with a persistent balance of payments surplus may will have an excess demand for its currency.
e) (b) and (d).

12. A country's currency will appreciate (gain in value) when:
a) the balance of payments is in a surplus.
b) the current account balance is in a surplus.
c) the financial account balance is in a surplus.
d) the balance of payments is in a deficit.
e) the current account is in a surplus and the financial account is in a deficit.

13. Which one of the following statements is true of the foreign exchange market?
   a) the Federal Reserve has official responsibility for conducting foreign exchange market intervention.
   b) when a country runs a balance of payments surplus under a fixed exchange rate system, its holdings of foreign exchange will decrease.
   c) Europe has plans to issue a new common currency named the "European currency unit" or "ecu."
   d) foreign exchange intervention may not be successful at changing a currency's value because the dollar amount of intervention is very small relative to the trillions of dollars traded on the foreign exchange market by private market participants.
   e) today, all countries participate in flexible exchange rate systems.

14. Which one of the following statements is NOT true?
   a) under the Bretton Woods system, all currency values were fixed in terms of an SDR (special drawing right).
   b) fixed exchange rate systems and the free (unrestricted) flow of capital are typically incompatible.
   c) for fixed exchange rate systems to work, countries must maintain similar inflation rates and interest rates.
   d) President Nixon effectively took the U.S. out of the Bretton Woods system.
   e) political events can sometimes lead to an international financial crisis.

15. Which one of the following statements is true of financial crises?
   a) they may result from an increase in the real exchange rate.
   b) they may result when foreign investors decide to move their funds out of the country.
   c) a devaluation of the crisis country's currency is often a first-stage remedy to a financial crisis.
   d) crisis countries may not have enough foreign reserves (currencies other than its own) to pay its foreign debts.
   e) all of the above.

VI. PRACTICE EXAM: ESSAY QUESTIONS

1. Suppose country X has a current account surplus of $251 billion and a financial account deficit of $178 billion. Assume the capital account equals zero. Answer the following questions:

   a. What is the dollar value of country X's balance of payments?
   b. Looking only at the current account balance, what must be true on the international market for Country X's currency?
   c. Looking only at the financial account balance, what must be true on the international market for Country X's currency?
   d. What does the balance of payments imply about the situation on the international market for Country X's currency?
   e. If this country has a **floating** exchange rate, what will happen to its exchange rate?
   f. If this country has a **fixed** exchange rate, what must the central bank do?

2a. Consider the market for Swiss francs (Sfr) where the current equilibrium exchange rate is $0.20/Sfr. What will happen to the exchange rate if the price of Swiss goods declined relative to the price of U.S. goods? Use supply and demand analysis to answer the question.

2b. Suppose that the U.S. and Switzerland wanted to prevent any change in the exchange rate, i.e. they want to keep it fixed at $0.20/Sfr. What will happen to Switzerland's balance of payments given your answer to (a)? What will the U.S. and Swiss governments have to do?

VII. ANSWER KEY: MULTIPLE CHOICE QUESTIONS

1. Correct answer: a.

Discussion: Since the exchange rate is expressed as francs/deutschemarks, the currency that is priced is the deutschemark; its price is 4.1 francs. If the exchange rate changes to 3.80, we would say that the price of a deutschemark has declined. It is now worth only 3.80 francs. That is, the deutschemark has depreciated in value. (See PET #1 above for review).

A depreciation in the value of the deutschemark means that the franc has appreciated in value. To see this, invert the exchange rate. In this case, the initial price of a franc would be 1 deutschemark/4.1 francs = 0.24 deutschemarks/franc and the new price would be 1/3.8 = 0.26 deutschemarks/franc. Thus, the franc is now worth more deutschemarks, not fewer deutschemarks. Thus, statement b is not correct. We could also say that the franc has appreciated in value. Statement c cannot be correct. A decrease in demand for francs would mean that the price of a franc would decline, i.e. it would depreciate in value. However, the change in the exchange rate implies that the franc has appreciated in value. Statement d cannot be correct. A decrease in the supply of deutschemarks would increase the price of a deutschemark, i.e. the deutschemark would appreciate in value. However, the change in the exchange rate implies that the deutschemark has depreciated in value.

2. Correct answer: b.

Discussion: Statement b is correct and requires that you understand that the increase in U.S. interest rates will increase the value of the U.S. dollar, say from 6 krona/dollar to 8 krona/dollar. At the current exchange rate, a Swedish vase costing 80 krona will, in terms of dollars, cost 80 krona/(6 krona/dollar) = $13.33. Since the increase in U.S. interest rates increases the value of the U.S. dollar, the dollar price of the Swedish vase will be reduced. If the exchange rate changes to 8 krona/dollar, the Swedish vase will cost, in terms of dollars, $10 (= 80 krona/(8 krona/dollar)).

Statement a is not correct. An increase in Swedish interest rates will increase the value of a krona (appreciate the krona) and decrease the value (depreciate) the dollar. That is, the exchange rate may change from 6 krona/dollar to 4 krona/dollar. In this case, the dollar price of the Swedish vase will increase from $13.33 to $20, not decrease. Statement c is not correct. The current dollar price of a Swedish vase is $13.33. Statement d is not correct. If a U.S. crystal vase costs $30 and the current dollar price of a Swedish crystal vase is $13.33, then Swedish crystal vases are less expensive than U.S. crystal vases, not more expensive.

3. Correct answer: e.

Discussion: A reduction in Japanese interest rates will reduce the attractiveness of Japanese financial assets to investors in the United States (and other countries, too). Consequently, the demand for Japanese financial assets (Japanese government and corporate bonds) by foreign investors will be reduced. If foreigners do not want to buy as many Japanese financial assets, the demand for yen which is necessary to pay for the Japanese assets, will also be reduced. Thus, statement a is correct. In terms of demand and supply analysis, this can be represented by a leftward shift in the demand for yen. A decline in the demand for yen reduces the price of yen. A decrease in the price of yen is also referred to as a depreciation of the yen's value. Thus, statement b is correct.

Statement c is not correct because the demand for yen decreases, not increases. Statement d is not correct. In fact, the supply of yen would increase since residents of Japan would seek to invest in financial assets outside of their country given the now reduced interest rates in their own country. Thus, Japanese residents, by increasing their demand for foreign (say, U.S.) financial assets would supply yen and demand dollars in exchange so as to be able to pay for the U.S. assets. Statement d is also not correct for the reason that a decrease in the supply of yen (assuming you thought that was correct) would actually increase the price of yen and appreciate it, not depreciate it.

4. Correct answer: e.

Discussion: If prices in Austria fall relative to those in the U.S, Austrian-made goods become relatively less expensive than U.S-made goods. This will increase the demand for Austrian-made goods and reduce the demand for U.S-made goods. Thus, Austria's net exports will increase and so statement d is correct. (Also, a decrease in the price of Austrian-made goods reduces Austria's real exchange rate. A lower real exchange rate is associated with an increase in net exports). To buy the goods, U.S. consumers must convert their dollars to Austrian shillings. That is, U.S. consumers will demand Austrian shillings (and correspondingly supply their dollars in exchange). Thus, statements c and d are not correct. The increase in demand for Austrian shillings will increase the price of a shilling (appreciate the shilling) and correspondingly decrease the price of the dollar (depreciate the dollar). That is, the shilling/dollar exchange rate will decline. Thus, statement a is correct.

5. Correct answer: c.

Discussion: For countries that experience hyperinflation, purchasing power parity calculations may provide a reasonable guide to setting an appropriate exchange rate.

Statement a is not correct; the U.S. multilateral real exchange rate (a weighted average of the real value of the U.S. dollar against a basket of other currencies) increased in value during the mid-1980s, not decreased in value. Statement b is not correct. The law of one price applies to goods that can be traded, but not to goods that cannot be traded. Statement d is not correct. An increase in the U.S. real exchange rate will be associated with a decline in U.S. net exports. This is because an increase in the real value of the dollar makes U.S. exports more expensive to foreign countries and U.S. imports from foreign countries less expensive. Thus, U.S. exports will decline and U.S. imports will rise. That is, net exports will decline.

6. Correct answer: c.

Discussion: Purchases of foreign assets are classified as a financial account transaction. A purchase of a foreign asset (e.g. a U.S. resident's purchase of a Japanese corporate bond) is considered as a financial outflow from the U.S. It is a financial outflow because some U.S. saving is flowing out of the country to purchase the Japanese bond.

7. Correct answer: c.

Discussion: When a foreigner wants to purchase any U.S. item, be it a computer, airplane, tobacco, or financial assets, will require that the foreigner convert their currency to U.S. dollars. That is, the foreigner will supply foreign currency to the international market and demand, in exchange, U.S. dollars.

Statements a, b, and d are all examples of transactions that would create a demand for foreign currency (and so too, a supply of U.S. dollars). For statement a, when we pay foreigners interest from U.S. financial assets they have acquired, foreigners will take the interest earnings in dollars and convert them to their own currency. That is, they will demand their (foreign) currency and supply (sell) dollars to pay for the foreign currency. For statement b, when we purchase a foreign good or service (an "import"), we must pay for it with foreign currency, not dollars. Thus, we will demand foreign currency and supply (sell) dollars to pay for the foreign currency. For statement d, when the U.S. provides aid to foreign countries, we convert dollars to foreign currency and then give the foreign currency to the country. Thus, U.S. aid to foreign countries creates a demand for foreign currency and a supply of dollars.

8. Correct answer: c.

Discussion: When a U.S. resident purchases a foreign asset, he/she must buy the foreign asset with that countries' currency. Thus, the U.S. citizen must convert his/her dollars to foreign currency before purchasing the asset. Thus, the U.S. resident supplies dollars (and correspondingly demands foreign currency).

Statement a is not correct. If a foreign resident has made an investment in the U.S. (i.e. purchased a U.S. asset), the investment income will be paid in terms of U.S. dollars (since it is a U.S. asset). The foreign resident, of course, will want to convert the U.S. dollar proceeds into foreign currency. Thus, U.S. dollars will be supplied and foreign currency demanded. Statement b is not correct. When a U.S. resident imports goods from a foreign country, the goods must be paid for with foreign currency. The U.S. resident must convert dollars to foreign currency to make the payment. Thus, imports into the U.S. create a demand for foreign currency and a supply of U.S. dollars. Statement d is not correct. When the U.S. gives foreign aid to another country, it gives the country aid in terms of the foreign country's currency. Thus, the U.S. government must convert U.S. dollars to foreign currency. That is, the U.S. supplies dollars and demands foreign currency.

9. Correct answer: b.

Discussion: If the U.S. has a financial account surplus, it is on net, borrowing foreign currency. That is, the U.S. is borrowing more from abroad than it is lending to foreign countries. (See PET #6 above). This means that, through financial account transactions only, foreigners are supplying their currency to the U.S. in excess of the U.S. demand for foreign currency. That is, there is an excess supply of foreign currency and correspondingly an excess demand for dollars arising from financial account transactions. Thus, statement d is not correct. The surplus on the U.S. financial account is used to finance a deficit on the U.S. current account. That is, a deficit on the U.S. financial account means that the U.S. demand for foreign currency exceeds the supply of foreign currency arising from current account transactions. The excess demand for foreign currency is alleviated through the U.S. financial account surplus (which generates the necessary supply of foreign currency). Thus, statement b is correct (and statement a is not). Statement c is not correct because a surplus on the U.S. current account corresponds to an excess demand for dollars (and an excess supply of foreign currency). This is because a current account surplus means that on net, foreigners are buying more U.S.-made goods and services than the U.S. is buying of foreign-made goods and services, i.e. the U.S. is a net exporter.

10. Correct answer: e.

Discussion: If the U.S. government believed that 135 yen/$ was too high, the government would take action to push down the exchange rate, i.e. reduce the (yen) price of a dollar say to 125 yen/$. A decrease in the price of a dollar could be accomplished by increasing the supply of U.S. dollars on the private market. That is, the government would sell dollars to the private market. At the same time, a decrease in the price of a dollar (which means an increase in the price of a yen) could be accomplished by increasing the demand for yen (i.e. buying yen). Thus, statements a and c will both work to reduce the exchange rate (i.e. reduce the yen price of a dollar).

11. Correct answer: e.

Discussion: Statement e is correct because both statements b and d are correct. A country with a persistent balance of payments deficit is a country where foreign currency is in excess demand (and the deficit country's currency is in excess supply) on international markets. The excess supply of its own currency indicates that the country may need to lower the price of its own currency and, correspondingly, raise the price of foreign currency. When a country takes these actions, it is said to 'devalue' its currency. Thus, statement b is correct. Statement d is also correct. Under fixed exchange rates, a country with a persistent balance of payments surplus will see an excess demand for its own currency. This happens because a country with a balance of payments surplus is selling more goods, services, and assets to foreign countries than they are buying from foreign countries.

Statement a is not correct since a country with a persistent balance of payments deficit will experience an *excess demand,* not supply, for foreign currency (and correspondingly, an excess supply of its own currency). Statement c is not correct since, under floating exchange rates, a country with a current account deficit will have a financial account surplus of the same amount (ignoring the capital account).

12. Correct answer: a.

Discussion: Statement a is correct. A country with a balance of payments surplus is a country that is selling more goods, services, and assets to foreign countries than it is buying from foreign countries. Consequently, there will be an excess demand for the surplus country's currency. An excess demand for currency leads to a rise in the price of currency – in this case, the surplus country's currency. Thus, we would say that surplus country's currency appreciates (or gains value). Based on this answer, statements b-e cannot be correct.

13. Correct answer: d.

Discussion: Statement d is true; there is limited evidence that foreign exchange market intervention can actually alter, in any substantial way, the value of one currency against another.

Statement a is not true. The U.S. Treasury has official responsibility for conducting foreign exchange market intervention although it may act in concert with the Fed. Statement b is not true. A country that runs a balance of payments surplus (sum of current account plus capital account) is on net earning foreign exchange. That is, the country's foreign reserves will increase, not decrease. Statement c is not true. While Europe does have plans to issue a common currency, the name of the currency is to be the "euro." Statement e is not correct. Some countries participate in fixed exchange rate systems. Many countries in Europe currently participate in a fixed exchange rate system known as the "exchange rate mechanism."

256 Chapter 19

14. Correct answer: a.

Discussion: Statement a is not true. Under the Bretton Woods system, all currency values were fixed in terms of the U.S. dollar (and the U.S. dollar's value was fixed in terms of gold, i.e. $35 per ounce of gold).

Statement b is true. For countries to successfully operate a fixed exchange rate system, it is often the case that they must also impose capital controls (taxes, etc.) on the movement of capital into and out of their countries. Statement c is true. Fixed exchange rate systems may break down when countries are not able to keep interest and inflation rates amongst themselves similar. Statement d is true. Nixon suspended convertibility of U.S. dollars into gold in August 1971 and thereby effectively ended the Bretton Woods system of fixed exchange rates. Statement e is true as the case study in your textbook about Mexico reveals.

15. Correct answer: e.

Discussion: Financial crises have a few characteristics that are common to each other. First, prior to the financial crisis, a country's foreign reserves (foreign currencies that it can use to pay for foreign goods, services, and loans) decline. The depletion of foreign reserves may arise because foreigners take their funds out of the country. Also, increases in the real exchange rate of the crisis-prone country, i.e. an appreciation of the real value of the crisis-prone country's exchange rate means that it is less costly for the country to import, and more expensive for it to export. Consequently, the increase in the real exchange rate also tends to create a current account or trade deficit. The trade deficit also leads to a loss of foreign reserves. Typically, in an effort to gain back foreign reserves, the crisis country will devalue its currency. However, this has costs since the devaluation makes it even harder for borrowers in the country to pay back on loans they owe to foreigners.

VIII. ANSWER KEY: ESSAY QUESTIONS

1. My answers to questions (1a) – (1f) are written below where I have reproduced each question. The starting point for the question was to suppose country X has a current account surplus of $251 billion and a financial account deficit of $178 billion (and the capital account was assumed equal to zero).

   a. What is the dollar value of country X's balance of payments? The balance of payments is in a surplus of $73 billion.

   b. Looking only at the current account balance, what must be true on the international market for Country X's currency? Country X's current account surplus of $251 billion implies an excess demand for country X's currency and correspondingly an excess supply of the other currency (US $).

   c. Looking only at the financial account balance, what must be true on the international market for Country X's currency? Country X's financial account deficit of $178 billion implies an excess demand for another currency (US$) and an excess supply of country X's currency.

   d. What does the balance of payments imply about the situation on the international market for Country X's currency? Given that the balance of payments is in a surplus, it means that on net, there is an excess demand for country X's currency (and correspondingly an excess supply of the other country's currency, US$).

   e. If this country has a **floating** exchange rate, what will happen to its exchange rate? Under floating exchange rates, Country X's currency would appreciate.

f. If this country has a **fixed** exchange rate, what must the central bank do? If country X has a balance of payments surplus, there is an excess demand for Country X's currency and correspondingly an excess supply of the other currency (US$). To keep the exchange rate fixed, the central bank of Country X must supply its own currency to the private market where it is in excess demand and buy up the excess supply of the other currency (US$). Consequently, Country X will gain foreign currency (US$).

2a. A decrease in the price of Swiss goods relative to U.S. goods will increase the demand for Swiss goods (from both Swiss and U.S. residents). The increased demand for Swiss goods by U.S. residents translates into an increase in the demand for Swiss francs (and correspondingly, an increase in supply of U.S. dollars on the foreign exchange market) since U.S. residents need the Swiss francs in order to purchase the Swiss goods. The increase in demand for Swiss francs will increase the price of the Swiss franc, i.e. the exchange rate expressed as $/Sfr will increase above, say, $0.20/Sfr. That is, the Swiss franc will appreciate (and the dollar will depreciate). For example, the Swiss franc may rise in value to $0.25/Sfr. The demand and supply diagram for Swiss francs below shows how the increase in demand for Swiss francs raises the price of the franc.

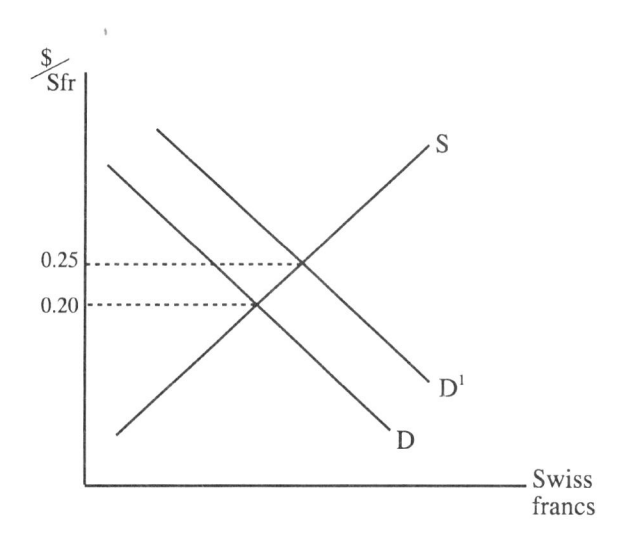

2b. Switzerland's balance of payments will (assuming it started at zero) move toward a surplus. The increase in demand for Swiss francs with the exchange rate fixed will create a situation of an excess demand for Swiss francs at the $0.20 price. (See diagram below). An excess demand for Swiss francs corresponds to a balance of payment surplus for Switzerland.

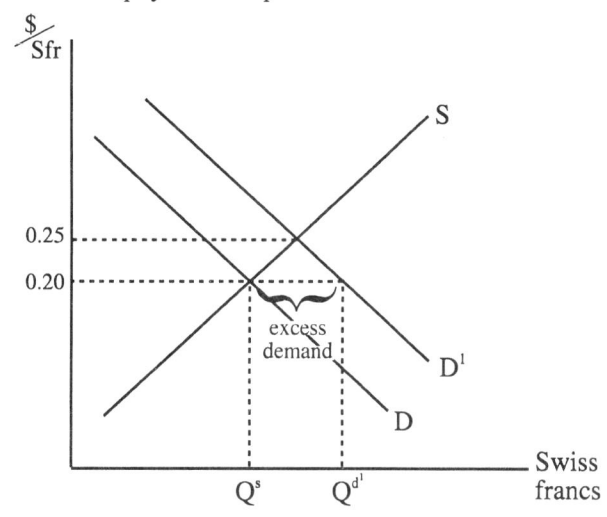

The governments must intervene in the foreign exchange market to prevent the Swiss franc from appreciating to $0.25/Sfr. They must take action to keep the exchange rate fixed at $0.20/Sfr. Since the demand for Swiss francs has increased (and correspondingly, the supply of dollars has increased), the governments must supply the market with the Swiss francs they desire (and buy up the supply of dollars, i.e. take dollars off of the market). Thus, the U.S. government will lose Swiss francs (since the U.S. government will be supplying them to the foreign exchange market (and taking in U.S. dollars). The Swiss central bank will gain U.S. dollars (since the Swiss government will be buying up the supply of dollars from the foreign exchange market (and giving out Swiss francs in return).

Take It to the Net

We invite you to visit the O'Sullivan/Sheffrin page on the Prentice Hall Web site at:

http://www.prenhall.com/osullivan/

for this chapter's World Wide Web exercise.